TWENTY-FIVE WOMEN WHO SHAPED THE EARLY MODERN HOLY ROMAN EMPIRE

"Through her well-chosen examples, Katrin Keller unlocks a multitude of previously hidden or partially obscured connections across the last three centuries of the vast Holy Roman Empire's existence, revealing not only how this complex entity functioned, but the important contributions made by women to its artistic, cultural, dynastic, economic, medical, political, religious, and scientific history. Fascinating and absorbing."

Peter H. Wilson, *University of Oxford, UK*

Challenging the conception that only men shaped the Holy Roman Empire, this book provides students and general readers with biographies of preachers, nuns, princesses, businesswomen, artists, scientists, writers, and social movers who exercised agency in the Holy Roman Empire.

Who was Maria Theresia Paradis, and have you ever heard of Empress Eleonora Magdalena? Numerous women achieved prominence or made important contributions to the life of the early modern Holy Roman Empire, but they are only gradually being rediscovered. Generations of historians had assumed that princely women were essentially limited to childbearing, or townswomen to running the household. And although it took a long time for higher education to become attainable to women, they also made their voices heard in the sciences, arts, and religion. Indeed, a closer look reveals that the history of the empire was also a history of the interaction of men and women and a history of women's self-empowerment. This book offers a biographical perspective on that past, as well as a fascinating panorama of women who left their mark on the Holy Roman Empire.

This book is the perfect introduction to anyone wishing to broaden their knowledge of women's history, the Holy Roman Empire, and early modern Europe.

Katrin Keller is Director of the Institute for Habsburg and Balkan Studies of the Austrian Academy of Sciences, Austria.

Twenty-Five Women Who Shaped... Series

The series *Twenty-Five Women Who Shaped...* looks at different periods in history and uncovers the women who helped to lay the cultural, political, social, or religious foundations of the time in question. The books offer accessible, well-researched introductions to influential female figures across the ages and around the world, enabling general readers to gain a reliable, richly detailed overview.

Twenty-Five Women Who Shaped the Italian Renaissance
Meredith Ray

Twenty-Five Women Who Shaped the Early Modern Holy Roman Empire
Katrin Keller

TWENTY-FIVE WOMEN WHO SHAPED THE EARLY MODERN HOLY ROMAN EMPIRE

Katrin Keller

Translated by Bernard Heise

LONDON AND NEW YORK

Designed Cover image: *Curiosity* by Gerard ter Borch
(1617–1681), oil on canvas, ca. 1660–62. *IanDagnall
Computing / Alamy Stock Photo*

First published 2024
by Routledge
4 Park Square, Milton Park, Abingdon, Oxon OX14 4RN

and by Routledge
605 Third Avenue, New York, NY 10158

Routledge is an imprint of the Taylor & Francis Group, an informa business

© 2024 Katrin Keller

The right of Katrin Keller to be identified as author of this work has been asserted in accordance with sections 77 and 78 of the Copyright, Designs and Patents Act 1988.

All rights reserved. No part of this book may be reprinted or reproduced or utilised in any form or by any electronic, mechanical, or other means, now known or hereafter invented, including photocopying and recording, or in any information storage or retrieval system, without permission in writing from the publishers.

Trademark notice: Product or corporate names may be trademarks or registered trademarks, and are used only for identification and explanation without intent to infringe.

British Library Cataloguing-in-Publication Data
A catalogue record for this book is available from the British Library

ISBN: 978-1-032–18104-2 (hbk)
ISBN: 978-1-032–18105-9 (pbk)
ISBN: 978-1-003–25287-0 (ebk)

DOI: 10.4324/9781003252870

Typeset in Sabon
by codeMantra

CONTENTS

List of Figures ix
List of Maps xii
Acknowledgements xiii
Note xiv

Introduction 1

The Sixteenth Century: Preachers, Nuns, and Dynastic Women 39

Caritas Pirckheimer (1467–1532): The Learned Nun 41

Katharina Zell (1497/98–1562): A Woman who Preached 52

Maria of Hungary (1505–1558): On Behalf of the Dynasty 61

Elisabeth of Brunswick-Calenberg (1510–1558): A Princess as Reformer 72

Anna of Saxony (1532–1585): Of Princely Domains and Good Medicines 83

Archduchess Maria of Inner Austria
(1551–1608): How a Mother Shapes her Children   93

The Seventeenth Century: Princesses, Businesswomen, and Artists   103

Polyxena of Lobkowicz (1566–1642): Between
Bohemia and Spain   105

Anna of Brandenburg (1576–1625): How
Prussia came to Brandenburg   115

Maria Magdalena Haidenbucher (1576–1650):
Abbess in Troubled Times   125

Catharina Regina von Greiffenberg
(1633–1694): The Poet in Exile   137

Maria Sibylla Merian (1647–1717): Science
and Painting   148

Glikl bas Judah Leib (1647?–1724): The
Experiences of a Jewish Businesswoman   158

Empress Eleonora Magdalena (1655–1720):
How to Care for Your Siblings   168

Maria Aurora von Königsmarck (1662–1728):
The Mistress in the Imperial Abbey   178

The Eighteenth Century: Scientists, Writers, and Social Movers   189

Erdmuthe Benigna of Reuß-Ebersdorf
(1670–1732): Women and the Pietist Movement   191

Maria Margaretha Kirch (1670–1720):
The Arduous Journey to the Sciences 200

Luise Adelgunde Gottsched (1713–1762):
More than the Woman at his Side 209

Dorothea Erxleben (1715–1762): A Medical
Doctor Prevails 219

Empress Maria Theresa (1717–1780): The Heiress 227

Anna Dorothea Therbusch (1721–1782): From
Innkeeper to Court Painter 238

Anna Barbara Gignoux (1725–1796): How to
Defend a Calico Manufactory 249

Sophie von La Roche (1730–1807): A Life as a
Female Author 259

Amalie Gallitzin (1748–1806): Philosophy,
Religion, and Conviviality 268

Maria Theresia Paradis (1759–1824): The
Blind Pianist 277

Henriette Herz (1764–1847): A Salon in Berlin 287

Index 297

FIGURES

1.1	Imperial eagle: the coronation of Empress Eleonora Magdalena of Palatinate-Neuburg in Augsburg in January 1690 *Austrian National Library*	1
2.1	Portrait of a Woman, Said to be Caritas Pirckheimer. This is a modern portrait made in the style of paintings by Albrecht Dürer *Alamy*	50
3.1	Strasbourg city view (1644) *Alamy*	52
4.1	Maria of Hungary. Copy of a lost portrait by Titian. This portrait was created in Augsburg in 1548, where Maria, Charles, Ferdinand, and their nephew Maximilian met, along with Christine of Lorraine and Dorothea of Denmark *Rijksmuseum Amsterdam*	67
5.1	Duchess Elisabeth of Brunswick-Calenberg, 1542 *Herzog-August-Bibliothek Wolfenbüttel*	74
6.1	Electress Anna of Saxony, after 1565 *Alamy*	85
7.1	Archduchess Maria of Inner Austria, 1577 *Kunsthistorisches Museum Wien*	93
8.1	Polyxena of Lobkowicz, ca. 1585 *The Lobkowicz Collection, Prague, Czech Republic*	107

x Figures

9.1	Electress Anna of Brandenburg, around 1605 *Stiftung Preußische Schlösser und Gärten Berlin-Brandenburg*	117
10.1	Maria Magdalena Haidenbucher, Abbess of Frauenchiemsee *Abtei der Benediktinerinnen Frauenwörth im Chiemsee*	130
11.1	Catharina Regina von Greiffenberg *Österreichisches Bundesdenkmalamt Wien*	138
12.1	Maria Sibylla Merian, 1679 *Kunstmuseum Basel*	151
12.2	The marvellous butterfly. Maria Sibylla Merian, *Metamorphosis Insectorum Surinamensium*, Amsterdam 1705, Table 53 *Alamy*	154
13.1	City view of Hamburg, ca. 1700 *Alamy*	158
14.1	Empress Eleonora Magdalena of Palatinate-Neuburg, 1690 *private ownership*	169
15.1	Maria Aurora von Königsmarck *Nationalmuseum Stockholm*	179
16.1	Erdmuthe Benigna of Reuß-Ebersdorf *Bildarchiv Foto Marburg*	193
17.1	Map of the southern starry sky surrounded by the representations of four great observatories: London, Copenhagen, Kassel, and Berlin. The latter is in the lower right corner (1742) *Bayerische Staatsbibliothek München*	200
18.1	Luise Adelgunde Gottsched, 1757 *Alamy*	209
19.1	Dorothea Erxleben *Alamy*	220
20.1	Maria Theresa and her family, 1764/65 *Alamy*	234
21.1	One of Therbusch's history paintings, entitled "Anacreon" *Stiftung Preußische Schlösser und Gärten Berlin-Brandenburg*	241

Figures **xi**

21.2	Anna Dorothea Therbusch, self-portrait 1782, signed "A. D. Therbusch née de Lisziewska par elle même / peintre du Roi 1782" *Germanisches Nationalmuseum Nürnberg*	244
22.1	Anna Barbara Gignoux *Kunstsammlungen und Museen Augsburg*	249
23.1	Sophie von La Roche, ca. 1774 *Freies Deutsches Hochstift / Frankfurter Goethe-Museum*	262
24.1	Princess Amalie Gallitzin, 1783 *Alamy*	270
25.1	Wax portrait bust of Maria Theresia Paradis *Wien Museum*	278
26.1	Henriette Herz as a 15-year-old, portrayed as Hebe, the goddess of youth, 1778. This is a work by the painter Anna Dorothea Therbusch *Alamy*	288

MAPS

1.1 The Holy Roman Empire after 1648   34
   Dominik Wieser, Wien

ACKNOWLEDGEMENTS

The idea for this book came about through a suggestion from the publisher, for which I am very grateful. It reached me just as a larger project on the empresses of the Holy Roman Empire had been completed. The empresses were preceded by smaller studies on princely women of the empire and on ladies of courtly society. On this occasion, I had looked more closely at the historiography on the Holy Roman Empire and found that until very recently it had focused essentially on the constitution and politics. This meant that women and their opportunities for action rarely came into view. Thus, the invitation to write the history of the empire through the biographies of women from different backgrounds and with very different life paths was most welcome, presenting a different image to contrast the "womanless" empire with a different image, at least in an exemplary way.

I would like to thank Bernard Heise, who translated my texts, always keeping a watchful eye on details of content and not shying away from the sometimes lengthy quotations. The Institute for Habsburg and Balkan Studies of the Austrian Academy of Sciences (Vienna), as well as many institutions that agreed to the publication of images, provided substantial support. William Godsey and Anna Spitzbart read parts of the text in advance, as did Wolfgang Schmale. I thank him both for constant support and for patiently listening for a long time to anecdotes and theories about empresses, electresses, and all the other "gals" with whom I share my scholarly life at times.

NOTE

The individual biographies always use the names by which the women generally appear in the scholarship. Often this is their married name, but there are also variations because of divorce or remarriage. In some cases, several different names are common, but this will not be addressed in detail here.

INTRODUCTION

FIGURE 1.1   Imperial eagle: the coronation of Empress Eleonora Magdalena of Palatinate-Neuburg in Augsburg in January 1690

Austrian National Library

Der Schutz- und Schatten-reich ausgebreitete Kaisers-Adler, Oder: Das Glorgrünende Römische Reichs-Zepter ..., s.l. 1690, Kupferstich, Österreichische Nationalbibliothek, Sammlung von Handschriften und alten Drucken, Signatur 77.Dd.660

DOI: 10.4324/9781003252870-1

On 19 January 1690, as suggested by the above picture created that same year, a woman stood at the centre of the Holy Roman Empire of the German Nation, one of largest polities of Europe, which existed from the tenth to the beginning of the nineteenth century.[1] The event depicted within the body of the imperial eagle, one of the empire's most important symbols, is the coronation of Empress Eleonora Magdalena, the consort of Emperor Leopold I. We see the ritual's most crucial moment, namely, when the elector and archbishop of Mainz, assisted by the two other ecclesiastical electors, the archbishops of Trier and Cologne, place the crown upon her head. The imperial crown is also shown between the two heads of the imperial eagle. On the very top of its wings are the portraits of the empress and her eldest son, Joseph, who would likewise be crowned in Augsburg just a few days later. Below them are the coats of arms of the seven electors,[2] the empire's highest-ranking princes, who had the right to elect the emperor. Finally, in the background we see a view of the Imperial City of Augsburg, where the coronation took place in 1690.[3]

Looking closely, one can identify more women inside the Augsburg Cathedral in the gallery, whereas the central interior space is occupied exclusively by men. Apart from the three aforementioned electors, the actors included the emperor himself, seen on the throne to the left of the empress, as well as numerous bishops and abbots of imperial monasteries, shown in the middle behind the empress. Also present were two of the four secular electors—the electors of the Palatinate and Bavaria—while the other two—Saxony and Brandenburg—had sent emissaries. The high-ranking spectators in the galleries were additional imperial princes and princesses, imperial counts and countesses, as well as many high officials of the imperial court and of the courts of the attending princes.

Prior to the event, the electors and imperial officials had negotiated the details of the traditional proceeding for days, adapting it to most fully represent the social distinctions of the various participants in the space of the coronation church, the festive procession to the town hall, and the coronation feast that took place there, so as to thereby manifest the order of the empire. Ritualistic stagings like this coronation depicted and thus repeatedly affirmed the imperial constitution: the emperor and the imperial estates—that is, the electors, princes, counts, and lords, as well as the imperial cities in their hierarchical order—were the most important "members of the empire".[4] In the procession to the church, the emperor appeared in the splendour of the imperial regalia, which contemporaries believed dated back to Charlemagne. After him came the attending electors as the highest-ranking imperial princes, followed in turn by the other imperial princes. The same applied to the empress's entourage, in which the imperial princesses and countesses participated in the procession.

Scholars have in recent decades shown great interest in how the Holy Roman Empire functioned and in the particularities of its constitutional history.[5] This has substantially broadened and differentiated the image of the workings of the empire and the ceremonial composition of its constitution and bodies. However, the actors dealt with in this regard have almost exclusively been men, for the imperial institutions were shaped by male rulers and their male representatives—jurists, councils, and emissaries. Women, on the other hand, even those of the social elite—that is, of an aristocratic or princely status—had virtually no place in the imperial constitution at all.[6]

This also held true for the empress. Although she was the focus of the coronation ritual, Eleonora Magdalena could only be crowned because she was the emperor's wife. Never would the electors have elected a woman as empress and thereby vested her with independent rights of dominion in the empire.[7] Eleonora Magdalena's coronation did not confer any additional rights on her, for the early modern imperial constitution did not provide for any such rights for an empress.

Gender hierarchies

Women were generally denied any part in the institutions of the Holy Roman Empire, and the reason for this was obvious to the people of the times. Their exclusion was based on the allocation of role models for women and men in Christian anthropology, on a hierarchisation of the genders.[8] Throughout Europe, females were deemed the weaker sex, burdened by the spread of original sin through Eve's disobedient violation of the divine commandment. "Female weaknesses" included, for example, profligacy, fickleness, and (according to many) lesser intellect and wit. These intellectual and moral-ethical deficits were combined with physical weakness as well.

These ascriptions had specific legal consequences that were associated above all with the concept of "gender guardianship",[9] which expressed that a woman's gender was precisely what limited her legal capacity and subordinated her to the comprehensive decision-making authority of men. Unmarried women were subject to the guardianship of their father or brothers, and married women to that of their husband. In many parts of the empire, widows and women without male relatives would be assigned a guardian, who was supposed to represent them in legal and economic matters.[10]

Admittedly, the relevance of this construct began gradually to wane in the Late Middle Ages. This started in the cities, where, given the commercial activities of married and unmarried women, the legal principle came up against practical limits. It was difficult to involve a male guardian in every business arrangement, and hence the legal norm was slowly relaxed, but without being fully rescinded. This applied more to the north-eastern German region (with the exception of the Hanseatic towns), the middle of the empire, and the Bavarian and Austrian region than it did to the south-west. Notwithstanding substantial regional differences, the construct of gender guardianship generally became less and less important as of the seventeenth century. But it continued to play a role until well into the twentieth century.

The legally fixed lower status of women entailed by this norm is also evident in inheritance law. Inheritance law is a very complex matter, which was differentiated by region and through legal traditions, as well as by individual decisions set down in wills. But the fact that land property, assets, and rights were primarily passed down to sons—often only to the oldest son—applied across all social groups. Daughters, on the other hand, tended to receive their share of the parental inheritance by way of their marriage endowment or as a payment after their parents' death. However, in the absence of male successors with inheritance rights, they could also inherit major assets and estates as "daughter-heirs". The same held true for widows, who in the absence of successors could inherit from their deceased husband. Thus although not without restrictions, in principle women had inheritance rights.

But while the early modern gender hierarchy appears very unequivocal at first glance, a closer look reveals that it was differentiated and simultaneously mitigated by various factors. In this respect, one must consider above all the organisation of society by estates. The society of the empire consisted of groups that were fundamentally unequal in terms of rights and obligations. They differed with respect to their types of income, lifestyles, and codes of conduct, as well as by their legal status and the position attributed to them within the system of government. This organisation affected both women and men. It allowed even most men to exercise political power only in a highly graduated manner and influenced their access to education and to privileged work in associations such as craft and merchant guilds. At the same time, the social order of estates was also the basis on which women of the princely or aristocratic rank were assigned more rights than, say, men of the peasant estate. Therefore the estate structure in a certain sense overlaid and modified the hierarchisation of men and women.

The organisation of society by estates thus resulted, on the one hand, in the differentiation of opportunities for action for both women and men according to their belonging to social groups. On the other hand, however, it also included a further differentiation that was effective across all genders, namely, that of familial status—that is, whether a person was single, married, or widowed. Each was associated with a different position within the family and thus also within the house. Integrated into the household or "house"[11] were not only family members but also workers (on farms or in skilled trade workshops) and domestic staff. As a nexus of work and life, the household was a central social institution in which power was exercised and hierarchies were generated and perpetuated until into the nineteenth century. And within the household, women held various positions, which in turn modified the hierarchies of gender and estate membership.

Regardless of social ranks, females as unmarried persons, as girls, hardly had any decision-making opportunities or scope for action but rather were very much subject to male agency (paternal, fraternal, etc.). Yet this was paralleled by the situation for young unmarried men, who were likewise subject to familial decision-making authority. The latter, however, was not exercised solely by men, for as a wife and mother[12]—that is, in a different personal status—women held substantially broader rights. Although the housewife remained legally subject to her husband as the male head of the household, at the same time she herself had authority over other members of the household, such as servants or artisanal workers—and naturally also over the children of the house, sons and daughters.

If the wife became a widow as a result of her husband's death, then her opportunities for action changed yet again. Although social consensus held that widows were supposed to lead a secluded and pious life[13] and they were also not juridically excluded from gender guardianship, in many respects they could nonetheless act in a relatively self-determined manner. Often enough, widows needed to continue economic operations in agriculture, skilled trades, or commerce to ensure the family's survival. As aristocratic or princely widows, they were responsible for the administration of larger and smaller territories or noble estates, which they might own as a widow's estate or manage as the guardian of underage sons. Admittedly, female guardianship was not the rule, and it was quite controversial among the affluent spheres of the nobility and urban patriciate. But throughout the empire, it was nonetheless a proven and widely practised method to secure property and assets, as well as the male succession of underage sons.

While one cannot, therefore, grasp the gender hierarchy in the early modern empire in overly strict bipolar terms, the legal status of women across all social groups established an essential commonality: because of their lesser legal status and the socially accepted gender hierarchy, they could not effectively act in institutions. This applied to the constitutional bodies of the empire as well as to city councils and rural communities. In recent years, feminist historians have used the term "intersectionality" to describe these complex overlappings of gender, law, and status.[14] Women could hold offices independently only in very specific contexts: for example, as appointed midwives in urban communities or as ladies-in-waiting within a narrow circle of princely women—thus in spaces designated as female. Hence, women were excluded from exercising power in and over institutions.

And this lower status had yet another serious consequence. Contrary to some widely held views, women were no more excluded from gainful activity in the Holy Roman Empire than in other European countries and regions. However, this was subject to a very substantial restriction: privileged work in the skilled trades, commerce, and agriculture remained closed to them. Commercial associations that were vested with production and sales privileges, such as artisan and merchant guilds, did not accept women as independent members. The only exceptions were a few "women's guilds", such as the Cologne silk makers, where women were the qualified producers.[15]

Also worth mentioning is the so-called widow's right, which was prevalent in many cities and trades. It provided for the widow of a guild craftsman to continue operating his workshop until the oldest son could take it over. In these cases, women had the right to engage in privileged work, but only as a proxy for a male family member and not in her own right. This broad exclusion from independent gainful employment, especially in the skilled trades, constituted a general trend in many vocations, one that can be observed as of the Late Middle Ages and which became quite pronounced in the early modern period.

What remained for women dependent on gainful employment was work in less secure occupations: day labourers, farm maids, washer women, domestic workers, unskilled labourers in commercial production facilities ranging from mines to early factories, shopkeepers, etc.[16] In addition, we can safely assume that while wives and daughters were unable to work independently in urban trades, they played an indispensable role as "assistants" of husbands, fathers, and brothers. Although they did not appear in town records or tax registers as workers, artisanal enterprises could hardly be sustained without their collaboration.

Because of their gender, women were also excluded from so-called learned professions, such as doctors or clerks, for they were only eligible for higher education in very specific cases.[17] In the "*Querelle des Femmes*", a debate on the gender hierarchy that persisted among scholars and the educated elite from the fifteenth to the eighteenth century,[18] the men who set the tone largely agreed that women had neither the intellect nor the patience to study scientific or philosophical texts in the scholarly language of Latin.

Naturally, female participants in this debate thought differently. As early as 1404, Christine de Pizan, the first woman to chime in with a text, eloquently argued that neither in their virtues nor in their intellectual capabilities were women inferior to men. Many other women, such as Moderata Fonte and Lucretia Marinella around 1600, concurred with her, and even some men commented in the same vein. Nonetheless, the view that women were inferior in intellectual and moral terms because of their sex continued to prevail.

Spheres of agency

The legally established hierarchisation of the genders had many different consequences for women's opportunities to act in the early modern empire. At first glance, this seemingly gloomy balance sheet appears to confirm earlier findings suggested by historical accounts of the empire: women played at best a marginal role for the empire as a political entity. At the same time, however, the above description already shows that women were by no means incapable of acting. Even though they remained excluded from participating in the Holy Roman Empire's institutional workings, there were many social sectors in which they could very well act.

One development whose significance in this respect can hardly be overestimated has been described by Heide Wunder for the empire as the "familialisation of work and life".[19] Already by the Late Middle Ages, the artisanal, mercantile, and farming sectors saw the development of the intra-familial working group, which provided social security to members of the household. In the household, the husband and wife constituted a "working couple", each with different directorial powers and responsibilities, through which they jointly—even though not on an equal footing—participated in securing an income, cultivating social networks, and looking after many other aspects of social and economic life.

Regardless of the legal and normative hierarchisation of the genders and without calling it into question, such division-of-labour processes occurred in all social groups. The master craftsman or farmer was responsible for production; his wife sold the products. In the absence of sufficient male staff (which was often the case), wives and daughters helped out in the workshop or on the farm. When a merchant was travelling, his wife would manage the accounts or take care of the business at home. Ever since the Reformation, as wives of Protestant pastors, women assumed tasks in providing social support to the congregation, just as wives and daughters assisted municipal office holders in their responsibilities. The image of the honourable housewife and her fields of activities also included using the household's resources as frugally as possible and ensuring the provisions for the family and personnel. In the upper classes, maintaining social status required the involvement of women in representative functions. And all women—from girls to widows—had to protect their family's honour by behaving appropriately.

One can list further facets of this familial division of labour. It not only enabled women's extensive integration into economic contexts but also to some degree their involvement in exercising power within the context of the household, the urban or rural community, the noble manor, or the principality. Hence, while the hierarchisation of genders undoubtedly existed, it was modified not only by one's estate as referenced above but also by the importance of joint collaboration in the process of the familialisation of life and work. Women remained excluded from participating in the institutions, regardless of whether these were imperial diets, guilds, or city councils. But the "house" as the fundamental structural unit of early modern society nonetheless enabled women to exercise power, especially if they belonged to a princely "house"—a dynasty. In this case, household rule could quasi be extended to an entire territory.

And hence one arrives again at the level of the Holy Roman Empire. Even if its most important institutions—the imperial and electoral diets—were not open to women, this did not apply to the imperial court system. Women could very well appeal to the imperial chamber court, which was first domiciled in Speyer on the Rhine and later in Wetzlar near Frankfurt am Main, as well as to the Aulic Council in Vienna. Both courts played a major role in mediating conflicts and in the juridification of governance in the empire. And repeatedly appearing before both of these courts were also women who in this way could successfully defend or enforce their rights.[20]

Beyond its institutional composition, the Holy Roman Empire comprised a conglomeration of numerous larger and smaller territories that were governed by dynasties of varying ranks: from the imperial house of Habsburg through the electoral houses of Hohenzollern, Wittelsbach, and Wettin, to imperial counts such as Hohenlohe, Castell, Erbach, Stolberg, and Nassau. And the dynasty—the "house"—was frequently a basis for women's participation in rulership. However, rulership could only be based on the woman's own rights if, as a daughter-heir, she brought together property and dominion rights in her own person.

Such cases were repeatedly used to legitimate rulership changes and personal unions in the territories of the Holy Roman Empire. Among the women presented here, this is exemplified by Anna of Brandenburg, who as the heiress of the Duchy of Jülich-Cleves-Berg and the holder of claims to the Duchy of Prussia brought substantial territories into the possession of the House of Hohenzollern. Brandenburg-Prussia's ascendance as a major European power would hardly have been imaginable without this inheritance. De jure, daughter-heirs like Anna of Brandenburg were supposed to transfer the exercise of power to their husband or son. But in her case we see that she was very actively engaged in securing and managing her inheritance. And this applied all the more so to Empress Maria Theresa, surely the early modern empire's most renowned daughter-heir, who is also covered in this volume. Contrary to the plans of her father, Emperor Charles VI, as the heiress of the vast territories of the House of Habsburg, she insisted after his death on exercising rule in these lands herself. As heiress, she was the queen of Hungary and Bohemia, the archduchess of Austria, the duchess of Styria, and the countess of Tirol, etc.; in contrast, as empress she was "only" the spouse of the elected emperor, Francis I.

Although daughter-heirs repeatedly existed in various larger and smaller territories of the empire, there were two other constellations in which princely women far more frequently participated in the practical exercise of power. On the one hand, there was a considerable number of custodial regents[21] who exercised rule as proxies, so to speak, for their underage sons or grandsons. Usually they were supported, but sometimes also hampered, by male co-guardians who sought to shunt them aside because of their lower status as women. Examples among the women discussed here are Elisabeth of Brunswick-Calenberg and Erdmuthe Benigna of Reuß, who both had to take responsibility for their dynasty and look after the territory because of a dynastic crisis triggered by the prince's early death.

Maria of Inner Austria, on the other hand, whom her husband also intended as the guardian of their children, was denied the right of regency by the men of the House of Habsburg. Then in 1711, however, when Charles VI became the sole male Habsburg, it was his mother, the Empress Dowager Eleonora Magdalena, who as regent represented her absent son for three-quarters of a year in the Habsburg hereditary lands. Legitimized by the will of the actual—the male—holder of power, such regencies were quite common for shorter or longer periods when the prince was absent or ill. The regency of Maria of Hungary also corresponded to this model—Emperor Charles V, her brother, who simultaneously was the Duke of Burgundy, appointed her as his deputy in the Netherlands for the period of his absence.

The other and probably most widespread form of women's participation in governance resulted from the joint collaboration of the princely or aristocratic working couple.[22] The aristocratic lady conveyed the decisions of her husband to the administrators of estates, or she supervised their management when her spouse was travelling or absent because of military service or official duties. The dynastic women could function as a regent, or as the addressee of supplications from subjects who asked her for assistance in all kinds of matters, or as an intercessor who encouraged her husband or male relatives to make decisions benefiting her petitioners. In her office as princess, however, she was also obliged to assist the poor and needy and to support the clergy. Various facets of this involvement in governance by women are found in the biographies of Elisabeth of Brunswick-Calenberg, Anna of Saxony, Maria of Inner Austria, Anna of Brandenburg, and Polyxena of Lobkowicz.

However, the empire was not held together merely by its constitution and governance. It was also characterised by numerous lines of communication on various levels, such as the correspondence between office holders and members of the aforementioned dynasties, as well as news media such as newspapers, journals, and pamphlets. These too have been intensively researched recently. It was a market for books that coalesced around the major trade fairs in Frankfurt am Main and Leipzig and the publishing centres of Nuremberg, Augsburg, and Strasbourg, a territory criss-crossed by numerous postal routes, and a scholarly discursive space for subjects such as imperial constitutional law.[23]

Historians have long studied the economic ties between the individual territories, between the many commercially developed regions, and between the trading cities of the empire. And when describing the Holy Roman Empire, one must also take broadly defined cultural contexts into account: contacts and exchanges between universities and scholars, between literati and readers, between court capitals and the itineraries and spheres of activity of painters, sculptors, and musicians, the connections between religious communities such as the Moravians and other Pietist groups. The list goes on and on.

Thus if one considers that the empire was more than the sum of its institutions, then women of various estates definitely had opportunities for action. They had the legal capacity to act, and they could participate both in communication networks and in economic and cultural developments. Admittedly, to date these fields of activity have been even less frequently related to the empire,[24] which is why most accounts of the empire's history have largely been written without women.

Twenty-five women

This book was written to make the importance of women in the history of the Holy Roman Empire visible for an interested readership. It is supposed to direct the gaze to the role women played in widely diverse fields in the political, cultural, and economic development of the empire as one of the oldest and largest political structures of early modern Europe.

Naturally, as individual people none of the women whose biographies are concisely presented in this book could really have changed Holy Roman Empire or influenced its development. But each one of them was selected to exemplify the opportunities for action sketched out in the first two sections above that were available to women.[25] This is also the reason why most of the biographies foreground a specific aspect of the life of the described woman, a particular field of action. This was the only way to bring together such a broad spectrum, such a large number of biographies, into a single volume. Even if we sometimes have very little material with which to reconstruct a woman's life path, often it is nonetheless still too much for the space that one book can offer for 25 women.

However, the women described here were chosen not just with an eye to the aforementioned opportunities for action but also with the goal of depicting the empire's diversity. The selection criteria therefore also considered the women's regional origin and main place of residence, and the inclusion of various confessions and different languages. Finally, the scope of available scholarship that could serve as a basis for the accounts of the individual persons also played a role, since biographies cannot be written without material.

The conditions governing the lives and actions of women in the Holy Roman Empire changed over the three centuries that we now refer to as the "early modern period", as did the empire itself—with regard to its borders, its economic interrelationships, and its cultural characteristics. The diversity of these changes cannot be comprehensively covered here; it is not without reason that the most recent books focusing on the history of the empire between 1500 and 1800 run to many hundreds of pages. Even so, from my perspective it seems necessary at the start to address the central aspects of the changes that can be identified for the Holy Roman Empire. Each of following seven sections are dedicated to one of these aspects, and at the same time they outline how the lives of the 25 selected women were tied to these changes. This hopefully will make it easier for readers to link the individual life descriptions with general trends and epochal events.

Rulership in the empire

Some of these changes pertained to the imperial constitution, the structures of the Holy Roman Empire itself. Until 1806, the Holy Roman Empire as a political entity[26] incorporated extensive parts of Central Europe and—albeit more loosely as "Imperial Italy"— Northern Italy. It constituted an association of many individual territories under the dominion of secular or ecclesiastic representatives, which met as so-called imperial estates at the imperial diets and had to pay taxes to the empire. Certain areas, such as the Netherlands or the Swiss cantons, that still belonged to the empire around 1500 would leave the association before 1806. And Alsace had to be ceded to France at the end of the seventeenth century as the result of military conflicts.

The head of empire was the emperor, who during the early modern period was almost always a member of the Habsburg dynasty. He was elected by the seven (later nine) electors and, until into the sixteenth century, crowned by the pope, but then as of 1531 was crowned by the elector of Mainz, the highest-ranking ecclesiastical imperial prince. Thus, the emperor did not receive his position and rights—at least in a legal sense—through dynastic succession, as was the case for the major European monarchies, but rather on the basis of the electors' decision. This was reflected, for example, in the oft-used set phrase, "emperor and empire".

During the seventeenth century, many princes as imperial estates increasingly strove for greater independence, but without wanting to leave the association of the empire. The Peace of Westphalia in 1648 fixed numerous sovereign rights for these princes, which over the long term strengthened their position vis-à-vis the emperor. Also important was the transition from an imperial diet that met at the emperor's invitation to the so-called Everlasting Diet, where from 1663 to 1806 the representatives of the imperial estates permanently negotiated the many different aspects of imperial politics and legislation.

Finally, the eighteenth century witnessed a significant decline in the capacity of imperial institutions to act, which was related not least to the competition between two powers within the empire. The empire's two politically and militarily strongest dynasties and their dominions—the Habsburgs with their hereditary lands (combined with Bohemia and Hungary) and the Hohenzollerns with Brandenburg-Prussia—increasingly oriented themselves politically according to European power constellations and less to the rules and borders of the empire. As of the mid-eighteenth century, this competition, which had already manifested itself in the War of the Austrian Succession between 1740 and 1748, intensified more and more into a conflict that gradually hobbled the work of the imperial institutions.

In a certain sense, the noticeable growth of the imperial princes' decision-making power during the course of the early modern period also benefited women of the princely estate because of their participation in the dynastic rights of dominion. However, this hardly applied to the few women who ruled in their own right over (usually very small) territories because they were the abbess of an imperial abbey.[27] There were around a dozen such imperial foundations, including Quedlinburg, Essen, Lower and Upper Münster in Regensburg, and Thorn.[28] By being elected to this office, the abbess as an ecclesiastical ruler became an imperial estate and was even entitled to representation in the Imperial College of Princes. However, in the early modern period most of these women came from imperial-estate families and hence were members of the ruling estate even before being elected. Among the exceptions is a case we look at here, namely, that of Countess Aurora von Königsmarck, who around 1700 sought election as the abbess of Quedlinburg.

Wars and crises

Power shifts between the ecclesiastical and seculars rulers of the empire, as well as the involvement of the imperial princes and the emperor in European politics, turned the Holy Roman Empire into a theatre of numerous military conflicts during the early modern period.[29] At the same time, to a greater and lesser degree, these conflicts were times of economic and social crisis, for war inevitably entailed not only destruction but also the payment of imposts, the disruption of trade networks, and the loss of harvests because of the passage of troops, which was furthermore often combined with the spread of epidemics such as pestilence, dysentery, and smallpox.

The Thirty Years' War, in particular, impacted large parts of the empire, where various European powers fought out hegemonic struggles and conflicts between 1618 and 1648. The western part of the empire was repeatedly afflicted by conflicts between France and the emperor and empire between 1672 and 1714. Between 1756 and 1763, the major powers France, Great Britain, Prussia, Habsburg, Russia, and Spain fought for European hegemony in the Seven Years' War. Primarily affected were large areas along the Rhine and in Saxony, Silesia, and Bohemia, even though the war also led to conflict in North America, the Caribbean, and India. Finally, the period between 1794 and 1815 was characterised by many different military conflicts between Napoleonic France and its allies, on the one hand, and Prussia, the Habsburgs, and Russia on the other, which to a large degree were fought on the empire's territories and contributed to its collapse in 1806. In contrast, the military conflicts with the Ottomans lasting from the fifteenth to the first half of the eighteenth century only directly affected regions in the south-eastern part of the empire, especially in the Habsburg hereditary lands. Other regions had to participate in the defensive war by raising troops, which led to financial burdens for the populations and to troop levies.

Several biographies gathered here show how war impacted the lives of women and how they reacted to the associated challenges. As the governor of the Netherlands, Maria of Hungary not only had to personally contend with conflicts with Denmark and concerning the Duchy of Guelders. Her brother Charles V also demanded income from the Netherlands to finance his wars against France and in North Africa. Maria of Inner Austria and Catharina Regina of Greiffenberg found themselves threatened by the Ottoman campaigns of conquest against Hungary and the Habsburg hereditary lands. While heavily pregnant in 1683, the Empress Eleonora Magdalena had to flee Vienna before the advancing

Ottoman troops. As abbess, Maria Magdalena Haidenbucher was responsible for the safety of her convent and its residents during the entire Thirty Years' War. Prussia's war against Austria in 1740 thwarted the desire of Dorothea Erxleben to study medicine together with her brother. Immediately upon ascending to power in 1740, Empress Maria Theresa became a decisive political actor, first in the War of the Austrian Succession and later in the Seven Years' War. The Leipzig author and translator Luise Gottsched, on the other hand, suffered deeply as a result of Prussia's invasion of Saxony, which began the Seven Years' War, and the battles that followed, which she had to watch from the side-lines. And Henriette Herz, the Berlin salonnière, was just one of many women who worked as assistants in military hospitals in 1813 in the war against the Napoleonic troops.

Reformation and confession

Military conflicts in the Holy Roman Empire from the sixteenth century down to the Thirty Years' War, especially small-scale struggles such as the Schmalkaldic War of 1546/47, were characterised by an amalgamation of political and confessional strife. This brings us to the Reformation, a fundamental process of ecclesiastical restructuring that split the Christian Church of Western and Central Europe into several confessions. The year 1517, with the publication of Luther's theses on indulgences, serves in this respect as the starting point, even though people had repeatedly contemplated church reform prior to this event. The Peace of Augsburg in 1555 then codified the new confessional situation in the empire for the time being.

It has long been known that women of various social classes played an important part in the church reform movements, above all during the early stages, for they were often among the first supporters and propagandists. Katharina Zell, for example, played such a role in Strasbourg during the Reformation[30] as one of the few women of the reformation movement who also published texts and even preached in public. But her need to defend herself against hostility throughout her life, and especially after the death of her husband, the Strasbourg reformer Matthäus Zell, shows that, when it came to theological knowledge and involvement in reform, the position with respect to women adopted by the new church was no less restrictive than that of the old.

However, the valorisation of married life, as promoted by Martin Luther and modelled by his own marriage, resulted in a new role for women in the church, which Katharina Zell, for her part, both shaped and propagated, namely, that of the Protestant pastor's wife. In supporting her husband and as part of the working couple in the parsonage, she took on responsibilities pertaining to the social care of congregation members. As late as the eighteenth century, this influential model helped allow the pastor's wife Dorothea Erxleben to practice as a doctor for years—precisely because she thereby expanded the responsibilities of care that were ascribed to her anyway as a pastor's wife.

Through engagement with the Bible, which was now available in German, as well as the reading of reformist pamphlets and spiritual writings, the Reformation in conjunction with the rapid expansion of printing facilitated access to theological knowledge. This at least applied to women who could read, which limited this circle mostly to aristocratic and bourgeois elites. At the same time, however, in Protestant territories the Reformation destroyed the traditional space for the female acquisition of knowledge, namely, the monastery. It threw the spiritual value of convent life fundamentally into doubt, and monasteries were progressively dissolved. Many ecclesiastical women reacted to this enthusiastically and left the convent, where often enough they had been brought by their families simply so they could be looked after. The example of Caritas Pirckheimer and her fellow nuns in Nuremberg, however, shows that there were also women who defended their spiritual life plan with its opportunity to acquire theological, philosophical, historical, and even medical knowledge.

In reaction to the emergence of new confessions—Lutheran and Calvinist—the papal church too underwent a far-reaching process of reform, the Counter-Reformation initiated by the Council of Trent, which concluded in 1563. The Counter-Reformation and catholic reform of the late sixteenth and first half of the seventeenth centuries precipitated many changes within the Catholic Church. Notable in this respect is not only the foundation of numerous new women's orders such as the English Ladies and Ursulines. At the same time, more and more restrictions were imposed on religious women. Under the auspices of the residency requirement and the supervision of female morality, religious women were ordered into strict seclusion, the likes of which was rare prior to the Reformation. As a result, they were also more isolated from intellectual influences, which no doubt further intensified the decline in importance of monasteries as a space where women could acquire knowledge, a decline that had already been set in motion by the dissolution of monasteries in Protestant areas. How this process of seclusion was advance by ecclesiastical and secular authorities and the problems this entailed for the agency of the abbess is shown by the example of Magdalena Haidenbucher, who served as the abbess of the Frauenchiemsee Benedictine monastery.

The transition from the early Reformation movement to the Reformation as the institutionalisation of the new church in the second half of the 1520s included the involvement of the rulers: princes and city councils now became a driving force and claimed the right to decide on the introduction or rejection of the new confession. In towns, women were still excluded from participating in this decision within the institutional context because they could not be members of city councils. But for some princely women, this transition resulted in manoeuvring room.[31] This is illustrated quite clearly by the example of Duchess Elisabeth of Brunswick-Calenberg. She converted to Lutheranism even while her husband was alive, and as the guardian of her son she ensured that the Reformation prevailed in the duchy.

Other princely women could not act so independently, but they occupied themselves with theological writings, backed up their husbands in confessional conflicts, and served as patrons for clergy. This obtained for Anna of Saxony, for example, who diligently supported the Lutheran faith in the conflict between the Lutherans and Calvinists that culminated after 1570. A few decades later, Electress Anna of Brandenburg did the same, thereby deliberately entering into a confrontation with her husband and son, who had adopted the Calvinist faith.

Analogous processes naturally occurred on the side of the Counter-Reformation: Archduchess Maria of Inner Austria supported her husband and later her son in their efforts to repress the Lutheran faith in their dominions in the southern part of the empire. To do so, she not only overtly displayed her Catholic piety in the largely Lutheran capital of Graz by participating in processions and pilgrimages. She also had a formative influence on her children and therefore ultimately on the Catholic piety of the House of Habsburg. And in situations of confessional conflict like those in Bohemia during the first half of the seventeenth century, women like Polyxena of Lobkowicz could likewise develop influence, namely, as benefactors of monasteries and donors of relics, and also as landowners who pressured their subjects to return to the Catholic faith.

This occurred against the background of an intensification of confessional differences in the empire as of the 1580s. Confessional differences that had already led to military conflicts and uprisings in the first half of the sixteenth century consequently became one of the causes of the Thirty Years' War, even though the latter should by no means be described as a war of religion. When it came to an end in 1648, the major confessions—Catholic and Protestant—largely had an equal status, which was contractually fixed in a multitude of regulations. While this did not eliminate conflict, it facilitated the peaceful co-existence of the confessions in the Holy Roman Empire.

All of the confessions, but especially the newly emerging Protestant ones, continued to evolve throughout the early modern period. Catharina Regina von Greiffenberg, for example, was a proponent of a Lutheranism influenced by mysticism. In the second half of the seventeenth century, this gave rise to religious revival movements, such as the small group of Labadists, which included Maria Sibylla Merian along with many other women. Maria Margaretha Kirch, who worked as an astronomer, was at the same time an early supporter of Pietism,[32] a movement that took shape in the empire in the 1670s to 1690s. Thus, without knowing each other, Merian and Kirch also shared a religious approach in their scientific studies, for in their observations of nature they both always searched for God's presence in nature at the same time. And like so many supporters of religious reform movements, they both accepted that they had to leave their home communities for the sake of their convictions. Merian moved from Frankfurt am Main to the Netherlands with her family; Kirch had to leave Electoral Saxony with her husband because the Lutheran clergy did not want to endlessly put up with the Pietists, who sometimes were critical of the established church.

Standing in here for many women who managed to achieve public visibility in Pietistic groups[33] is above all Erdmuthe Benigna of Reuß, who had already been deeply influenced by Pietist ideas in her youth. As a guardian regent of the small principality of Reuß-Ebersdorf in Thuringia, she was able to implement some of her reform ideas directly, and through her children she had a lasting effect on the development of the religious movement of the Moravian Church.

For the Catholic world, Amalie Gallitzin can serve as an example of the re-emergence of piety and confessional bonds after the secularising tendencies of the Enlightenment period. And Henriette Herz, who achieved great influence as a Jewish salonnière in Berlin in the late eighteenth century, converted to Lutheranism in 1817 and therefore illustrates the influence of a "new" emotionally charged, romantic piety at the end of the Enlightenment in a different way.

Educational movements: humanism and the Enlightenment

In its early stage, the Reformation in the Holy Roman Empire was linked in part to the Renaissance, the first of two cultural renewal movements in the early modern period that were of general societal importance. The Renaissance was a European phenomenon, which reached the territory of the Holy Roman Empire at the end of the fifteenth century. At first primarily associated with humanism, it was focused on the recovery of ancient knowledge and skills, starting with literature and the visual arts.[34] Only since the nineteenth century has the term also been used to designate an epoch that saw the emergence of a culture that, based on the reception of antiquity, propagated a new image of humanity of earthly perfection, combined with specific political, social, and economic circumstances and conditions.

In Italy a relatively large number of women took part in this development as patrons, writers, or painters, but far less so in the empire. It is no coincidence that women with humanist interests are represented in this book particularly by Caritas Pirckheimer, a highly educated nun from Nuremberg's upper class, and Queen Maria of Hungary. The men and women able to pursue their interests in ancient literature and art came almost exclusively from the educated and affluent upper classes. This already followed from the fact that knowledge of Latin and Greek was virtually indispensable for humanistic readings and correspondence. And women had great difficulty achieving these skills because their sex prevented them from gaining access to institutions of higher learning. The new conception of humanity did not change gender roles. But even so, humanism spread the idea that women could develop and cultivate an interest in scholarship and literature even outside of monastic seclusion.

The most influential educational movement of the eighteenth century was the Enlightenment, which began sweeping through the empire in the late seventeenth century. The first verifiable use of the German term "Aufklärung" occurred in 1691—and by 1760 it had already become a buzzword that subsumed all progressive ideas and ambitions. The movement's goal was to critically analyse authorities, traditions, and hierarchies against the background of a newly defined reason, and to abolish them if they contradicted its laws. The entire lifeworld was supposed to be reorganised according to these laws. In the empire, the movement ultimately affected almost every aspect of life, but without having determined all of the century's ideas and developments. One reason for its relatively large practical relevance in the territories of the empire is that, in contrast to Western European countries, Enlightenment proponents extensively cooperated with the authorities and the latter demonstrated an openness to numerous changes, but without this redefining the principles of government, for example.[35]

Like everywhere else, in the empire the Enlightenment was primarily a movement of the educated elite and thus of academically educated men, who pursued the goal of an "improvement of reason" for wide groups, although by no means in the same way for all people. For women, the gradual expansion of the Enlightenment meant the growing importance of literary education (which, however, was still almost impossible for them to receive at schools of higher learning) as well as the strengthened legitimacy of literary and artistic production. As illustrated here by the examples of Amalie Gallitzin and Henriette Herz, aristocratic and bourgeois women played a significant role in Enlightenment associations like salons and reading societies, but not so much in Masonic lodges and so-called economic societies.

Women with scientific interests were by no means entirely new in the eighteenth century, nor were female artists, writers, and musicians. Their presence in the sixteenth century is demonstrated, for example, by Anna of Saxony with her pronounced medicinal and alchemical interests[36] and by Caritas Pirckheimer, a humanist thinker and historian of her monastery. Examples from the seventeenth century include the poet Catharina Regina von Greiffenberg, the painter and naturalist Maria Sibylla Merian, and the calendar maker Maria Margaretha Kirch, as well as the accomplished author Countess Königsmarck. Various princely and aristocratic women were active as composers, whose educational canon included music.[37]

But not until the eighteenth century was there a noticeable increase in the number of women active in the arts and sciences and who claimed their place as educated women or artists.[38] This sharply distinguished the Holy Roman Empire from Italy, where women appeared particularly as musicians and painters as early as the late sixteenth century, and from Great Britain and France, where commercially successful female authors already existed in the second half of the seventeenth century. Dorothea Erxleben, Anna Dorothea Therbusch, Sophie von La Roche, and Maria Theresia Paradis are presented here as examples of women who were influenced by and promoted the Enlightenment and at the same time used the opportunities that, in certain constellations, arose for women as a result of Enlightenment educational aspirations.

However, all of these cases reveal how greatly the scientific and artistic work of women—especially if it was meant to be long-term and received public recognition—still depended on the support of men. As the examples show, an unmarried status was by no means a prerequisite for scientific or literary activity. Rather, the combination of marriage, family, and scientific or literary work was almost taken for granted; in fact, it often was an important legitimating element for female work in this area. This was not least because men played an important role as teachers and supporters in conveying theoretical and practical knowledge, for this was the only way women could gain a "higher" education, for example, through home learning as in the cases of Kirch, Gottsched, and Erxleben. And the collaboration with men—especially with one's husband, as was the case for Maria Magdalena Kirch and Luise Adelgunde Gottsched—gave scientific and sometimes also literary work a legitimate basis.

In this respect, the gradual development of "modern" science also tended to have negative implications for the involvement of women[39] because of its detachment from familial (as evident with Merian and Kirch) and representative contexts. The growing integration of science into the university system and the combining of empiricism and theory excluded women because they had no access to universities until the late nineteenth century and only rarely received a formal education in the natural sciences. With respect to research in the natural sciences, as of the late eighteenth century women tended to appear more as audience members (for example, at scientific lectures in salons) than as researchers.

The Enlightenment ideal of a society of equal and free persons pertained first and foremost to men, and, as indicated, primarily to those of the bourgeois and aristocratic elite. Another factor is that the Enlightenment also brought about the "scientification" of traditional gender roles.[40] Consequently such roles were ascribed much more strongly to the biological characteristics of two sexes, whereby the "nature" of women was understood as passionate, devoted, and focused on motherhood. This gradually rendered older, estate-specific distinctions obsolete. Women remained women, regardless of whether they were day labourers or electresses.

Upon initial reflection, this sounds like a model of equality, but such an articulation of gendered characters offered welcome points of attack for reducing women's scope of activity by ignoring their integration into the estate system precisely because all women were equally determined by the "nature" of their sex. Women were supposed to be defined through the man, and they were increasingly consigned to the inside of the house, while men had to contend with the outside—and therefore also the political—world. Hence, the end of the eighteenth century witnessed the gradual development of an understanding of privacy that had not existed in the past—a female privacy in the house that was set off against the public of politically active men. Starting in the late eighteenth century, with their reduction to the house as a private space, women "vanished" more and more from political, public space. Thus the consequence of the Enlightenment's moral revaluation of women was their political and social relegation.

So the answer to Joan Kelly-Gadol's famous question, "Did Women have a Renaissance?"—which Ruth Dawson similarly posed with regard to the Enlightenment[41]—is ambivalent for the Holy Roman Empire as well. Women doubtless played a part in these large movements, but under no circumstances could they shape them to the same degree as men. At best, the positive consequences and negative effects balanced themselves out.

However, here one must again recall the difference in opportunities for action based on one's estate. As patrons or book collectors, princely and high-ranking aristocratic women could support the art and science of the Renaissance. Through conversions, or by supporting clergy or religious orders, they could send a signal or even clear a path for the Reformation. Bourgeois women, as supporters of the Reformation and especially of movements such as Pietism, could play an important role in its dissemination and impact. A farm woman or day labourer, on the other hand, might have experienced the Reformation as an individual experience of faith—and a convent sister of the sixteenth century as an existential threat.

Enlightenment men definitely made it possible for women to acquire education, and women knew quite well how to exploit the opportunities for development that arose from the fundamental moral principles of reason and equality. There was a significant growth in number of female painters, authors, actors, and singers in the empire who were acknowledged by a public interested in literature and the arts. And in the last third of the eighteenth century, there was a brief window of time during which alternative life plans for women became apparent, not only because of the effects of the Enlightenment but also because of historical events such as the American and French Revolutions.[42] This moment is represented here by Amalie Gallitzin, Dorothea Therbusch, and Maria Theresia Paradis, who shaped their lives separately from their husbands or in independent cohabitation.

It is also represented by Henriette Herz, who, influenced by the Jewish Enlightenment—the Haskalah[43]—created fields of action for herself as a salonnière and teacher that had largely remained closed to earlier generations of Jewish women. The goal of the Haskalah was to achieve legal and social ameliorations for people of the Jewish faith, and, through the acquisition of education, to mediate effectively between Jewish and Christian elites. Henriette Herz represented many of the aspects this implied. And yet for a long time she was denied the scope of action enjoyed by bourgeois women of the Christian faith. Her life path clearly shows that equal rights for various religious faiths in the empire was not yet part of the Enlightenment programme. To be sure, confessional conflict subsided during the course of the Enlightenment, at least among the empire's elite. But freedom of worship remained restricted to Christian confessions. It excluded Jews as well as Muslims, who are repeatedly encountered, for example, as merchants, slaves, or refugees.

Networks

Even beyond such pan-European developments like the Reformation and Enlightenment, the territories of the Holy Roman Empire were integrated into transregional and intercontinental processes of exchange and communication. These had many different levels and cannot be described in detail here. However, emerging from the biographies of this volume are a few elements where one can identify the inclusion of women in such networks.

One, for example, is travel. Migration in the spatial sense was important both for the social networking of individual persons and for that between the territories of the empire, and it was far more widespread and extensive than one had long assumed. This also applied to women. Labour migration, which was probably the most important kind, shows up in our examples only in a few distinct forms: the merchant Glikl bas Judah Leib travelled to exhibitions and distant trading cities to conduct her business. The painter Therbusch and musician Paradis travelled widely to publicise their prowess and gain contracts. This similarly applied to the travels of Luise Gottsched, which she undertook as her husband's escort, for example, to Vienna. And even the longest journey taken by the women described here, namely, Maria Sibylla Merian's trip to Suriname, was strictly speaking taken for professional purposes—that is, for the acquisition of animals and plants as trade goods and to continue her scientific studies as an insect researcher.

Women of aristocratic and even more so those of princely origins travelled relatively often in connection with their marriages, which then marked a permanent change in their main place of residence. But this did not mean that they could not later return to the place of their childhood. Rather, there was a brisk flow of travel between larger and smaller capitals for the purpose of neighbourly relations, maintaining connections within the princely house, and for sightseeing and hunting.[44] Until the mid-seventeenth century, princely women also repeatedly travelled to Frankfurt am Main, Augsburg, or Regensburg for imperial and princely diets, as in the case of Anna of Saxony as her husband's escort, or Maria of Hungary, who met her brothers Charles V and Ferdinand several times on such occasions.

For a long time princely women—and even more so, unmarried aristocratic women—travelled almost exclusively accompanied by their husband or father. Travelling on one's own—naturally with a socially appropriate retinue—only began to occur more frequently in the second half of the seventeenth century. And not until the second half of eighteenth and in the early nineteenth century could women of the social elite participate in the educational tourism typical of the Enlightenment period. This is exemplified not only by Sophie von La Roche and Amalie Gallitzin, but also by Henriette Herz with her journey to Italy.

Of course, such travels often combined several aspects: Maria Aurora von Königsmarck travelled to Wolfenbüttel, Hanover, and Dresden not only to participate in courtly life but also to deal with family matters. Maria Theresia Paradis travelled to France, England, and the empire to perform as a musician, but she also wanted to get to know other musicians and potential patrons. She also visited people she already knew through correspondence or whose own artistic work had impressed her, like that of Sophie von La Roche. Princess Gallitzin received numerous male and female visitors in Münster, including renowned theologians and scientists, as well as authors such as Johann Wolfgang von Goethe, whom she in turn visited in Weimar. All told, it is apparent that the interconnections between women active in literature and art and their male colleagues increased during the eighteenth century. The Enlightenment's culture of correspondence and travel clearly included women and made this possible.

But social networking, representation, and amusement were not the only reasons for travel. Itinerancy could also be forced upon people by external circumstances. This included fleeing from the events of war or from epidemics, as well as emigration for religious reasons, which at times was especially pronounced. During the uprising of the Protestant estates in 1618, Polyxena of Lobkowicz had to leave Prague and Bohemia because she was a proponent of the emperor and the Catholic cause. In 1663, Catharina Regina von Greiffenberg fled with her mother from Lower Austria to Nuremberg because of an advancing Ottoman army. Years later, she definitively immigrated to the imperial city because, as a Protestant, she was subject to numerous restrictions in Catholic Lower Austria.

Correspondence constituted a further networking element that extended beyond the empire's territories. Although women's letter exchanges have often barely survived, this does not alter the fact that they were often conducted for decades. Their content was varied and can hardly be generalised—economic issues could be just as central as religious or political questions, or the exchange of ideas about literature and painting or illness and health. Letters were often accompanied by an exchange of gifts to strengthen the bonds and commitments between the corresponding parties, men and women alike.

Gifts and letters were a means to maintain connections particularly when family members lived in distant regions. Maria of Hungary wrote and received a multitude of letters, through which she remained in contact with her royal siblings, who were under way between Vienna and Lisbon, Brussels, and Tunis. Polyxena of Lobkowicz corresponded for decades with her sisters, whose marriages had brought them to Spain and Italy. Hence the correspondence of women was also a medium of cultural contact on a European scale. This is illustrated above all by the example of Princess Lobkowicz, who functioned as a mediator between Spain and Bohemia throughout her life. But it is also shown by women such as Luise Gottsched and Henriette Herz, who translated French and, respectively, English literature, thereby making it accessible to larger readerships in the Holy Roman Empire.

Economic developments

It was therefore nothing unusual for women of the early modern empire to be integrated into communication processes—by letter, literarily, verbally. Opportunities for this were also more likely to arise if they chose to live in cities, like most of the women dealt with here.[45] The large towns in which they lived—imperial cities, trade fair centres, and ports—were nodes for processes of cultural change, communications, and transfers. Networks and transfers were in this respect often linked to the economic developments of the early modern period, which influenced the living and working environment of men and women.

The sixteenth century[46] was characterised by the extension of European trade networks, an expansion of markets, as well as new types of organisations (such as trading companies), which in conjunction with European discoveries and conquests conducted an increasingly intercontinental trade. The territories of the empire tended to be rather indirectly involved, for the princes of the empire hardly figured in the global campaigns of conquest.

The empire's merchants usually relied on Spanish, Italian, and Dutch harbours and traders as middlemen.

Previously the large towns in the northern part of the empire had played a central role in the Hanseatic League, which had facilitated important connections in the Baltic and North Sea region in the Late Middle Ages. But these connections gradually lost their significance, especially in the eighteenth century. The same was true for the key positions still held by cities like Augsburg and Nuremberg in the sixteenth century for Europe's north–south trade with Italy and the Mediterranean. In the eighteenth century, it was cities like Hamburg (through its connections with England and the Netherlands and to trans-Atlantic trade) and the trade fair cities of Frankfurt am Main and Leipzig that played a major role in the empire's internal trading network and in its integration into transregional and transcontinental exchange processes.[47]

Associated with the expansion and change of trading ties was a stronger connection between trade and commercial production. The significance of skilled crafts and trades, which were organised in guilds, evolved even as they remained vitally important for supplying towns and rural regions with quotidian consumer goods. But mass products such as linen or cotton textiles, as well as luxury goods such as mirrors, silk, sugar, porcelain, and the like were increasingly produced outside the guilds and for very distant markets. This occurred in part in so-called manufactories, large-scale commercial facilities that either centralised certain stages of production or entire manufacturing processes or where entire manufacturing processes were carried out by different persons in separate work stages. This developmental phase of commercial production is also called "proto-industrialisation" because it exhibits the first signs of the later emergence of modern industries.

In these cases, the economic involvement of women is much more difficult to follow than that of men, and only recently have historians given it more attention.[48] It has been possible here to shine a light on various dimensions of early modern economic activity by way of a few examples: Electress Anna of Saxony nicely exemplifies the economic involvement of many aristocratic and princely women. Their role in the management of large aristocratic properties and thus for agriculture—the "oeconomie" per se according to the understanding of the sixteenth and seventeenth century—has still not been well illuminated. But for the electress, it can be shown that she was actively involved in the improvement of livestock breeding and the sale of products from the estates. This income was a major part of the princely finances. And in seventeenth-century Bohemia, Polyxena of Lobkowicz not only knew how to manage her own estate but was also substantially involved in the successful expansion of the family's properties.

Glikl bas Judah Leib, a Jewish trader and putting-out merchant of the seventeenth century, stands here as a representative of merchants' wives who, as part of a working couple or as a widow, participated in organising the business. After her husband's death, Glikl was able to further advance the enterprise during difficult times while simultaneously supporting the businesses of her sons and sons-in-law. Anna Barbara Gignoux, a craftsman's daughter from Augsburg, similarly took over the cotton printing works of her husband, who had previously inducted her in the production techniques. Her conflicts with her second husband over her right to have a say in the enterprise illustrate the problems many women no doubt had to struggle with in their economic activities. The fact that Gignoux ultimately prevailed and managed to operate the manufactory for decades indicates both legal and entrepreneurial manoeuvring room and capabilities.

Much larger than the number of successful female merchants and entrepreneurs was admittedly the number of women from the lower classes who were offered work in the towns and countrysides of predominantly commercial regions. Beyond the confines of the guild system, women—married and unmarried—were an important labour force in the production of textiles and many other sectors, where they also appeared as intermediaries. As a result, the expansion of commercial production to the countryside entailed the development of new livelihoods less dependent on marital status. In certain regions—such as the Ore Mountains and in parts of Bohemia, Silesia, and Swabia—there were many single women, including those with illegitimate children.

To be sure, their existence remained economically fragile because of their insecure income, but new life plans became conceivable. At the same time, commercial activity and the income it provided could also create a basis to overcome the restrictions on marriage that prevailed in various parts of the empire for men and women from the lower classes.

Unfortunately, the book provides no individual examples of precisely these innumerable women and girls who in agricultural enterprises, as textile workers, day labourers, traders, etc. maintained an economic life together with their husbands, fathers, brothers, daughters, and sisters. There are no examples of newspaper readers, book dealers, and all of the women who in conversations took part in the political and intellectual debates of their respective times, nor of the women who took sides during peasant rebellions (such as the Peasants' War of 1524–1526) or urban uprisings (dozens of which occurred in the early modern period, especially from the late sixteenth to the seventeenth century and in the late eighteenth century), backing up their husbands or even taking the initiative themselves.[49]

Forgetting

Common to them all is a problem that is difficult for a biographically oriented work to overcome: their life stories are difficult to reconstruct and inevitably require painstaking archival work. In most cases, their stories must remain very fragmentary because women rarely appeared in the sources as individuals and because material has been lost. This especially limits the reconstructability of biographies of women from the middle and lower social classes and renders the kaleidoscope on offer here incomplete.

However, the "forgetting" of women in accounts of the history of the Holy Roman Empire and its territories and the early modern period as a whole is by no means merely the result of inadequate sources. Instead, it also characteristically applies to many of the women presented here. Only a few of them, such as Maria of Hungary and above all Empress Maria Theresa, have consistently figured in the history of the empire as written by men. Others, like Amalie Gallitzin, Henriette Herz, and Luise Adelgunde Gottsched, at least found their way into nineteenth-century historical portrayals in passing. They were often included because they left behind written work or had biographical aspects that could be used by historians to outline a pre-history of the bourgeois era, which in the German-language historiography was elaborated above all in the second half of the nineteenth century. In the process, many of these women were reframed: Amalie Gallitzin became a figurehead of the new Catholicism, Anna of Saxony appeared in accounts written in the nineteenth and early twentieth centuries as the ideal of a bourgeois housewife, and Aurora von Königsmarck symbolised the licentiousness of court society. Because of insisting on her inheritance, Anna of Prussia was transformed from a responsible duchess to a narrow-minded denier of reality, while Maria of Inner Austria became a Catholic fundamentalist.

But there are at least as many cases where not even the names of the women described here were remembered prior to mid-twentieth century. This applies, for example, to Katharina Zell, Polyxena of Lobkowicz, Empress Eleonora Magdalena, and Anna Dorothea Therbusch. Such names and histories have only come to light again because of the interest in women's history that has emerged since the 1970s. Since then, we have come to know about so many women that, along with the persons selected here, many others could have been presented as examples of active regents, successful authors, early scientists, or advocates of religious reform. Thus, certain prominent examples might be absent, such as Martin Luther's wife Katharina von Bora, Landgravine Amalie Elisabeth of Hessen-Kassel, or Anna Maria van Schurmann, as well as Duchess Luise Dorothea of Saxe-Gotha, Johanna Eleonora Petersen, the singer Gertrud Elisabeth Mara, the composer Josepha Barbara Auernhammer, the theatre director Friederike Caroline Neuber, the author Anna Louisa Karsch, Dorothea Schlegel, and others. This notwithstanding, our collection should make it possible to take a fresh look at the Holy Roman Empire as a region and a highly complex political entity whose visage was also shaped by the activity of women.

34 Introduction

MAP 1.1 The Holy Roman Empire after 1648

Dominik Wieser, Wien

copyright by Domik Wieser

Introduction 35

Notes

1 Henceforth the book uses the slightly abbreviated term "Holy Roman Empire". On the empire, see also one of the sections of this introduction, "Rulership in the Empire".
2 Prince-electors or electors were the members of the electoral college in the Holy Roman Empire. The constitutional structure of the empire was fixed by the Golden Bull of 1356, which also established the seven electors who had the privilege to elect the next monarch of the empire. This number was later increased to nine. For more information on this and other key terms, see Pavlac, B.A., and Lott, E.S. (eds.) (2019) *The Holy Roman Empire: A Historical Encyclopedia*. Santa Barbara, California: ABC-CLIO, and *Encyclopedia of Early Modern History Online*. Available at https://brill.com/view/db/emho?language=en.
3 On her person, see the relevant chapter in the present volume; on the coronation, see Keller, K. (2020) *Die Kaiserin: Reich, Ritual und Dynastie*. Vienna: Böhlau pp.133–141.
4 This has been shown above all by Barbara Stollberg-Rilinger in her book *The Emperor's Old Clothes: Constitutional History and the Symbolic Language of the Holy Roman Empire*. New York and Oxford: Berghahn Books 2015 (in German: *Des Kaisers alte Kleider: Verfassungsgeschichte und Symbolsprache des Alten Reiches*. Munich: Beck, 2008).
5 For an English-language overview, see Whaley, J. (2012) *Germany and the Holy Roman Empire*, vol. I: *Maximilian I to the Peace of Westphalia 1493–1648*, vol. II: *The Peace of Westphalia to the Dissolution of the Reich 1648–1806*. Oxford: Oxford University Press, and Wilson, P.H. (2016) *Heart of Europe: A History of the Holy Roman Empire*. Cambridge Mass.: Harvard University Press; see also Coy, J.P., Marschke, B., and Sabean D.W. (eds) (2010) *The Holy Roman Empire, Reconsidered*. New York: Berghahn; Evans, R.J.W., Schaich, M. and Wilson, P. (eds.) (2012) *The Holy Roman Empire, 1495–1806: A European Perspective*. Leyden: Brill; Stollberg-Rilinger, B. (2018) *The Holy Roman Empire: A Short History*. Princeton: Princeton University Press; in the German language, most recently Schnettger, M. (2020) *Kaiser und Reich: Eine Verfassungsgeschichte (1500–1800)*. Stuttgart: Kohlhammer, and in French Bretschneider, F. and Duhamelle, C. (eds.) (2018) *Le Saint-Empire: Histoire sociale (XVIe–XVIIIe siècle)*. Paris: Fondation MSH.
6 On imperial princesses, see below.
7 See the chapter on Empress Maria Theresia.
8 See Wunder, H. (1998) *He is the Sun, She is the Moon: Women in Early Modern Germany*. Cambridge Mass.: Harvard University Press (in German: *"Er ist die Sonn', sie ist der Mond": Frauen in der Frühen Neuzeit*. Munich: Beck, 1992), with its focus on the empire; Karant-Nunn, S. (2012) "Is There a Social History of the Holy Roman Empire", in Evans, R.J.W., Schaich, M., and Wilson, P. (eds.), *The Holy Roman Empire, 1495–1806: A European Perspective*. Leyden: Brill, pp. 245–262; for Western Europe, most recently Capern, A.L. (ed.) (2019) *The Routledge History of Women in Early Modern Europe*. London: Routledge.

9 For an overview of the legal aspects, see Gerhard, U. (ed.) (1997) *Frauen in der Geschichte des Rechts: Von der Frühen Neuzeit bis zur Gegenwart*. Munich: Beck 1997.
10 Examples of this in Westphal, S., Schmidt-Voges, I., and Baumann, A. (2011) *Venus und Vulcanus: Ehen und ihre Konflikte in der Frühen Neuzeit*. Munich: Oldenbourg.
11 Wilson, *Heart of Europe*, pp. 508–510; Wunder, H. (1997) "Herrschaft und öffentliches Handeln von Frauen in der Gesellschaft der Frühen Neuzeit," in Gerhard U. (ed.), *Frauen in der Geschichte des Rechts: Von der Frühen Neuzeit bis zur Gegenwart*. Munich: Beck, pp. 27–54; Eibach, J. and Schmidt-Voges, I. (eds.) (2015) *Das Haus in der Geschichte Europas: Ein Handbuch*. Berlin and Boston: De Gruyter; Eibach, J. and Lanzinger, M. (eds.) (2020) *The Routledge History of the Domestic Sphere in Europe, Sixteenth to Nineteenth Century*. Abingdon: Routledge.
12 Westphal, S. et al. (2011) *Venus und Vulcanus: Ehen und ihre Konflikte in der Frühen Neuzeit*. München: Oldenbourg, pp. 132–142; Wunder, "Herrschaft".
13 Ingendahl, G. (2006) *Witwen in der Frühen Neuzeit: Eine kulturhistorische Studie*. Frankfurt am Main: Campus; Kruse, B. (2007) *Witwen: Kulturgeschichte eines Standes in Spätmittelalter und Früher Neuzeit*. Berlin: de Gruyter.
14 On the concept of intersectionality, see Crenshaw, K. (1989) "Demarginalizing the Intersection of Race and Sex: A Black Feminist Critique of Antidiscrimination Doctrine", in *The University of Chicago Legal Forum*, pp. 139–167; Hill Collins P. and Chepp V. (2013) "Intersectionality" in Waylen G. et al. (ed.), *The Oxford Handbook of Gender and Politics*. Oxford: OUP, pp. 58–87.
15 Illustratively shown in Werkstetter, C. (2001) *Frauen im Augsburger Zunfthandwerk: Arbeit, Arbeitsbeziehungen und Geschlechterverhältnisse im 18. Jahrhundert*. Berlin: Akademie-Verlag.
16 Wunder, H. and Vanja C. (eds.) (1996) *Weiber, Menscher, Frauenzimmer: Frauen in der ländlichen Gesellschaft 1500 bis 1800*. Göttingen: Vandenhoek & Ruprecht; Wunder, *He is the Sun*, pp. 85–99.
17 Hohkamp, M., and Jancke, G. (eds.) (2004) *Nonne, Königin und Kurtisane: Wissen, Bildung und Gelehrsamkeit von Frauen in der Frühen Neuzeit*. Königstein/Taunus: Ulrike Helmer Verlag.
18 Most recently, Opitz-Belakhal, C. (2020) *Streit um die Frauen und andere Studien zur frühneuzeitlichen Querelle des femmes*. Roßdorf bei Darmstadt: Ulrike Helmer Verlag.
19 Wunder, *He is the Sun*, pp. 66–84; Spicksley, J.M. (2021) "Work in Countryside, Cities, and Towns", in Capern, A.L. (ed.) *The Routledge History of Women in Early Modern Europe*, London: Routledge, pp. 135–180.
20 Westphal, S. (ed.) (2005) *In eigener Sache: Frauen vor den höchsten Gerichten des Alten Reiches*. Cologne: Böhlau.
21 Puppel, P. (2004) *Die Regentin: Vormundschaftliche Herrschaft in Hessen 1500–1700*. Frankfurt am Main: Campus; Woodacre, E. (2021) *Queens and Queenship*. Amsterdam: Amsterdam University Press, pp. 73–82.

22 For an introduction, see Keller, K. (2016) "Frauen und dynastische Herrschaft: Eine Einführung", in Braun, B., Keller, K. and Schnettger, M. (eds.) *Nur die Frau des Kaisers? Kaiserinnen in der Frühen Neuzeit.* Vienna: Böhlau, pp. 13–26; on aristocratic women more generally, see Bastl, B. (2000) *Tugend, Liebe, Ehre: Die adelige Frau in der Frühen Neuzeit.* Vienna: Böhlau, and Hufschmidt, A. (2001) *Adlige Frauen im Weserraum zwischen 1570 und 1700: Status – Rollen – Lebenspraxis.* Münster: Aschendorff.
23 With literature references on this, Schnettger, *Kaiser und Reich*, pp. 244–249 and Behringer, W. (2012) "Core and Periphery: The Holy Roman Empire as a Communication(s) Universe", in Evans, R.J.W., Schaich, M., and Wilson, P. (eds.), *The Holy Roman Empire, 1495–1806: A European Perspective.* Leyden: Brill, pp. 347–358.
24 Keller, K. (2022) "Hidden Figures: The Holy Roman Empire as a Realm of the Ladies" *Central European History* 55, pp. 339–354.
25 Merkel, K., and Wunder, H. (eds.) (2000) *Deutsche Frauen der Frühen Neuzeit: Dichterinnen, Malerinnen, Mäzeninnen.* Darmstadt: Wissenschaftliche Buchgesellschaft; Frindte, J. and Westphal, S. (eds.) (2005) *Handlungsspielräume von Frauen um 1800.* Heidelberg: Winter.
26 For an overview of the constitution and the state and territorial structures, see Schnettger, *Kaiser und Reich*; Stollberg-Rilinger, *Holy Roman Empire*; Whaley, *Germany*; Wilson, *Heart of Europe*.
27 An imperial abbey was an ecclesiastical institution with the status of imperial immediacy and directly subject to the emperor. The abbess of such an abbey had territorial sovereignty within its domains.
28 Küppers-Braun, U. (2002) "Dynastisches Handeln von Frauen in der Frühen Neuzeit", in Wunder, H. (ed.), *Dynastie und Herrschaftssicherung in der Frühen Neuzeit: Geschlechter und Geschlecht.* Berlin: Duncker & Humblot, pp. 221–238; Schröder-Stapper, T. (2015) *Fürstäbtissinnen: Frühneuzeitliche Stiftsherrschaften zwischen Verwandtschaft, Lokalgewalten und Reichsverband.* Cologne: Böhlau.
29 On this, see above all Whaley, *Germany*.
30 Schattkowsky, M. (ed.) (2016) *Frauen und Reformation: Handlungsfelder – Rollenmuster – Engagement.* Leipzig: Universitätsverlag; Stjerna, K.I. (2009) *Women and the Reformation*, Malden, MA: Blackwell.
31 Gehrt, D., and Osten-Sacken, V. (eds.) (2015) *Fürstinnen und Konfession: Beiträge hochadliger Frauen zur Religionspolitik und Bekenntnisbildung.* Göttingen: Vandenhoeck & Ruprecht.
32 Whaley, *Germany*, vol. 2, pp. 310–320.
33 See also Wustmann, C. (2008) *Die "begeisterten Mägde": Mitteldeutsche Prophetinnen im Radikalpietismus am Ende des 17. Jahrhunderts.* Leipzig: Edition Kirchhof & Franke.
34 Whaley, *Germany*, vol. 1, pp. 102–116; Wilson, *Heart of Europe*, pp. 262–264.
35 Whaley, *Germany*, vol. 2, pp. 330–336, 447–452.
36 In general, see Rankin, A.M. (2013) *Panaceia's daughters: Noblewomen as Healers in Early Modern Germany.* Chicago: University of Chicago Press.

37 Rode-Breymann, S., and Tumat, A. (eds.) (2013) *Der Hof: Ort kulturellen Handelns von Frauen in der Frühen Neuzeit*. Cologne: Böhlau.
38 For recent work on this, see, for example, Krimmer, E., and Nossett, L. (eds.) (2020) *Writing the Self, Creating Community: German Women Authors and the Literary Sphere, 1750–1850*. Rochester: Camden House, and Deiulio, L.C., and Lyon, J.B. (eds.) (2019) *Gender, Collaboration, and Authorship in German Culture: Literary Joint Ventures, 1750–1850*. New York: Bloomsbury Academic.
39 For a systematic account, see Ceranski, B. (2006) "Transition toward Invisibility: Women's Scientific Activities around 1800", in Gleixner, U. and Gray, M.W. (eds.), *Gender in Transition. Discourse and Practice in German-speaking Europe, 1750–1830*. Ann Arbor: University of Michigan Press, pp. 202–217.
40 Opitz-Belakhal, C. (ed.) (2000) *Tugend, Vernunft und Gefühl: Geschlechterdiskurse der Aufklärung und weibliche Lebenswelten*. Münster: Waxmann; Ulbrich, C. (2015) "Ständische Ungleichheit und Geschlechterforschung" in Füssel, M., and Weller, T. (eds.), *Soziale Ungleichheit und ständische Gesellschaft: Theorien und Debatten in der Frühneuzeitforschung*. Frankfurt am Main: Vittorio Klostermann, pp. 85–104.
41 Dawson, R. (2006) "'Lights out, lights out!' Women and the Enlightenment", in Gleixner, U., and Gray, M.W. (eds.) *Gender in Transition: Discourse and Practice in German-Speaking Europe, 1750–1830*. Ann Arbor: University of Michigan Press, pp. 218–245.
42 Frindte and Westphal, *Handlungsspielräume*; Opitz-Belakhal, *Tugend*.
43 Whaley, *Germany*, vol. 2, pp. 480–483.
44 Cremer, A.C., Baumann, A., and Bender, E. (eds.) (2017) *Prinzessinnen unterwegs: Reisen fürstlicher Frauen in der Frühen Neuzeit*. Berlin: de Gruyter 2017.
45 See Map 1.1.
46 North, M. (2000) "Von der atlantischen Handelsexpansion bis zu den Agrarreformen" in North, M. (ed.) *Deutsche Wirtschaftsgeschichte: Ein Jahrtausend im Überblick*. Munich: Beck. pp. 107–191; Whaley, *Germany*, vol. 1, pp. 122–129.
47 Whaley, *Germany*, vol. 2, pp. 270–276, 494–507.
48 Lepp, C. (2007) "Verdeckt von Sombarts 'smarten Männern'? Bedingungen und Merkmale von Unternehmerinnen von der Mitte des 17. bis zum Anfang des 20. Jahrhunderts", *Archiv für Kulturgeschichte* 89 (1), pp. 91–112; Ogilvie, Sheilagh (2004) "Women and Labour Markets in Early Modern Germany", *Jahrbuch für Wirtschaftsgeschichte* 45 (2), pp. 25–60; Wunder and Vanja, *Weiber*.
49 Allweiler, S. (2001) *Canaillen, Weiber, Amazonen: Frauenwirklichkeiten in Aufständen Südwestdeutschlands 1688–1777*. Münster: Waxmann; Wunder, *He is the Sun*, 180–184; Whaley, *Germany*, vol. 1, pp. 136–139.

The Sixteenth Century

Preachers, Nuns, and Dynastic Women

CARITAS PIRCKHEIMER (1467–1532)

The Learned Nun

Barbara Pirckheimer, the oldest of 12 children and named after her mother, was born in 1467 in Eichstätt, where her father was an episcopal counsellor. But she probably grew up in Nuremberg, where the Pirckheimers worked for decades as successful merchants. The girl's grandfather and father, however, had first studied in Italy, and the inquisitive girl, too, received an early education in Nuremberg from an unmarried aunt: Katharina Pirck-heimer had pronounced scholarly interests, which is evidence that the family did not view the education of girls as a secondary matter.

Barbara therefore probably entered the Convent of St. Clara in Nuremberg in 1479 primarily out of this desire for learning, since girls in the Middle Ages and Early Modern Period could only acquire higher education—meaning above all instruction in Latin, the language of theology and science—at home or in ecclesiastical institutions. City schools and universities remained closed to them and were only accessible to boys and men. The Convent of St. Clara had a school where girls of affluent Nuremberg families were not only taught Latin but also learned about the writings of the Church Fathers and read the Bible and ancient authors. These were essential elements of a classical humanist education.

The abbess of the convent told one of the girl's uncles about her outstanding Latin skills as early as 1481—Barbara had evidently found her purpose in the study of theological and scholarly writings. Her decision to take the vows of the Poor Clares and

DOI: 10.4324/9781003252870-3

permanently join the convent was presumably motivated by two reasons: it was an expression both of her piety and aspiration to lead a godly life as well as her desire to continue working with books and texts. Had she left the convent as a young woman, she would undoubtedly have become the wife, mother, and governess of a large household of a well-to-do citizen of Nuremberg. But it would have been much more difficult to pursue her scholarly interests—that is, if her husband did not in fact forbid her from doing so.

It was presumably 1495 when Barbara took the vows and at the same time changed her name to Caritas. As a canonical sister, she consequently chose a life of poverty, chastity, and obedience. A large part of the day was devoted to prayer and religious song; some of the sisters were also responsible for making luxurious fabrics and embroideries, which decorated churches in Nuremberg and elsewhere. Others—Caritas among them—dedicated themselves to the reading of religious texts and the copying and production of manuscripts in the convent library. Under the supervision of a Franciscan monk, Caritas was soon involved in the creation of a convent chronicle and working as a teacher in the convent's school (novice mistress).

Associated with the vows, however, was a general seclusion from the outside world. Caritas and her fellow nuns could now only meet and speak with their relatives at a small and mostly covered window. But in her case, this certainly did not mean that she lost her connection to family, especially since one of her sisters, Clara, had also joined the convent. After Caritas's father died in 1501, she remained closely connected above all with her only brother Willibald—through visits, but also especially through letters.

It was also Willibald who spread the reputation of his sister's erudition within the tightly networked group of German humanists—after all, it was particularly her interest in studying that most strongly preserved their bond. As an educational movement emanating from Italy, in the second half of the fifteenth century humanism had also achieved great importance in the German-speaking world, with Nuremberg as one of its centres. History and language were cultivated especially deeply here as scholarly fields, and Willibald Pirckheimer was one of the most prominent proponents of humanism in the imperial city.

Hence he did not find it difficult to spread the word to other humanists about the erudition of his sister Caritas, whom he viewed in a certain sense as his student and supported by regularly sending her books. The poet and geographer Conrad Celtis, for instance, subsequently dedicated a work to her in 1502, in which he published Latin texts of the scholarly medieval canoness Hrotsvitha von Gandersheim. Caritas Pirckheimer thanked him for this—wholly in humanistic style, with a perfectly formulated letter in Latin. In it, she first referred to her own imperfection and naivety. But this was no doubt primarily due to the norms of the time and the Poor Clares' commandment of humility, because later the text clearly reveals how Caritas really saw the relationship between the sexes with regard to scholarship: God made no distinction and endowed both sexes with the same intelligence.

An expression of this conviction was also her long-time correspondence with the humanistically educated Provost of St. Lawrence in Nuremberg, Sixtus Tucher. Even though Caritas and Tucher most likely never met in person, they were connected through an intimate correspondence, of which only Tucher's letters survive, however. The two of them exchanged thoughts about personal matters as well as theological issues. At the same time, they strengthened each other's piety and did this on an equal footing. Tucher was not tutoring a naive woman; rather, two intellectually affiliated human beings "spoke" about their ideas and worldviews.

And Celtis was not alone in contributing to the contemporary public fame of Caritas as a learned woman. Albrecht Dürer, the most famous German painter of his time, dedicated his *Life of the Virgin* series (1511) to her and described her with the words: "Avid governess of attentive maidens. The Latin books that you, woman, assiduously read, make you treasured and lauded by us".[1] Even Erasmus of Rotterdam, the "Prince of Humanists", praised Caritas in a 1518 text[2] for her erudition.

In her letters—only a few of which survive, however—Caritas Pirckheimer expressed herself with a striking self-assurance and presented opinions of her own that reflect her intense engagement with theological texts. At the same time, she was reticent about any idealisation of her person. And the attention she received in humanist circles as a learned woman and nun met elsewhere with disapproval, as evidenced by a determination made by the Nuremberg Franciscans. As chaplains for the Convent of St. Clara, they had the authority to issue directives to the nuns. In 1503, they used it to forbid Caritas from using Latin in her correspondence. This deeply appalled Willibald Pirckheimer—he therefore described the Franciscans as "wooden footed people",[3] by which he meant that the monks' wooden sandals matched their rigid, simplistic views. But his sister complied and henceforth wrote to her learned brother in German.

However, after December 1503 Caritas had much less time anyway to spend on books and reading. This was the month that the 60 or so nuns elected her abbess of the convent. This meant that she now had to look after all of the convent's spiritual and secular concerns, from communications with the Nuremberg Council through to managing the finances and complying with the order's rules. After her election, her brother Willibald wrote: "I should congratulate you, but I pity you."[4] This suggests that Caritas, too, viewed the election as an expression of her fellow nuns' appreciation but was also very much aware of the office's challenges.

She met them with success. During her first years in office, she managed to catch up on many neglected building projects. The construction was financed through support from the Nuremberg Council and the sale of flowers and spices from the convent's garden. Caritas Pirckheimer also managed to obtain indulgences[5] from Rome, which were sold for the benefit of the convent and did much to secure the financial situation, which had long been strained. Her fellow sisters deeply appreciated the abbess's administration, for her dealings with them were marked by affection and cheerfulness without this calling into the question the strict observance of the order's rules.

But the greatest challenge of her tenure, which did not end until Caritas Pirckheimer died in 1532, would be the Reformation. Martin Luther had already voiced fundamental criticism of convent life early on, and this soon led to the dissolution of monasteries and the flight of monks and nuns who had discovered the new teachings for themselves. In autumn 1518, a group of influential men who sympathised with Luther and the Reformation was formed in Nuremberg. It included Caspar Nützel, for example, the first person to translate Luther's theses—so central to the start of the Reformation—into German. At the same time, Nützel was commissioned by the Nuremberg Council as the overseer of the Convent of St. Clara. He thus became the convent's most important secular administrator, and Abbess Caritas Pirckheimer had to work with him directly on an ongoing basis.

That this would lead to conflict was obvious. At first, however, everything still ran as before, particularly since the Convent of St. Clara had also shown an initial interest in reforming the traditional church. But in the convent, this soon turned into disapproval, as was formulated by Caritas Pirckheimer in 1522 in a letter to the theologian Hieronymus Emser in Saxony, and which the Nuremberg Council used, in turn, as an opportunity to accuse the abbess of insubordination and unwarranted critique. By 1523, when Martin Luther inveighed against convents as institutions that held young women against their will, the situation for the Poor Clares in Nuremberg had slowly become more precarious.

Abbess Caritas watched all of these developments with concern and started keeping a chronicle in which she wanted to record current events in and related to the convent. Entitled *Denk-würdigkeiten* (Memorabilia), she dictated this chronicle to several scribes in the years between 1524 and 1532. The text begins with a reference to an old prophecy of a catastrophe that Caritas Pirckheimer related directly to the Reformation:

And, although this [the prophecy] has generally been understood as a flood, experience has taught us that the stars did not indicate water as much as misery, fear and distress, and later, bloodshed. In the year noted above [1524] it happened that many things were changed by the new teachings of the Lutherans and much dissension befell the Christian faith. The ceremonies of the Church have been done away with in many instances and the clerical class has been almost completely destroyed in many areas. ... During the day many of the powerful as well as simple people came to their relatives who resided in our cloister. They preached to them and spoke of the new teachings and argued incessantly that the cloistered were damned and subject to temptation.[6]

The threat became very real for Caritas Pirckheimer and her nuns in February 1525, when a Nuremberg woman demanded that her daughter leave the convent: she was supposed to come home and listen to Lutheran sermons. But the girl refused, and Caritas explained to the mother and several of the male relatives escorting her that, in her view, she could only let her fellow nun go if this was what she herself wanted, which was not the case. Almost at the same time, in March 1525, the so-called Nuremberg Religious Colloquy was held in the city, which dealt with nothing less than the question of which religious orientation was true and accurate and should therefore in future be adopted by the Nuremberg Council. As most people expected, it concluded with a council decision in favour of the Lutheran faith.

This threatened not just one individual nun but rather the existence of the entire convent, and the first major intervention soon followed: the council forbade the Franciscans from preaching in the women's convents and listening to confessions—that is, from giving the cloistered women spiritual guidance.[7] Nor did the way in which the council told the Poor Clare nuns about this measure give them reason to expect anything good. In mid-March 1525, two envoys of the council forced their way into the conclave, an area of the convent reserved solely for the sisters. As abbess, Caritas vigorously protested against the deprivation of pastoral care, and all of the present nuns supported her against the two envoys, but to no avail.

Her appeal to Caspar Nützel as the convent's overseer also led nowhere. During his visit to the convent, the sisters even fell at his feet in support of their abbess, but this only intensified the conflict. Although she apologised for this commotion in a letter, Caritas remained firm on the matter, insisting on the rights of the sisters to their convent life, as well as on their right to pastoral care. Of course, the council saw these rights as guaranteed, since, after all, Lutheran sermons started being held in the convent's church the week of Easter 1525, and they had to be attended by the convent's nuns.

This tense situation reflected the problematic position of an abbess facing secular authority. Without the support of men like the overseer or clergy, there was little Caritas could do. This support came, however—namely, through the mediation of Willibald Pirckheimer. To be sure, Caritas's brother was neither a champion of the Reformation, nor a defender of the traditional church. However, the moral coercion that de facto was being inflicted on Caritas and her fellow sisters by the push to dissolve the convent clashed with his humanistic convictions and those of the abbess herself. She documented this not only in writing but also by having her convent continue to sound its bells according to the liturgy of hours that signified the traditional church—hers was the only institution in the city to do so. As a result, the Poor Clare nuns repeatedly had to reckon with insults and nocturnal assaults, for everyone in the city naturally understood this ringing of the bells to be an act of resistance, a rejection of the new confession.

Willibald Pirckheimer, on the other hand, used his scholarly connections to enlist Philipp Melanchthon, one of the Lutheran movement's leading figures, as a mediator. However, another scandal engulfed the Convent of St. Clara before he arrived. In June, the relatives of several nuns forced them to leave the convent and demanded that the abbess release the nuns from their vows. Caritas refused, but three nuns were practically kidnapped from the convent. The overseer Caspar Nützel, moreover, increased the pressure on the abbess by having Wenzeslaus Linck, a preacher and adherent of Luther, deliver theological lessons to the intractable abbess. The abbess answered this with a clear written response in which she insisted on being allowed to ponder spiritual questions independently and without coercion, just like Paul had suggested to the early Christians. With this defence of freedom of conscience, Caritas built on scholarly positions she had already formulated earlier: freedom of conscience, she insisted, applies equally to all human beings—men and women, nuns and secular persons.

Philipp Melanchthon finally turned up in Nuremberg in November 1525, though not specifically to support the Poor Clares but rather to set up a school. But he did, in fact, visit the convent and had a discussion with Caritas Pirckheimer. Both were evidently impressed by each other and identified many commonalities, above all their rejection of violence and coercion with regard to one's confession of faith. Naturally, one might say, Caritas could not convince the Lutheran of her position on monastic vows, but she nonetheless summed up: "He was more moderate in his speech than any Lutheran I had ever heard. He was deeply offended that our people were being subjected to force. He left us on friendly terms."[8]

Following up on this discussion, Melanchthon intervened against the actions of the Nuremberg Council with regard to the convent, and the abbess too subsequently referred in several letters to her discussion with Melanchthon and his position in favour of the nuns. Thereupon the preacher Wenzeslaus Linck ceased his polemics, and the overseer Caspar Nützel went back to a neutral administrative approach. But this only temporarily secured the convent's existence because the council still saw to it that no novices could join and forbade the Franciscans from giving the sisters pastoral care.

Caritas Pirckheimer's final years in office were therefore overshadowed by concerns about her convent's prospects, which at the very least were unclear. But this did not, of course, prevent the 50 or so still remaining nuns from marking their esteemed abbess's 25th anniversary in office with a big celebration. Willibald Pirckheimer contributed a barrel of wine and splendid tableware; the jubilarian played on dulcimer—a string instrument—and, emotionally moved, accepted the tribute.

In summer 1532, the convent's remaining residents mourned the death of Caritas Pirckheimer as deeply as they had enthusiastically celebrated her when she was alive. An abbess register of the convent noted that "she was a women of the Latin language, almost expert and well spoken, then wrote many Latin letters, which still survive, was elected as abbess in 1503, headed the cloister for 29 years, and died anno 1532 ... She had a magnificent library".[9] Following her as abbess was first her sister Clara, then her niece Caritas (Katharina) Pirckheimer, until the convent finally closed upon the death of the last nun in 1590.

Caritas Pirckheimer, just as famous to her humanist contemporaries as she was notorious to Nuremberg Protestants, was forgotten for many years. Her memory was only revived upon the rediscovery of a manuscript of her *Denkwürdigkeiten*, published in 1852 by Konstantin Höfler. Her life and works can be aligned with at least two important developments that deeply influenced the shaping of the early modern Holy Roman Empire: first, the spread of humanism as part of the Renaissance, which would dominate culture and learning throughout Europe until the early seventeenth century. And second, the Reformation as a religiopolitical development, which would have long-lasting effects on the evolution of the empire. The work of Caritas Pirckheimer, both as a teacher and scholar and as an abbess and defender of her convent, allows us to identify the fields of action of women. But it also reveals the limits of women's agency, whether in theological or political respects. Caritas had to accept the boundaries set by others—for example, by Franciscan pastors, the Nuremberg Council, and the overseer of the convent. But she also set some boundaries herself so that could lead, as desired, a scholarly as well as pious life within the convent walls.

It has long been underappreciated that, in doing so, she formulated theological convictions that seem quite modern. With her view that every monastic nun must personally come to terms with her faith, with her defence of religious freedom of conscience, and with the emphasis she placed on the mediation of Jesus Christ, she had many points of agreement with her Protestant contemporaries. But even so, she defended her way of life and the monastic practices of faith against coercion from outside—also against the pressure to be subordinate as a woman, which she avoided in certain respects through her seclusion from the world.

FIGURE 2.1 Portrait of a Woman, Said to be Caritas Pirckheimer. This is a modern portrait made in the style of paintings by Albrecht Dürer

Alamy

Metropolitan Museum of Art, https://www.metmuseum.org/art/collection/search/438844

Notes

1 Quoted in Bezzel, *Pirckheimer*, p. 35.
2 "Colloquia familiaria" [1518] (1972), in Halkin, L.E., et al. (eds.), *Opera omnia Desiderii Erasmi*, vol. I–3, Leiden: Brill.
3 "Xylopodes" in the original Greek. See Hess, U. (2000) "Caritas Pirckheimer (1467–1532)", in Merkel, K., and Wunder, H. (eds.), *Deutsche Frauen der Frühen Neuzeit: Dichterinnen, Malerinnen, Mäzeninnen*. Darmstadt: Wiss. Buchges, p. 33.
4 Quoted in Bezzel, *Pirckheimer*, p. 27.
5 According to the early-church doctrine, indulgences were an act of grace that remitted temporal punishments for sin. They were routinely used as a source of income in Catholic regions. Payments for such acts of grace were frequently shared between the papacy and institutions like convents (as in this case) to help finance them.

6 MacKenzie, P.A. (ed.) (2006) *Caritas Pirckheimer: A journal of the Reformation years, 1524–1528*. Cambridge, England: D.S. Brewer, p. 11.
7 Deichstetter, G. (ed.) (1984) *Briefe der Äbtissin Caritas Pirckheimer des St. Klara-Klosters zu Nürnberg*. Transcribed by B. Schrott. St. Ottilien: EOS.
8 McKenzie, *Caritas Pirckheimer*, p. 141.
9 Quoted in Bezzel, *Pirckheimer*, p. 105.

Selected bibliography

Bezzel, A. (2016) *Caritas Pirckheimer: Äbtissin und Humanistin*. Regensburg: Pustet.

Mouris, K. (2012) *From Reform to Reformation: The Life and Times of Abbess Caritas Pirckheimer (1467–1532)*. Washington: The Catholic University of America.

Wiesner-Hanks, M. (1998) *Convents Confront the Reformation*. Milwaukee: Marquette.

KATHARINA ZELL (1497/98–1562)

A Woman who Preached

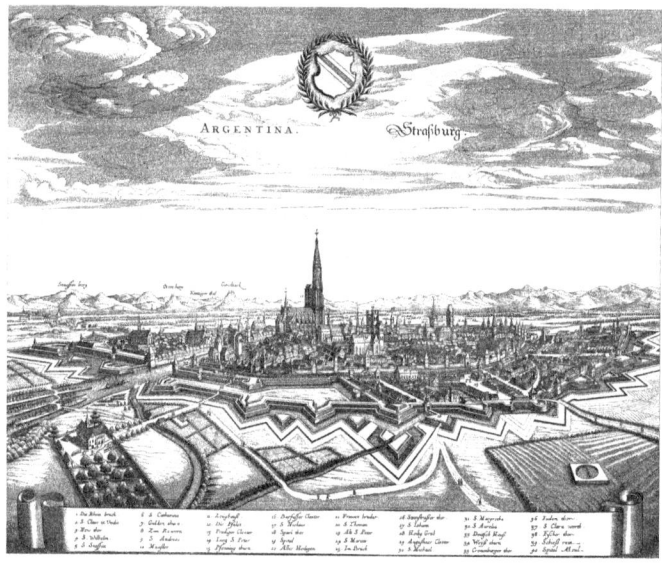

FIGURE 3.1 Strasbourg city view (1644)
Alamy
Matthäus Merian, Topographia Alsatiae, Frankfurt am Main 1647, Tafel 33

Katharina Schütz was born between mid-1497 and spring 1498 in Strasbourg, the largest city in Alsace. Even just the uncertainty of her date of birth indicates that she did not stem from any of the town's very affluent families, for whom such records would

DOI: 10.4324/9781003252870-4

have been customary. She was the daughter of a cabinetmaker, who earned a good living for his family but did not belong to the wealthy elite.

What she had common with Caritas Pirckheimer of the previous generation is that she was already interested in theological issues at an early age. However, in her case she was driven primarily by the search for forms of proper belief and a pious life. As she herself reported, Katharina was already eagerly attending religious services as a ten-year-old. Unsettled by many dangers such as war and disease, the girl was seeking out opportunities to secure her salvation and threw herself into ascetic exercises and pious works.

In contrast to Pirckheimer, the Clarisse nun from Nuremberg who found her way to God through an early decision for monastic seclusion and the study of theological writings, for Katharina Schütz it was the Reformation that eliminated her doubts. Upon hearing sermons in Strasbourg in 1521 that were informed by Luther's teachings, she felt "I had been drawn up out of the depths of the earth, yes, out of grim bitter hell, into the sweet, lovely kingdom of heaven."[1] Whereas, for Caritas Pirckheimer, the Reformation constituted a threat, Katharina Schütz experienced it as a liberation.

After this foundational experience, it was only a question of time before she definitively committed herself to the Reformation. In her case, this was simultaneously linked to another life decision. In early December 1523, she married Matthäus Zell, who since 1518 was working as a pastor in the Strasbourg Cathedral and figured among the imperial city's reformers. Thus, Katharina was one of the first women who, as part of the Reformation, collaborated as a pastor's wife in shaping a new religious and social role for women. Previously, celibacy had naturally also applied to secular clergy, who sometimes lived together with women but were unable to affirm the relationship through the sacrament of marriage, a practice that was more or less tolerated.

But now the married couple working in the parsonage became a hallmark of the Protestant Church. Pastors' wives were responsible for managing the household and family, just like any other housewife. But they also had to take on responsibilities for social welfare in the congregation. Consequently, they took over more or less clearly defined fields of work within pastoral care, even if these were not pastoral activities in a narrower sense. In addition, the households of Protestant pastors wanted and were meant to exemplify a good marriage according to the new confession. What the Luthers did in Wittenberg in this regard, the Zells and others did in Strasbourg. As a result, Katharina quickly became a central figure in the network of new pastors' wives in the Alsatian city, which also included, for example, Agnes Roettel, a friend from youth who likewise married a first-generation Protestant theologian, Wolfgang Capito. The fields of action and self-conceptions of the "pastor's wife" were worked out through the collaboration and exchanges of this group of around ten women, who backed each other up in their role as pastors' wives and on a personal level, in some cases for decades.

However, Katharina Zell was the only one in this network who, already the year after she married, felt moved to also raise her voice in writing in the disputes about the new confession of faith. She sided with the Reformation by writing to the Strasbourg bishop in 1524, evidently in rather strong terms. Printed that very same year was a book of consolation, which she formulated as a letter to Protestant-minded women in Kenzingen in the Breisgau. Around the same time, she also wrote a pamphlet vigorously defending her husband's abandonment of celibacy through their marriage. Tellingly, the point for her in both cases was to encourage the faithful to stay true to the new confession despite massive changes in church practices as well as banishments. However, the Strasbourg City Council prohibited the printing of this text and for a time banned the strident pastor's wife from writing and publishing.

In a way that was unusual for women, Katharina Zell thus combined her activities at her husband's side in the Strasbourg church with making independent written statements on religious issues. Support from her husband was crucial for her ability to explore both areas of action. Until the death of Matthäus Zell in early 1548, their relationship was marked by immense trust and mutual support in acting for the benefit of the new confession. As a married couple, the Zells described each other as "helpers", thereby exhibiting a self-understanding that researchers have since labelled with the concept of the "working couple".

Shortly after getting married, Matthäus and Katharina Zell together opened their home to religious refugees who had fled to Strasbourg after being banished for their Protestant beliefs. But it was Katharina who, with other women and men—mostly from the Strasbourg elite—created a committee ("deacons of the exiles") that dealt with accommodating and providing for these religious refugees. They managed to convince the city council, for example, to have the shut-down Dominican monastery set up as a shelter. In 1543, together with Margarethe Hedio, another pastor's wife, and Amelia Meyer, the wife of a councilman, Katharina also successfully arranged for the conversion of the Wilhelmer monastery into a school.

During the plague epidemics of 1531, 1541, and 1553, Zell dedicated herself above all to being a caregiver in the households of other clergymen. As a childless woman (her two children died young), she had flexibility in this respect, which she regularly used to benefit not only other pastors' wives, her siblings, nieces, and nephews, but also members of the community in general. Throughout the entire city, she was known not least as a deathbed comforter who spoke and prayed with the dying and read them edifying texts. Katharina saw works of charity as a sure sign of belonging to those people whom God had blessed with faith. And at the same time, they were an aspect of the pastoral work that was meant to emanate from the parsonage.

While the death of her husband in January 1548 was not a decisive turning point for her social welfare work, it indeed was one for Katharina as a person. One reason is that she now felt as if half of herself was missing, as she put it. Another reason, however, is that she thereby lost the social and legal backing for her activities that marriage to a respected churchman had provided. She was still highly esteemed throughout the city in general and among her husband's official colleagues. But for legal transactions, she now needed to draw on the help of a guardian. In accordance with the norms in many territories of the empire, a woman could not act independently before the courts but rather needed to be represented by a gender guardian (Geschlechtsvormund).[2] Hence at the end of the 1550s, Katharina's guardian was Jacob Meyer, who negotiated in court to have her disabled nephew Lucas Schütz, whom she had long looked after in her house, accommodated and cared for in a hospital.

Katharina's personal situation after 1550 also changed because, as trusted theologians emigrated or died, her public work became more difficult. She also suffered more frequent illnesses. And the political–religious environment in Strasbourg changed with the Interim concluded by the imperial diet in Augsburg in 1548. In this compromise paper, the Protestant princes of the empire, after their military defeats against Emperor Charles V, had to agree to the reversion of ecclesiastical conditions to their pre-Reformation status. This obliged Strasbourg and many other imperial cities to allow Catholic religious services, which then occurred starting early February (Candlemass).

All these factors made it more difficult for Katharina Zell to advocate publicly for her positions. However, this by no means kept her from doing what she had done before. For not only had Zell always campaigned for Strasbourg citizens and religious refugees alike in social welfare matters, but she had also continued to take sides in her writing. Thus from 1534 to 1536, she published a hymnal consisting of cheap booklets that contained songs of the Moravian Brethren (Unity of the Brethren), a confessional group that had been founded in Bohemia in the fifteenth century by the theologian and reformer Jan Hus. Katharina Zell valued the pious nature of the songs and wrote the hymnal to disseminate Protestant songs and texts among the common people. In 1548, as a long-planned journey of the Zell couple to Wittenberg drew near, their friend, Pastor Wolfgang Capito, wrote about Katharina to a friend living there: when the trip finally takes place, "you will clearly hear personally that our women are not at all silent. But she is good and devout."[3]

However, she also raised her voice in public in the truest sense of the word. This probably first took place with the eulogy she delivered at the grave of her husband during his interment in January 1548. The eulogy survives in a manuscript written in her own hand, which was likely meant to be printed. Even more unusual was that, shortly before dying, she delivered two further eulogies, this time for women who had belonged the Schwenckfeldians.[4] Katharina and her husband had always stood in vehement opposition to the old faith, but without ever clearly adopting any of the various Protestant creeds. They therefore also sheltered Caspar von Schwenckfeld, the founder of this group, in Strasbourg when he had to leave Silesia in 1529. Katharina remained friendly with his Strasbourg supporters until the end of her life without directly belonging to the group herself. But when Felicitas von Andernach was supposed to be interred without clerical support because she had been a follower of Schwenckfeld, Katharina Zell took it upon herself to deliver a commemorative speech at her grave. This not only shows her non-dogmatic approach to Protestant beliefs and her energetic presence within the city, but also that she retained her function as comforter of the sick and dying.

Between 1555 and 1557, Katharina seized the opportunity to speak out in other ways as well, such as politically and theologically when she engaged in a written controversy with Ludwig Rabus. The latter had been an employee and then the successor of Matthäus Zell as a preacher at the Strasbourg Cathedral; but because of a conflict with the council, he had transferred to Ulm as a superintendent. From there he soon inveighed sharply against deviating Protestant currents, such as the Schwenckfeldians, and criticised Katharina herself and her deceased husband, finding neither of them sufficiently Lutheran. In 1557, Katharina Zell published this correspondence, together with a letter of her own to the citizens of Strasbourg, in a text that she herself described as "the confession of my faith".

Rabus had been one of the city's most prominent churchmen, and the Strasbourg Council viewed Zell's polemics against the former cathedral preacher with displeasure. She was asked to stop selling her work and to turn over all remaining copies to the council. That said, compared to the publication ban imposed on her by the council 30 years earlier, the warning should be considered a rather restrained reaction on the part of the authorities. Evidently, Katharina Zell enjoyed great respect in the city and consequently had enough social backing to lead the council to proceed with moderation. This respect manifested itself one last time when Katharina Zell died in September 1562: her burial was attended by large numbers of the Strasbourg population.

The life of Katharina Zell was thus widely shaped by the Reformation. In the movement launched by Luther, she not only found the key to her own assurance of salvation. As the wife of a Protestant theologian and preacher of the early Reformation, she also played a role in shaping the office of the pastor's wife, which would remain important for centuries in the Protestant territories of the Holy Roman Empire and allowed women to collaborate in pastoral duties. The diversity and scope of Zell's social commitment served as an example to other women.

Katharina Zell's propensity to make statements on theological and religiopolitical issues in written form and public speech was rather unusual. Admittedly, there were other theologically untrained women who, just like men, spoke out during the Reformation period with pamphlets, confessions of faith, or songs. One of the most famous was Argula von Grumbach, whose pamphlets from 1523/24 were printed in many editions. But as far as we know, the woman on the side of the Reformation with the most works available in print was Katharina Zell. However, her texts were primarily known in Strasbourg and its surroundings, because she essentially spoke out about events and people that mattered in this environment. In her wide-ranging texts she nonetheless developed outlines of her own theological positions, in that she composed arguments from Biblical and scholarly texts she was familiar with and presented and published them. At the same time, she purposefully referred to the roles of women in Biblical texts and used them as referential figures for her own actions.

Katharina did not receive a comprehensive education as a child but rather simply learned to read and write in the girls' schools of Strasbourg. She did not know Latin. But during the course of her life, she used various sources to glean a theological education, obviously with considerable success. She keenly attended religious services and doubtless adopted suggestions from the sermons of her husband and other churchmen. And, even before her marriage, she was an avid reader of the Bible, who later also discussed her readings with her theologically educated husband. Moreover, many prominent theologians socialised in the Strasbourg parsonage, and Katharina sought discussions with them; she also corresponded with them over shorter or longer periods of time. Zell no doubt made similar use of the couple's several journeys. Having accompanied her husband on a trip to Wittenberg in 1538, Katharina also met Martin Luther, and the conversation with him apparently made a lifelong impression. The reading of numerous Reformation works also played a role.

She wrote about this herself in her dispute with Ludwig Rabus in the late 1550s:

> I heard their [the older reformers] sayings and sermons, read their books, received their letters with joy, and they received mine with joy. ... In summary, I am writing all this because I must show how in my younger days, I was so dear to the fine old learned man and architects of the church of Christ ... They never withheld from me their conversation about holy matters and they gladly (from the heart) heard mine.[5]

She thereby not only justified her public position vis-à-vis Rabus but also put the younger man in his place—and at the same time disclosed important sources of her theological education.

Yet it must be noted that Katharina obviously also knew and acknowledged the boundaries imposed upon her by her gender, even though she reached for the quill and made public statements more frequently than any other woman of the Reformation period. This becomes especially clear in her graveside speech for her husband, which she prefaced by saying that she only saw herself called to give such a speech because she was the person most impacted by his death, not because she wanted to place herself "in the office of the preachers and apostles".[6] Even in her conflict with Ludwig Rabus, she noted that, as a woman, she would have preferred to stay silent, but since the men who should have been opening their mouth in this situation were not saying anything, she herself had to raise her voice. She maintained, however, that she had never done anything unbefitting for her as a woman.

This notwithstanding, even while her husband was alive, some contemporaries viewed her involvement with reserve. The fact that Matthäus Zell allowed her time for reading and theological discussions, as well as for her extensive social commitment, soon led to accusations that the Zell household was under "woman's rule". Even a close friend of the couple, the Strasbourg reformer Martin Bucer, criticised the way Matthäus Zell allowed his wife too many liberties. But this is precisely what no doubt formed a basis for their trusting collaboration for the benefit of the Protestant church, whose servant Katharina Zell felt she was, as suggested by her self-description as a "church mother",[7] a woman who provides maternal care for the church.

Notes

1 McKee, E.A. (1999) *Katharina Schütz Zell* (2 vols.). Leiden: Brill, vol 1, p. 226.
2 See the Introduction, p. 1.
3 McKee, *Katharina Schütz*, vol. 1, p. 102.
4 This was a movement within Protestantism that followed a spiritualistic theology and was soon subjected to persecution.
5 McKee, *Katharina Schütz*, vol. 2, p. 172.
6 McKee, *Katharina Schütz*, vol. 2, p. 71.
7 McKee, *Katharina Schütz*, vol. 1, p. 420.

Selected bibliography

Jung, M.H. (2002) "Katharina Zell geb. Schütz (1497/98–1562): Eine Laientheologin der Reformationszeit?", in Jung, M.H. (ed.), *Nonnen, Prophetinnen, Kirchenmütter: Kirchen- und frömmigkeitsgeschichtliche Studien zu Frauen der Reformationszeit*. Leipzig: Evangelische Verlagsanstalt, pp. 121–168.

Stjerna, K.I. (2009) "Katharina Schütz Zell, 1498–1562—A Publishing Church Mother in Strasbourg", in Stjerna, K.I., *Women and the Reformation*. Malden, MA: Blackwell, pp. 109–131.

MARIA OF HUNGARY (1505–1558)

On Behalf of the Dynasty

Archduchess Maria was only ten years old when she stepped before the altar as a bride in Vienna's St. Stephen's Cathedral on 22 July 1515. Her grandfather, Emperor Maximilian I, had negotiated an alliance with King Vladislaus II of Bohemia and Hungary, which was supposed to be secured by a double marriage. Maria wed Louis, the crown prince of Bohemia and Hungary, and his sister Anna wed Maria's brother, Ferdinand. But this by no means brought Maria's childhood to an end—rather, together with her sister-in-law, she continued to be raised at her grandfather's court until 1521, first in Vienna and later in Innsbruck.

Maria was born in Brussels in 1505, one of six children of Philip the Handsome and his Spanish wife, Joanna. She was little more than one year old when the news of her father's death arrived from Spain, where he had travelled with his spouse. Her eldest brother, Charles, thus became the Duke of Burgundy, and later he would also govern Spain and the Holy Roman Empire as Charles V. Even though her mother would not die until 1555 in Tordesillas, the girl never saw her again. Until 1513, Maria grew up in Brussels under the supervision of her aunt Margaret, who had been the governess of the Netherlands since 1507. Maria, whose mother tongue was French, had already learned Spanish and Latin at an early age, and then in Vienna she learned German as well. The small archduchess also certainly drew plenty of inspiration from her aunt, who was very interested in music, painting, and literature. In Innsbruck, her grandfather Maximilian, an avid

DOI: 10.4324/9781003252870-5

hunter, had her introduced to hunting, an activity she would later pursue with great enthusiasm.

As early as 1518, the Venetian envoy Gasparo Contarini reported from Innsbruck that Queen Maria was admittedly somewhat gaunt and not as charming as her sister-in-law, Anna, but "of great intellect and very promising".[1] This would be confirmed when she finally made the journey to Hungary and actually became queen. She arrived in Buda on 11 July 1521, where her 15-year-old spouse, Louis II, awaited her. New research has shown how quickly Maria learned to secure a clientele among office holders and nobles in order to strengthen her position as queen. To this end, she also used her income from the extensive properties at her disposal through the morning gift[2] and other donations from the king or which she acquired by purchase. Monetary payments, offices, and intercessions with her husband made noble office holders beholden to the queen. Her coronation in 1522 in Székesfehérvár likewise helped solidify her position in the country, which was politically turbulent and threatened by the Ottomans. By contrast, the young couple stayed in Bohemia, her husband's second kingdom, only once, namely, in winter 1522–1523. During this time Maria was crowned as queen here as well, in the St. Vitus Cathedral in Prague.

Soon after they returned to Hungary in 1523, the danger of an Ottoman attack became acute again. The Ottoman Empire had been steadily expanding northwards for decades; the army of Sultan Suleiman I had conquered Belgrade in 1521. Ever since then, Louis II of Hungary had been trying to create a league of Christian powers to prevent further conquests. Finally, in summer 1526, he led an extensive army against the sultan. On 29 August 1526, a battle was fought at Mohács, which ended with a devastating defeat for Hungary. King Louis himself died in the battle, and his fleeing army dissolved. In the following weeks, the Ottomans were able to occupy large parts of the kingdom. As a result, Hungary faced a dynastic and political catastrophe.

In this initially very unclear and dangerous situation, the young widow Maria proved to be resourceful.[3] She left Buda, which was occupied by the Ottomans just a few days later, and from Bratislava (Pressburg) in what was then Upper Hungary tried to save anything she still could. Despite antagonistic noble factions, Maria managed to secure the election of her brother, Ferdinand, as king of Hungary in 1527, not least thanks to the networks she had created during her few years as queen. Although this election remained disputed for a long time, the widow queen thereby demonstrated perseverance and a political will to act. It also became clear how she thought to use them: in favour of securing the kingdom of Hungary, but also to benefit her dynasty of origin, the House of Habsburg.

In the following years, she stayed mostly in the Bratislava region, but was repeatedly forced to move from place to place due to her financial problems—towns and nobles were usually only willing to support the widow queen and her court for a short time. In autumn 1529, Maria had to flee to Linz and Passau, for a massive Ottoman army was moving through Hungary towards Vienna in order to conquer the city—a plan that admittedly failed. To be sure, her brother Ferdinand had gladly come to Maria's assistance in Hungary, but, due to his own financial worries and military endeavours, he found himself unable to ensure regular income for his sister from her Hungarian and Bohemian possessions. Even so, she vehemently objected to having Charles, her eldest brother and the emperor since 1519, contemplate a second marriage for her. A reunification of Charles and Maria in Innsbruck in 1530 would have long-term consequences for the young widow, for it no doubt led to his decision a few months later to make Maria the successor of their recently deceased aunt Margaret as governess of the Netherlands.

Charles V was especially fond of this part of the vast Habsburg possessions, which during his rule extended from Hungary and Bohemia through the empire to Spain and its overseas possessions in Latin America and Asia. He was born in this region and, like Maria, spent his early years there. Moreover, although the sections of the Duchy of Burgundy still belonging to the Habsburgs were part of the empire, at the same time they lay in the zone of conflict between the empire, France, and England and therefore in a hotspot of political disputes. Due to the conflicting interests of cities and nobles in the interior, they were not easily governed, but they were rich in revenue and consequently an important source of money for Habsburg rule.

As a result, 1531 became another turning point in Maria's life. In a letter of 3 January 1531 from Cologne, in which he told her about aunt Margaret's death, Emperor Charles V asked his sister to succeed Margaret as governess.[4] At the same time, in the letter he respected her desire not to marry again. And he emphasised his complete confidence in her in religious matters and welcomed her decision to part (at his request) with attendants with questionable religious commitments.

Of course, this reference to religion must be placed, on the one hand, in the general context of the Reformation, which had been spreading through the empire since 1517. As is well known, the emperor used all available means to oppose its advance. On the other hand, the reference also pertained to Maria personally, even if Charles was not explicit. In Hungary, which by the 1520s already had many Lutherans, the queen had showed quite an interest in the Lutheran creed and evidently had even read Luther's writings. Like many other contemporaries, she too probably felt that the Church needed to be reformed. Her court chaplain, Johannes Henckel, maintained, at the very least, contact by mail with Lutheran theologians. This interest even drew attention in Wittenberg, and Martin Luther himself took it into account by dedicating a book of consolation to the newly widowed queen of Hungary in 1526.[5] But at least by the time she took over in the Netherlands—and even though, throughout her life, she remained more willing than her brother to compromise on religious issues—Maria accepted the logic of their dynasty: the House of Habsburg was and would remain loyal to the pope.

Maria and the emperor travelled separate routes to the Netherlands, meeting there in April 1531. Over the next few months, Charles and his sister proceeded through the provinces—he wanted thereby to demonstrate his confidence in Maria to his office holders and subjects in the Netherlands and thus provide an all the more solid footing for her governorship. On 5 July 1531, they both participated in an assembly of the general estates in Brussels, where Charles introduced his sister as governess to the representatives of the nobility and towns. The year that Maria and Charles spent together in the Netherlands, and during which Maria certainly learned much about the everyday practice of government, deeply shaped their lifelong trusting relationship.

Prior to leaving Brussels in January 1532, the emperor admittedly set clear limits to her independent decision-making.[6] Maria was generally supposed to make decisions only after consulting with advisors; Charles retained the final say regarding personnel decisions and reserved for himself the granting of privileges and acts of mercy in the event of severe crimes. In addition, he left behind numerous directives for dealing with France, England, Guelders, and Cleves, neighbours with whom more or less open conflicts had been simmering for years. Maria was also supposed to undertake regular visitation journeys throughout the land and make reports. As a result, despite the restrictions, she had far more extensive rights—especially in financial administration—than her aunt Margaret had ever been able to claim. This once more illustrates Charles's confidence in his deputy.

Maria always signed her many letters to her brothers Charles and Ferdinand with "your very humble and very obedient sister Maria". In these letters, she also often regretted her "incompetence", which she insisted almost made her come undone when faced with her brothers' demands; she wrote about her "foolishness", or that she had a "crazy head". But we can confidently categorise this as rhetoric she used to ensure that the two princes did not feel slighted or aggrieved by her quick and direct responses. And the empty phrases reveal Maria's deep awareness of her problematic position as governess. She held power only at the behest of her eldest brother and, as much as he trusted her, he could also dismiss her at will. At the same time, as his sister, she was also very closely tied to him, and her years in Hungary doubtless helped make her aware of her organisational skills and ability to exercise power. Yet, as a woman, she held no direct rights of rulership of her own in the territories.

Maria's letters, especially those to Charles, were sometimes very short, and sometimes elaborate with many specific details. Those written after she assumed power clearly reveal the everyday governmental routines of a regent, for Maria consulted on many individual issues—she and Charles exchanged 239 letters in 1532 alone, while there were an additional 69 letters between Ferdinand and Maria. Reports were made about awarding offices, for example. Loyal office holders were crucial for securing Maria's long-term ability to act, and she was evidently very successful in balancing the large aristocratic families. In this area, she could often prevail against Charles's ideas and interventions through her tenacity. But reports were also made about the construction of fortresses and work on the North Sea dikes; messages were passed on and pension payments were arranged for allies. The regent forwarded requests with regard to money, offices, and honours from a wide array of people, as well as files on many different kinds of issues. She recruited soldiers in the name of the emperor and obtained money for his military campaigns, settled disputes between noble families, and tried to resolve conflicts with the towns of the Netherlands.

Maria was not successful in every respect—for example, she could only resolve the unrest in Brussels in 1532 and Ghent in 1539 with difficulty or by involving Charles V. She repeatedly made her brothers aware that, despite the affluence of the Netherlands, taxes and levies could not be immeasurably increased. However, the financing of Charles's military campaigns in France, Italy, North Africa, and the empire, as well as Ferdinand's conflicts with the Ottomans, was consistently one of the greatest challenges of Maria's regency. Another problem was the armed conflicts that affected the Netherlands directly, such as the disputes with France and the duke of Cleves, who was allied with France in the 1540s. And finally, in the Netherlands Maria had to fight not just for money and troops but also increasingly about the religious confession. The number of Protestants continually grew in parts of the territory, and Charles expected resolute action against them without regard for economic or political consequences, which Maria regularly warned against.

For more than a quarter century, Maria of Hungary was her imperial brother's confidant and pillar of support in a stormy time and sometimes under difficult circumstances. At times she seems to have been overwhelmed by the burden of government affairs; several times, she asked Charles V to discharge her. But we can assume that such requests were more likely aimed at reminding her brother, who was often absent for long periods and preoccupied with plans for his global empire, about the conditions in the Netherlands and Maria's situation, rather than reflecting a serious desire to retire. Despite the burden of the office, and notwithstanding protestations to the contrary, Maria was a regent in heart and soul.

FIGURE 4.1   Maria of Hungary. Copy of a lost portrait by Titian. This portrait was created in Augsburg in 1548, where Maria, Charles, Ferdinand, and their nephew Maximilian met, along with Christine of Lorraine and Dorothea of Denmark

Rijksmuseum Amsterdam

Rijksmuseum Amsterdam, http://hdl.handle.net/10934/RM0001.COLLECT.10359

Of course, managing war and peace in the Netherlands was not Maria's only field of action. She was continuously in contact with her brother Ferdinand regarding Hungarian matters, primarily because of the transfer of money she was supposed to receive from Hungary. Ferdinand's financial distress and legal ebbs and flows concerning Maria's control over the Hungarian estates to which she was entitled as widow queen meant that income arrived sporadically. But at least in the 1540s, she nonetheless drew substantial sums from there, which helped her maintain her court in the Netherlands. Not until 1548 did Maria finally agree to have her estates fall to Ferdinand in exchange for a fixed pension.

What is interesting here is that Maria's demands were partially justified, but sometimes quite excessive, and yet they were repeatedly affirmed—evident here are the strategies of princely financial policy, which both Maria and Ferdinand had mastered. Namely, it was their mutual affirmation of high claims that created the external creditworthiness used by Maria and Ferdinand to secure each other.

Maria's correspondence with Ferdinand[7] reveals a relationship that was significantly less hierarchical than the one with Charles, for although Ferdinand was her brother, he was not the supreme head of the House of Habsburg. And until Charles V abdicated, Ferdinand was "just" a king—and she a widow queen. Hence with him she sometimes took the liberty of expressing much clearer criticism, such as regarding the selection of an envoy, for which she recommended someone who, in her view, was a suitable gentleman. "It is better to use such people than, as you have often done, to entrust important business to unsuitable envoys who are just good enough to break what was not yet broken."[8] But she definitely expressed criticism or admonishments to Charles as well, particularly calling for prudence with regard to his sometimes grandiose military campaign projects. In 1538, the emperor was evidently dreaming about a crusade by the European powers against the Ottomans, whereupon Maria sent him a memorandum in which she tried to bring him back to the solid ground of facts: "The route to the Levant is far, and one must be doubly equipped; that is something quite different than Tunis, so close to the harbours of Sicily. ... Successes are not to be gained here in quick seizures but only in years, and that costs an endless amount of money."[9]

However, her ties to her siblings and thus at the same time to the House of Habsburg did not just move Maria of Hungary to put her political capabilities as regent in the service of her brother. Like her aunt Margaret, she also functioned as a "substitute mother", in her case for the children[10] of her sister Isabella, who died young. In 1523, Isabella had been forced to flee Denmark with her deposed husband, Christian II, and had found refuge in Brussels. Starting in 1548, Maria's court was also a safe haven for her widowed sister Eleonora, who had been married to King

Francis I of France, because his son and successor, King Henry II, no longer wanted to tolerate her in Paris.

Evidence still somewhat visible today of the close bond between the royal siblings is a collection of family portraits from Spain, Portugal, Italy, France, and Austria that Maria collected in her Brussels palace. On the one hand, Maria's collection was dedicated to the memory of siblings, nephews, and nieces, for, given the large distances, they rarely saw each other. On the other, the gallery also served as a representation of Maria's dynastic relationships, which of course reached far beyond the empire.

For the representation of the House of Habsburg, the regent also repeatedly used magnificent festivals, which she organised in Brussels and in her palace in Binche—for example, in 1541 on the occasion of the marriage between her niece Christine and the duke of Lorraine in Brussels, in 1544 during a visit from Queen Eleonora of France, and especially in 1549, when Maria held a legendary festival in Binche in August for her eldest nephew, Philip II of Spain. And like the festivals, Maria's extensive collection of tapestries was not used merely to furnish her palaces in a way that befitted her social status. At the same time, she used them in accordance with Burgundian tradition to represent political and military success, often in the form of ancient heroic stories. The great series "Hunts of Maximilian" and "The Conquest of Tunis", which decorated a hall in Brussels, glorified the House of Habsburg and Charles V—and thus probably also Maria herself as a Habsburg and the sister of the emperor.

In addition, the specific character of the way she held court speaks volumes about Maria as a person. That her court consisted of around 150 people was merely in keeping with her status as a queen and regent. But the fact that, apart from ladies of the court, guards, and clerics, these people also included grooms and the members of a court orchestra points towards her two great passions: Maria was an enthusiastic and indefatigable rider and hunter who also routinely reported on her accomplishments to the emperor, himself an avid hunter. The English envoy John Hutton noted in this regard: "I have often accompanied her on her excursions, and the man who wants to be able to follow her day after day needs a strong horse and a strong heart."[11]

Apart from hunting, music was her favourite pastime. As a child she was educated in singing and composition and learned to play several instruments. And, finally, Queen Maria was also a passionate builder. From 1533 to 1537, she had the Palace of Coudenberg in Brussels remodelled according to her ideas. After 1545, she had the castles of Binche and Mariemont converted into a manor house and hunting lodge, respectively. Binche thereby became one of the earliest Renaissance palaces north of the Alps and was greatly praised and admired by contemporaries.

The close bond above all with her eldest brother and Maria's unshakeable commitment to the House of Habsburg constituted, therefore, a determinative factor for the life of Maria of Hungary. This became quite apparent again during her final years: as a sick and disillusioned Charles V abdicated in 1556 and ceded the title of emperor to his brother, Maria, together with her sister Eleonora, accompanied him to Spain. In the last months of her life, Charles and his son Philip II urged her, however, to return to the Netherlands again as regent—Philip, who had taken over the governorship there, had to concede, although very reluctantly, that he was actually unable to come to grips with circumstances and that the religiopolitical conflicts were still intensifying. Maria struggled with herself for a long time, but, as a loyal pillar of support for her brother, ultimately agreed in the awareness that it was up to her to preserve the Netherlands for the House of Habsburg. However, this time she could no longer fulfil the task, for in October 1558 she unexpectedly died at her Spanish home in Cigalés, just a few weeks after Eleonora and Charles. Today her mortal remains rest in the El Escorial.

Her funeral oration said the following about her work as regent: "In her council there was never a man who knew better than her how to debate the pros and cons of a problem and how to draw a more accurate conclusion."[12] While she did not by any means always enjoy political success, Maria of Hungary nonetheless determined the history of the provinces of the Netherlands for decades. And without the backing that Charles V received from Maria's regency, the political and confessional developments in the empire would doubtless have taken on a different shape.

Notes

1 Tamussino, *Maria*, p. 49.
2 Particularly in Germanic cultures, a gift given by the husband to his wife after the consummation of their marriage.
3 Songs about the death of the king and the widow's situation circulated throughout all of the German-speaking regions and show that the public at the time was aware of the catastrophe and followed the fate of the queen; see Tamussino, *Maria*, pp. 129–133. The same is shown by a text by the famous humanist Erasmus Rotterdam, whose published treatise *De Vidua Christiana* is dedicated to Maria of Hungary.
4 See the print in Gorter-van Royen, L., Hoyois, J., and Stratenwerth, H. (eds.) (2009) *Correspondance de Marie de Hongrie avec Charles Quint et Nicolas de Granvelle*, vol. 1: *1532 et années antérieures*. Turnhout: Brepols, no. 17a.
5 *Vier tröstliche Psalmen* (1526) in Luther, M. (1897) Weimarer Ausgabe: Schriften, vol. 19. Weimar: Böhlau, pp. 542–615.
6 For detail, see Gorter et al., *Correspondance*, no. 24.
7 Laferl, C. et al. (1912–2015) *Die Korrespondenz Ferdinands I* (6 vols. thus far). Vienna: Böhlau.
8 Quoted in Gorter, "Korrespondentin", pp. 57–58.
9 Tamussino, *Maria*, p. 210.
10 Dorothea of Denmark, Electress of Palatinate; Christine of Denmark, Duchess of Milan, later Duchess of Lorraine, and Johann of Denmark.
11 Tamussino, *Maria*, p. 195.
12 Quoted in Gorter, "Korrespondentin", p. 52.

Selected bibliography

Fuchs, M., and Réthelyi, O. (eds.) (2007) *Maria von Ungarn (1505–1558): Eine Renaissancefürstin*. Münster: Aschendorff.

Gorter-van Royen, L. (2007) "Maria von Ungarn als Korrespondentin", in Fuchs, M., and Réthelyi, O., *Maria von Ungarn (1505–1558): Eine Renaissancefürstin*. Münster: Aschendorff, pp. 47–58.

Réthelyi, O. (ed.) (2005) *Mary of Hungary: The Queen and her Court 1521–1531*. Budapest: History Museum.

Tamussino, U. (1998) *Maria von Ungarn: Ein Leben im Dienst der Casa de Austria*. Graz: Styria.

Walsh, K. (2006) "A Habsburg who received a dedication from Martin Luther: The Reformation sympathies of Maria, Queen of Hungary and Archduchess of Austria", in Clarke, H.B. (ed.), *Ireland, England and the Continent in the Middle Ages and Beyond: Essays in Memory of a Turbulent Friar, F. X. Martin, O.S.A.* Dublin: University College Dublin Press, pp. 272–229.

ELISABETH OF BRUNSWICK-CALENBERG (1510–1558)

A Princess as Reformer

Born in 1511 as the daughter of Elector Joachim I of Brandenburg and his wife Elisabeth of Denmark, Elisabeth deserves recognition because she took an active role in the political and religious restructuring of the Reformation period. She did this, on the one hand, as the driving force behind the reforming of the Duchy of Calenberg and, on the other, as a female author who specifically grappled with her period's confessional and political questions.

As a 14-year-old she was married off to Erich I of Brunswick, 40 years her senior, whose Duchy of Calenberg covered substantial portions of today's Lower Saxony. Their age difference makes the marriage seem unusual from today's perspective but, in her time, this was by no means the case. The duke, whose first marriage never produced any children, hoped his younger wife would give him descendants, especially a son as the heir of the duchy. And so it was: Elisabeth brought four children into the world: Duke Erich II, born in 1528, as well as three daughters, Elisabeth, Anna Maria, and Katharina.

Elisabeth's father and his younger brother, Archbishop Albert of Mainz, campaigned vigorously against Luther and the Reformation. In contrast, her mother Elisabeth—born a royal princess of Denmark—turned to the new creed with full conviction as early as 1527. This left Elector Joachim feeling mortified as a husband and diminished in his authority as a prince, and he threatened to have her walled away if she did not return to her old faith. As a result, the electress fled to Saxony in 1528, where she lived under the protection of her uncle, Elector Johann of Saxony,

DOI: 10.4324/9781003252870-6

until her husband died in 1535, and she also had personal contact with Martin Luther in Wittenberg.

The mother's early and decisive change of faith probably had a major impact on the daughter and several of her siblings. We must at least assume that this strengthened Elisabeth's interest in Luther's writings. A few years later, in 1534, the young duchess visited her mother in Wittenberg, where she also attended a sermon by Martin Luther. Over the years, Elisabeth of Brunswick therefore drew closer to the Protestant faith. Her mother's influence in this process can also be deduced from the fact that Elisabeth's conversion in 1538 was preceded by a visit from her mother and her brother Johann, who was already Lutheran. The reading of Lutheran texts also played a role here: an inventory of the duchess's books from 1539[1] shows that, already back then, she owned a significant number of such written works, from the Luther Bible through to writings by Philipp Melanchthon and Caspar Hedio, a prominent theologian from Strasbourg.

In contrast, Duke Erich I of Brunswick remained committed to the old creed until his death, but felt that, since his wife left him unmolested in his faith, he also wanted to leave her confession up to her. When the duke died in summer 1540, Elisabeth herself was thus a Protestant. Entirely new opportunities for action in the realm of politics and confessionalism now arose for her, because her only son, Erich II, the heir of the duchy, was only 12 years old and hence could not lead the government on his own. As was common in most German principalities, the duke had appointed his spouse—the heir's mother—as legal guardian. Together with advisors and related and/or friendly princes, she was supposed to lead the government until the heir could take over himself.

To be sure, like every other princely woman, Duchess Elisabeth had already previously been responsible for certain tasks of government.[2] And she had also displayed skill and perseverance in a conflict with her husband. Soon after their wedding, Duke Erich I had resumed contact with his long-time concubine Anna Rumschottel[3]—naturally, to Elisabeth's disapproval. Despite her husband's resistance, in 1534/35 she managed to see to the concubine's banishment. To settle the marital conflict, the duke ultimately also declared his willingness to grant Elisabeth free disposition over her wittum, the domain of Münden.[4] Strictly speaking, a wittum was meant to provide for a widow after her husband's death, but Elisabeth now presided over the domain during her husband's lifetime. Consequently, Elisabeth had direct responsibility over a fairly large dominion already prior to 1540, which also gave her a significant source of income.

FIGURE 5.1 Duchess Elisabeth of Brunswick-Calenberg, 1542

Herzog-August-Bibliothek Wolfenbüttel

Christliche/ Bestendige vnnd in der Schrifft vnd Heiligen Veteren wolgegrünte Verklerung vnd Erleuterung/ der furnemesten Artikel vnser waren Alten Christlichen Religion/ Fur Arme Einfeltige Pfarrherrn/ Jnn den Druck gegeben, Erfurt: Sachsse 1542, Herzog-August-Bibliothek Wolfenbüttel, Signatur AB M: Th 2938

This doubtless helped ensure that she already had practical governing experience by the time her husband died. However, it was only by prevailing in protracted disputes that she ultimately managed to lead her son's legal guardianship until 1545 largely on her own. Her main adversary here was her co-guardian, Heinrich the Younger of Brunswick-Wolfenbüttel, who put obstacles in her way and sought to secure for himself the broadest possible access rights to both the young prince and the territory. Until the birth of Elisabeth's son, Duke Heinrich was considered the heir of the Duchy of Calenberg, and he now wanted to use the legal guardianship to expand his rights of rule in the neighbouring territory. In addition, he was and remained Catholic and found himself in confrontation with Elisabeth and the other (Protestant) guardians, Landgrave Philipp of Hessen and Elisabeth's brother Elector Joachim II of Brandenburg.

After 1540, Henry and Elisabeth faced each other as opponents, neither wanting to concede an inch: Elisabeth strove for broad independence and the implementation of the Reformation; Henry wanted to prevent both. The duchess widow, however, managed to secure the long-term support of her co-guardians from Hessen and Brandenburg and also retain the loyalty of the duchy's nobility to her and her son. As an influential representative of the empire's adherents to the old faith, Henry, on the other hand, won the favour of Emperor Charles V. Only after a long showdown did the duchess finally gain the upper hand in spring 1542, not least because Henry's threat of military action prompted the duchy's territorial estates to side clearly with the young duke and his mother.

Another factor was that the duchess was able to convince her brother Joachim to promise his military support to King Ferdinand I in the fight against the Ottomans only on the condition that Elisabeth was confirmed as the legal guardian of her son. And the Schmalkaldic League, the military alliance of Protestant imperial princes, resolved in summer 1542 to attack Duke Henry, as the last prince of the old faith in the northern empire, and drive him out of his duchy, which ultimately brought about the final decision. The struggle for power in the duchy linked the level of the territory—that is, the negotiation of the relationship between the territorial estates and regent—with that of the empire—the positioning of the duchess between the emperor and the territorial princes and simultaneously between the Roman Catholic and Protestant powers. The same applied to the establishment of the Reformation, one of the duchess's key concerns.

Elisabeth had already introduced the Reformation to her Münden domain in 1538. Immediately after her husband's death, she had her son take communion with bread and wine, which clearly signalled to contemporaries his belonging to the Protestant faith. After 1542, she took the initiative of imposing the Reformation on the entire duchy, although towns like Göttingen, Hameln, and Northeim had already decided earlier in favour of the Lutheran faith. Protestant preachers were brought into the territory; the court and organisation of the church and convents were restructured. Thus Duchess Elisabeth classically imposed the reforms from the top as a "princely Reformation". This had also occurred in other territories of the empire—for example, in the Duchy of Saxony and the Landgraviate of Hessen. But in the case of the Duchy of Calenberg, it was a princess ruling as a regent that legally and organisationally paved the way for the new creed.

An important spiritual advisor to the duchess and later superintendent of the Duchy of Calenberg was Antonius Corvinus, who had already come from Hessen to Münden in 1538. In 1542, Elisabeth arranged for the publication of a church order he had formulated and for which she herself had written a foreword, in which she explained the motives and basis for her actions in detail. She also did the same in her visitation instructions, a directive she wrote herself for the review and reformation of the monasteries. She elucidated them again in 1544 because abbots and other heads of the monasteries were not complying with her directive. This explanatory text was printed in 1545 as *Ein Christlicher Sendbrief* (A Christian open letter), which at same time marked Duchess Elisabeth's debut as a Protestant author.

The *Sendbrief* was probably created in collaboration with Antonius Corvinus and presents thoughts on individual and institutional religious practices and on princely rule. Here and in her foreword to the church order, it becomes clear that Duchess Elisabeth took her role as "Landesmutter" (mother of the people) very seriously and legitimated it in two ways: she explained that her conversion to Lutheranism should by no means be seen only as a personal decision but rather at the same time arose from an obligation towards her subjects. From her perspective, her own salvation and that of her subjects were closely linked, for Elisabeth, as a princely authority, felt herself responsible for guiding her subjects and promoting their piety.

As regent, she therefore acted very independently, resolutely, and in keeping with her convictions at the confessional level—and this produced consequences for the duchy's political position in the empire. Elisabeth repeatedly had to fight for the security of the Duchy of Calenberg, not least because, even after 1542, she was politically caught in the middle between her co-guardians: whereas Duke Heinrich of Wolfenbüttel persisted in the old faith, Landgrave Philipp of Hessen was a leader of the Protestant League, and her brother Joachim of Brandenburg positioned himself as a mediator. And she tacked between the aforementioned Schmalkaldic League, which attracted her because of her conviction as a Lutheran, and the emperor. Demanding that she support his side, Charles V made reference to the decision of Duke Erich I, who had decided for the (Catholic) Nuremberg League, which had been initiated by the emperor. In the end, Elisabeth had to restrain herself from committing to any such alliances and had to leave the decision on the duchy's political affiliation to her son as the legitimate holder of power.

Along with her confessional policy measures, however, Elisabeth of Brunswick was also on a mission for her faith as a writing princess, which she pursued until the end of her life. Apart from the aforementioned *Sendbrief* of 1545, the duchess wrote other texts as well: also in 1545, a "Fürstenspiegel" (manual on government) for her son Erich II; and a small book on marriage for her daughter Anna Maria written in 1550, the year of the latter's marriage. In both she presented her ideas about living and governing according to Christian principles. The advice and instructions in the text are always placed in a Biblical context and founded on the word of God. That they were at the same time determined by the Lutheran faith is obvious. The same applied to the book for the consolation of widows of 1555 and to several songs and shorter writings.[5]

In addition, Elisabeth repeatedly compiled extracts from the Bible on certain topics or formulated prayers in situations where she herself needed consolation—not all of these texts have survived. Just like this authorial practice, her letters show her as a competent reader of theological texts. This is particularly clear in her correspondence with her son-in-law Albert of Prussia.

The latter kept her up to date from 1551 on a theological debate about the contentious views of the theologian Andreas Osiander, who taught first in Nuremberg and then in Königsberg. The theological content of this "Osiandrian controversy", which involved many theologians and believers throughout the empire, cannot be discussed here. But Elisabeth of Brunswick took an active role in it, insofar as she repeatedly read texts produced as part of the controversy and stated her position regarding their content to the duke of Prussia. She also repeatedly offered to act as a mediator between the participating theologians and attempt a conciliation. Although in the end this never came about, her letters clearly show that she was well-versed in theological issues and readily presumed to participate in and moderate a theological debate.

Elisabeth's characteristically Lutheran religious thought plays a major role in other texts she wrote as well. More than a third of the manual on governance for her son consists of discussions about religious issues and practices. But its other sections constitute a compendium of practical advice and explain what a prince should and should not do: how to select officials, what their duties and necessary qualifications should be, how much confidence one should have in their work (not much), when to introduce new taxes (rarely, since this turns the hearts of subjects away from the prince), how to deal with monasteries (with caution), whether to trust alliances (never). Here she doubtless summarised many lessons she had been forced—or was able—to learn herself, first in Münden and then during her regency as her son's legal guardian.

The assumption of government by her son Erich II and Elisabeth's remarriage in 1546 to Count Poppo of Henneberg symbolically and de facto marked the end of her guardianship, in that she turned over power to her son and began a new life as a wife. However, these steps heralded difficult times for Elisabeth of Brunswick.

Her son took part in the Schmalkaldic War in 1547 on the emperor's side and banished Protestant preachers from his domain. Despite his Protestant upbringing by his mother, the young duke converted back to the old faith in 1548 and began reintroducing Catholicism to his duchy. His mother commented on this with the words: "I would truly have sooner predicted the fall of the heavens than such disloyalty of my own child."[6] In this respect, she more or less openly opposed him and vehemently tried to protect the pastors of the Münden domain. Together with the territorial estates, she pressed for the duke's promise to safeguard the Lutheran confession, which Erich II then provided in 1553 because he needed money for a military campaign. However, both the recatholicisation and his sporadic willingness to compromise on confessional matters remained half-hearted. All told, Duke Erich II spent little time in his duchy, which he viewed primarily as a source of revenue. Instead, he waged war for the emperor in Spain, the Netherlands, and Italy, and died in his house in Pavia, Northern Italy, in 1584.

Perhaps Elisabeth had foreseen the kinds of problems with her son that emerged when he assumed power on his own, for in her manual on governance she had always demanded his obedience to her as his mother and extensively justified this from the Bible. "Dear son, since from God you have no other authority to which you must be subject with obedience other than the emperor, your lord, and me, your dear mother, thus you should properly and duly obey him in all things that are not against God and concern only body and property. ... So, my son, such obedience and honour towards me as your mother also does not stop, regardless of whether you have just set aside the years of childhood."[7]

In the course of this conflict with her son, Elisabeth also lost Münden, her widow's estate. In 1545 she had secured her usage of Münden for the rest of her life—that is, even after her remarriage, which was highly unusual. Normally a princely women lost such entitlements if she remarried because her new husband was henceforth responsible for providing for her. Elisabeth, however, evidently highly valued her economic security and independence, and she initially prevailed with regard to her control of Münden. But as early as autumn 1550, Erich II, who by then no doubt very clearly understood the level of income derived from Münden, tried not only to take action against the Lutheran preachers there but also to totally deprive his mother of access to the domain. The duchess defended herself, which included calling upon the Imperial Chamber Court in Speyer and appealing to the emperor. But she lost in both instances.

During the military developments in summer 1553, Münden was occupied by the troops of Heinrich the Younger of Brunswick-Wolfenbüttel. Even after the territory was returned, her son only allowed Elisabeth to receive a fraction of her earlier payments because he wanted to use the rest of the substantial income from Münden to cover his own debts from his military expeditions. Moreover, he blamed his mother for his disastrous campaign in summer 1553, during the course of which Münden was initially lost, and he absolutely wanted to prevent her from still having access to the domain and therefore a voice in the duchy. As a result, Elisabeth had to live with her younger daughter Katharina in impoverished circumstances in Hanover. She received no money, neither from her son nor from her husband, and appealed everywhere for support, but above all to her son-in-law in Prussia.

An agreement regarding support payments was finally reached in 1555, after which Elisabeth usually lived in Ilmenau or Schleusingen in Thuringia. Her husband, Poppo of Henneberg, had not got involved in Elisabeth's last dispute with her son. But in Ilmenau, conflicts soon developed between Elisabeth, who was used to her autonomy, and her husband. It went so far that Poppo—resolved to assert his rule in Ilmenau against his wife—separated from his spouse "at the table and in bed",[8] as she herself put it. Only after considerable pains could amity between them be restored, under the condition that Elisabeth was to restrain herself and leave the governance to Poppo, in keeping with "her womanly profession", that is, as per the female gender norms.[9]

The life of Elisabeth of Brunswick can therefore be divided into several phases, which were also—but not only—linked to her respective status as a girl, wife, and widow, and marked by various distinctive opportunities for action. As a girl and young wife, she quite obviously subordinated herself in large part to her father and husband. But when her husband disrespected her person and origin—after all, she was the daughter of an elector and a royal princess of Denmark—by consorting with a concubine, Elisabeth fiercely defended herself. Thus a new phase of life began for her in 1535: although reconciled with her husband and acting with his authorisation, she gained a noticeable independence as the mistress of the profitable domain of Münden. She also made use of it to further her engagement with the new Lutheran confession and to finally publicly convert in 1538.

After the death of Duke Erich I in 1540, she together with male relatives assumed the legal guardianship over her son Erich II. At the same time, as she had already started doing in Münden in 1538, she implemented the Reformation throughout the entire duchy. She viewed the imposition of the new confession (at least on an administrative level) and the governmental reforms as her duty as a ruler, Christian, and mother. She turned over power to her son in 1545, but at first reserved the domain of Münden for herself. When she definitively lost the latter in 1555, her second husband, Poppo of Henneberg, exploited the change in his spouse's situation to secure his own position as master of the house. As a result, Elisabeth's final years of life may have been very sobering for the energetic duchess, not least because she now had to forgo her independent exercise of rule, which she had been accustomed to since 1535. The duchess had returned to the earth of the early modern gender hierarchy, so to speak.

Unlike other women who published writings during the Reformation, such as Katharina Zell, Elisabeth as a princely woman and custodial regent could put very direct force behind her religious convictions (albeit, not without resistance). And unlike many of her male princely counterparts, she also explained her motivations and convictions in the aforementioned texts—in this respect, she can be described in a double sense as a "Reformation princess".

Notes

1 Schlotheuber, E. et al. (2011) *Das Bücherinventar der Elisabeth von Calenberg: Edition und Anmerkungen*, Wolfenbüttel. Available at http://diglib.hab.de/edoc/ed000082/start.htm.
2 See the Introduction.
3 On this in detail, Lilienthal, *Fürstin*, pp. 44–54.
4 Today Hannoversch Münden.
5 For a list of her writings see Schlotheuber, *Herzogin Elisabeth*, pp. 281–283.
6 Mengel, I. (ed.) (1954) *Elisabeth von Braunschweig-Lüneburg und Albrecht von Preußen; ein Fürstenbriefwechsel der Reformationszeit*. Göttingen: Musterschmidt, p. 84.

7 Tschackert, P. (ed.) (1899) *Herzogin Elisabeth von Münden (gest. 1558), geborene Markgräfin von Brandenburg, die erste Schriftstellerin aus dem Hause Brandenburg und aus dem braunschweigischen Hause, ihr Lebensgang und ihre Werke*. Berlin: Giesecke & Devrient, p. 33. Available at https://gdz.sub.uni-goettingen.de/id/PPN533605687.
8 Mengel, *Elisabeth*, p. 285.
9 Quoted in Lilienthal, *Fürstin*, p. 178.

Selected bibliography

Lilienthal, A. (2007) *Die Fürstin und die Macht: Welfische Herzoginnen im 16. Jahrhundert: Elisabeth, Sidonia, Sophia*. Hannover: Hahnsche Buchhandling.

Schlotheuber, E., et al. (eds.) (2011) *Herzogin Elisabeth von Braunschweig-Lüneburg (1510–1558). Herrschaft—Konfession—Kultur*. Hanover: Hahnsche Buchhandlung.

Stjerna, K. (2009) "Elisabeth von Brandenburg, 1485–1555, and Elisabeth von Braunschweig, 1510–1558—Exiled Mothers, Reforming Rulers", in *Women and the Reformation*. Malden, MA: Blackwell, pp. 87–108.

ANNA OF SAXONY (1532–1585)

Of Princely Domains and Good Medicines

On 22 November 1532, the bells rang out in the castle of the Danish town of Haderslev: the first child of the young ducal couple Christian of Schleswig-Holstein-Hadersleben and Dorothea of Saxe-Lauenburg had been born. The father of the baby girl, who was given the name Anna, was the eldest son of King Friedrich I of Denmark and Norway, whom he succeeded in 1534 as Christian III. In 1537, Anna's parents were crowned as king and queen in Copenhagen. Since both had been members of the Lutheran faith since the 1520s, the ceremony was performed by Johannes Bugenhagen as an envoy of Martin Luther. It was the first Protestant coronation in history.

Anna and her four younger siblings—Friedrich (later Danish king), Magnus, Johann, and Dorothea—were likewise raised in the Lutheran faith. The siblings' mother tongue was German, but they also spoke Danish. As is often the case for women, we know little about Anna's education. However, her library, which consisted of well over 400 volumes[1] when she died, indicates a broad range of interests, many of which probably accompanied her throughout her life. She read the classics of ancient literature, such as Thucydides, Caesar, and Aesop, as well as contemporary Italian texts, albeit both in German translation, and she owned numerous medical books and historical works. Two-thirds of her library, however, consisted of religious writings. They included many texts by Martin Luther, quite a few of them in multiple editions, the biography of Luther by Johannes Mathesius, various anthologies of sermons, and an entire collection of prayer booklets.

DOI: 10.4324/9781003252870-7

During Anna's youth, the members of the Danish royal house cultivated a rather modest lifestyle compared to their princely contemporaries, but they were naturally conscious of their status and tied into many different political and dynastic networks. Princely women played an important role in elaborating such networks, with marriage, of course, being a proven method for creating and shaping these connections. Accordingly, a marriage plan was developed in 1547 through which the Danish royal house established an association with one of the most important princely houses of the Holy Roman Empire—Anna became engaged to August of Saxony, the younger brother of Elector Maurice of Saxony. The marriage took place in 1548 at the Torgau castle and was one of the most splendid festivals of the period. In Saxony, the event was celebrated as a success in two respects: Duke August, as his brother wrote, had received "a beautiful virtuous young lady"[2] as a wife. Above all, however, through this marriage with a royal daughter, the Saxons had emphatically underscored their great political ambitions, which Elector Maurice was supposed to keep pursuing in the years that followed.

The young couple first took up residence in Weißenfels, where their first son was born in 1550. But just a few years later, the situation dramatically changed. In 1553, Elector Maurice of Saxony died from wounds received on the battlefield. Since he left no son behind, his brother August succeeded him as elector. Thus Anna became the electress of Saxony, one of the highest-ranking ladies of the empire, and the house mistress in the resplendently expanded Dresden palace, where the family—now growing in almost yearly intervals—resided. By 1575, Anna had given birth to a total of 15 children, only four of whom, however, reached adulthood and survived her: her son Christian I succeeded his father as elector in 1586; her daughter Elisabeth married Count Palatine Johann Casimir in 1570; Dorothea married Duke Heinrich Julius of Brunswick-Wolfenbüttel in 1585; and Anna married Duke Johann Casimir of Saxe-Coburg in 1586. The electress's only daughter-in-law, Sophie, was a daughter of the elector of Brandenburg.

These family connections alone illustrate the political importance of the electoral house and its alliances with other ruling houses of the Holy Roman Empire. For the electress, this is further reflected by her correspondence with numerous princes and princely women, aristocratic men and women, as well as with office holders of the Dresden and Copenhagen courts. More than 15,000 letters have survived, which allow us to trace these correspondence relationships and identify many aspects of the life and work of Anna as an electoral consort. She maintained longstanding contacts with quite a few of her correspondents, which only came to an end with her death on 1 October 1585.

FIGURE 6.1 Electress Anna of Saxony, after 1565

Alamy

Lucas Cranach the Younger, Full-lenght portrait of Anna of Denmark, Electress of Saxony, Oil on canvas, The Picture Art Collection

As a princess, Anna of Saxony had many different responsibilities and opportunities for action, which she pursued with great dedication and energy. Naturally, she was a wife and mother, and her letters exhibit a constant concern with the wellbeing of her spouse and children. She evidently had a trusting and loving relationship with Elector August for a long time. This meant, among other things, that Electress Anna accompanied her husband on all of his trips. They travelled together several times to Kolding and Copenhagen in Anna's homeland; they visited Emperor Maximilian II in Prague and Vienna; they travelled to imperial diets in Augsburg, Frankfurt am Main, and Regensburg. But there were also numerous meetings with princes and princely women of neighbouring territories, such as in Kassel, Kostrzyn nad Odrą, Güstrow, Wolfenbüttel, and Munich. And in Saxony itself, Anna accompanied her husband, an avid huntsman, to places like Stolpen, Torgau, Annaburg, and Augustusburg.

The electress's areas of responsibility also included helping coordinate life at court. Her clothing, the hosting of guests, the furnishings of the numerous palaces where the family stayed during the year, the gardens—such matters did not depend solely on the princess's taste. Rather, they were also aspects of the representation of the family's power and influence, and consequently they had a significance that reached beyond one's own court. Magnificent and status-appropriate, but not wasteful—this is how one could describe the basic principle of the electress in this respect.

She herself did not consider it sinful for women to wear makeup to appeal to their husbands, and she meticulously looked after her hands and hair. With regard to her clothing, Anna largely remained true to what she knew from Denmark. When preparing for the wedding of her eldest daughter Elisabeth in 1570, she told the invited princely women that they should appear in "German" clothing. The electress felt that "in this honest attire" one would "probably derive just as much glory from this and do just well as if we dressed ourselves right away in Italy's unusual naughty costumes and styles."[3] Did Anna's rejection of "naughty costumes" arise from her aversion to plunging necklines, so common in Italy at the time?

In the collaborations of the princely couple, however, the electress did not remain restricted to the parameters of the court, that is, her household in a broader sense. As Johannes Bugenhagen had already noted during the coronation of Anna's mother, a consort's job was also to appear with her husband as a facilitator and advocate. But Anna was also in demand as a facilitator for the Danish royal house. Her brother Friedrich had been king since 1559, and she maintained close contact with him by mail throughout her life. In the 1560s, she energetically took on the important and politically relevant task of brokering a marriage for him and her youngest brother Johann. But then during the Northern Seven Years' War between Denmark and Sweden from 1563 to 1570, the electress also arranged loans for her brother and took part in the initiation of peace negotiations.

An important concern for the electress, both in her work as the electoral consort in Saxony and in her networks throughout the empire, was always the protection and strengthening of the Lutheran confession. To be sure, by her time the great battles of the Reformation had already been fought; her brother-in-law Maurice and then her husband August had played major roles in establishing the 1555 Peace of Augsburg within the empire. But during the following decades, clerics and princes of all faiths sought to consolidate their own respective confession and recover lost positions wherever possible. During this time of contentious religious peace, contemporaries expected a princely woman to provide "maternal" protection and care for her respective church.

Anna was especially prepared to fulfil this expectation, for her deeply felt faith and piety were the foundations of her life. And this was not just because Lutheranism was the confession of her parents and spouse. Rather, as shown not least by her library, by no later than the end of the 1560s the electress was also dealing substantively with the theological controversies of her time. She encouraged court chaplains and theologians at the University of Wittenberg to translate theological texts; court chaplains such as Nikolaus Selnecker and Georg Listhenius dedicated theological publications to her. She was interested in the various religious discussions and, as an advocate of Lutheranism, sent polemical theological pamphlets to other princely women.

For very few female consorts of the early modern empire is it possible to trace the many facets of their actions within the framework of family, principality, and empire with as much nuance as for Electress Anna. Her extensive correspondence offers a rich resource that is far from thoroughly explored. She not only knew broad parts of the Holy Roman Empire from her many travels, but by way of correspondence was also associated with many princely and noble men and women, as well as with theologians and office holders. Through her involvement in confessional matters, arrangement of marriages, and advocacy, she influenced many smaller and larger decisions that helped determine the development of the empire and many of its territories.

In Saxony, however, she is remembered to this day above all for her impact as a "Landesmutter" (mother of the people), as a princess who worked very intensely and in various ways for the wellbeing of her subjects. This widespread image is no doubt idealised and based in some respects on historical accounts of the nineteenth century, which stylised the electress as a kind of bourgeois "super housewife". But, as often happens, it also contains a kernel of truth, which in Anna's case lies, on the one hand, in her actual identifiable and successful involvement as the administrator of the electoral estates, and, on the other, in her undeniable passion for the production of medicines and interest in healing.

It was not uncommon for princely, aristocratic, and bourgeois women to be knowledgeably involved in the administration of country estates. Indeed, it was often absolutely necessary, for when men held offices, performed military service, or were sick they could not look after properties and income on their own. We can even find cases, such as those of Anna of Brandenburg-Prussia and Juliane of Hessen-Kassel, where consorts helped reorganise the princely revenues—and this also applies to Anna of Saxony. For decades, the electress personally managed a large estate directly before the gates of Dresden, whose products benefited the kitchen of the electoral court or were sold in the market. She was evidently so successful that Elector August assigned to her (probably in 1570) the management of all 70 manors owned by the elector—the so-called chamber estates. Consequently, Anna of Saxony was responsible for a substantial portion of the electorate's revenue. The intensity with which she took up this task is shown by the large number of letters that Anna henceforth exchanged with managers and officials.

The main objective of the restructuring of the estates under Anna's management was to increase their income, which was accomplished in part by keeping more livestock and marketing yields more effectively. The electress procured large numbers of cattle from Poland, Denmark, Switzerland, and Italy to improve her stocks through breeding. She supervised the training of the maids who were responsible for caring for the livestock and producing cheese and butter. Many of her measures were evidently successful, since the income from the estates increased, and many years later agricultural textbooks were still praising the electress's expertise. Some contemporaries, however, reacted to the economic success and Anna's dedication with a lack of understanding. A woman residing in Sangerhausen, for example, came under investigation for allegedly making disparaging remarks about how the electress ran around in the cattle sheds, made butter and cheese, and sold them—"one calls her a Danish dairy mistress".[4]

During her lifetime, Anna was also known for her interest in medicines and their production, as well as in alchemy. She had extensive facilities at her disposal in several places in Saxony for the production of medicines—so-called distillation houses—where she often personally lent a hand. The largest was at Annaburg Castle. It was equipped with a vast number of various receptacles, along with several distillation apparatuses, scales, stills, etc., and it allowed for the performance of complex chemical processes. The electress had gained the requisite knowledge from a wide range of sources over the years. She collected recipe books and often had other princely and noble women send her such books or transcribe them for her. Her aforementioned library contained many printed herbal books and medicinal texts, including those of the physician Paracelsus, who is still famous today.

For the practice of making medicines, however, experience and advice were at least equally important. Anna of Saxony obtained it through quite an extensive network that connected her with like-minded women and men. They included, for example, Dorothea of Mansfeld and Anna of Hohenlohe-Langenburg, themselves both experienced pharmacists. But the group also included Abbess Margarethe von Watzdorf of the Clarissan convent in Weißenfels, the elector's personal physician Johann Neefe and his wife Appolonia, the erudite nobleman Hans Ungnad von Sonnegg, and many others.

The electress and her workers produced various oils and salves, distilled spirits and powders, as well as sweets that were attributed with healing effects. Particularly sought-after was evidently her "aqua vitae", a distillate of more than 300 herbs and other ingredients, which was supposed to help against a large number of diseases and ailments. As she did with many of her other products, the electress used it for gifts to relatives and princely and aristocratic friends. But, when asked, she was also willing to issue medical advice, above all with regard to female disorders, and to recommend or send over medicines.

Electress Anna was thus indeed an experienced apothecary and had an extensive understanding of medicines. But she was very well aware of the limits of her knowledge. Especially in the second half of her life, she doubtless had plenty of practical experiential knowledge, which grew through the lively exchange of ideas about recipes and illnesses. But, notwithstanding her plentiful reading and contacts with doctors, she had no knowledge of academic medicine, which was a male domain because it was taught in universities, and, like all women of her time, Anna had no access to the academic world. Moreover, since she also had no Latin skills, she could hardly take note of any specialised medical literature.

Her awareness of the limitations this entailed is reflected by, among other things, her description of her knowledge—despite having made many successful suggestions and medicines—as "common peasant arts".[5] And at the request of Empress Maria in 1574 for medical advice for her sister Joanna of Portugal, the electress first stated: "Although we indeed know that Your Majesty [Empress Maria] and no doubt also the royal dignity [Joanna] of Portugal are provided with excellent highly acclaimed doctors, hence we should probably have reservations about helping here with our womanly arts. But since God also grants grace to the humble and gives them the experience that often many people are helped by valuable medicine that does not come from the very erudite, [and] we also duly acknowledge being most humbly obedient to Your Majesty in many more matters, we are all the less shy about loyally disclosing and conveying to Your Majesty our science and experience."[6] Here she referred, on the one hand, to the experience-based origins of her "womanly arts" and to her lack of academic medicinal knowledge. On the other hand, she took pride in already having helped many people and at least eased their suffering on the basis of this experience.

Anna's passion for making medicines did not, of course, remain limited to concerns for the wellbeing of her family and princely and noble acquaintances. She also dispensed medicinal advice and had medications distributed to the inhabitants of Saxony. Also especially dear to her was the training of midwives. When an outbreak of the plague loomed in 1566, she hastily arranged for the production and generous distribution of substantial quantities of her *Giftpulver*, an antitoxic powder that was supposed to help prevent and heal infectious diseases. The fact that her inventory in Annaburg featured many medicinal supplies "for the poor, sick people"[7] shows that such medicinal support was not just provided during times of the plague.

Electress Anna served the sick because she possessed extensive experiential knowledge in pharmaceuticals and medicine and because supporting and caring for the sick and poor was part of the contemporary ideal of the housewife and good princess. The distribution of medications and health advice was part of her understanding of her God-given office as "Landesmutter". This was also true for many other princely women of the sixteenth century. Apart from the women already mentioned above, we also know that Dorothea of Prussia, Juliane of Schwarzburg, Magdalena of Hohenlohe-Langenburg, and many other women manufactured medications and generously distributed them to members of the court and other princely personages.

Anna was no doubt quite successful in this area, but, above all, her production was particularly large-scale. In addition, she was more broadly interested than many other women in pharmaceutical work as a form of experimental practice. Yet it was an interest she also shared with other princely contemporaries, such as Dorothea of Mansfeld, Anna of Hohenlohe-Langenburg, Anna Maria of Württemberg and others, some of whom she also collaborated with over years. These women participated in a development that stood between the medieval and modern understanding of the natural sciences. As she did with many other things, Anna engaged in the production of medications with remarkable thoroughness and efficiency, probably because she was able to pursue her personal interests and proclivities. And while her extensive distribution of medications to common people may have been unusual, in terms of her work with medicines she was by no means an exception.

Notes

1 See: Sächsische Landes- und Universitätsbibliothek Dresden, Registratur uber S. Frauen Annes Churfürstin zu Sachsen Bücher, Signatur Bibl.Arch.I.Ba,Vol.24.a https://digital.slub-dresden.de/werkansicht/dlf/109368/1. Hale, B.J. (2014) "Anna of Saxony and her Library", *Early Modern Women: An Interdisciplinary Journal* 9, pp. 101–114.
2 Quoted in Keller, *Kurfürstin*, p. 19.
3 Quoted in Keller, *Kurfürstin*, p. 51.
4 Quoted in Keller, *Kurfürstin*, p. 119.
5 Quoted in Keller, *Kurfürstin*, p. 168.
6 Quoted in Keller, *Kurfürstin*, p. 168.
7 Quoted in Rankin, *Daughters*, p. 28.

Selected bibliography

Arenfeld, P. (2005) *The Political Role of the Female Consort in Protestant Germany, 1550–1585: Anna of Saxony as "Mater Patriae"*. Florence: EUI.

Keller, K. (2010) *Kurfürstin Anna von Sachsen (1532–1585)*. Regensburg: Pustet.

Rankin, A. (2013) *Panaceia's Daughters: Noblewomen as Healers in Early Modern Germany*. Chicago: University of Chicago Press.

Schlude, U. (2009) "Naturwissen und Schriftlichkeit: Warum eine Fürstin des 16. Jahrhunderts nicht auf den Mont Ventoux steigt und die Natur exakter begreift als die 'philologischen' Landwirte", in Ruppel, S., and Steinbrecher, A. (eds.)*"Die Natur ist überall bey uns": Mensch und Natur in der Frühen Neuzeit*. Zürich: Chronos, pp. 95–108.

ARCHDUCHESS MARIA OF INNER AUSTRIA (1551–1608)

How a Mother Shapes her Children

FIGURE 7.1 Archduchess Maria of Inner Austria, 1577

Kunsthistorisches Museum Wien

Cornelis Vermeyen, Erzherzogin Maria von Innerösterreich, 1577, Kunsthistorisches Museum Wien, GG 3102

DOI: 10.4324/9781003252870-8

On 9 September 1571, Archduchess Maria entered the city of Graz for the first time, where, except when making various journeys, she would spend the following decades until her death in 1608. Together with her husband, Archduke Karl II of Inner Austria,[1] she was greeted before the town gates by the state captain of Styria, the bishop of Seckau, as well as numerous prelates and aristocratic men and women. Accompanied by celebratory gunfire and fireworks, the entry of the archducal couple marked the conclusion of an entire string of festivals that celebrated their marriage, first in Vienna and then in the Inner-Austrian capital of Graz.

This brought to a close a long process that had started with protracted negotiations that preceded the marriage, and during which it had not always been certain that these two persons would actually wed. Maria was the eldest daughter of the Bavarian ducal couple Albert V and Anna, the latter a daughter of Emperor Ferdinand I. Deeply Catholic and having grown up in the splendid Munich residence, Maria had been the subject of various marriage projects that had been pursued since she was 15 years old. At first, her father had his eye on Lorraine. And in 1566, Electress Anna of Saxony suggested to him a marriage with her brother, the king of Denmark and Norway. Although the king was Lutheran, the marriage plan was taken quite seriously, for it was joined with the hope that Maria would later bring her husband back into the fold of the Catholic Church.

Not until 1570 was this plan finally dropped in favour of another. Duke Albert had probably already earlier contemplated a marriage of his daughter to Archduke Karl, the youngest brother of Emperor Maximilian II and Albert's own wife. For a long time, however, Karl had been under discussion as a marriage candidate for Queen Elizabeth I of England. Only once this plan of the emperor had been shelved did the path open up for an enquiry from Vienna to Munich. The duke and duchess evidently quickly agreed to this proposal, especially since they "sensed" that their daughter was "not unwilling to do this".[2]

And this marriage between uncle and niece would prove to be a successful project in every respect. Already in November 1571, Karl personally wrote to his father-in-law in Munich: "Your Beloved should know that your dear one [Maria] acts towards me such that I cannot give enough thanks, first to God and thereafter to Your Beloved, that you have provided me with such a spouse."[3] As late as 1585, the nuncio in Graz reported to Rome that the archducal couple were devoted to each other in an almost unbelievable way and actually did not want to be apart for even an hour. The 15 children born between 1572 and 1590 were further signs of their mutual affection—throughout her marriage Maria was almost always pregnant or had just survived giving birth.

Of course, this did not prevent her from pursuing activities in many areas. She was very interested in music, collected exotica (following the example of her father and brother in Munich),[4] and was an enthusiastic hunter. Above all, however, she supported her husband, who indeed faced immense challenges. Defending against Ottoman attacks on the borders of his territories and thus the empire, and overcoming the resistance of the almost completely Lutheran nobility in Styria and Carinthia, were two highly complicated and closely intertwined tasks for the archduke.

To defend the borders, Archduke Karl needed the nobles and towns, but above all he required their money. To this end, however, he found himself forced to make assurances regarding the continued existence of Lutheranism, even though he actually strove for a counter-reformation, consequently a repression of the Protestant creed. The alarm bells sounded in Rome and in the Munich of Karl's Catholic father-in-law at the end of 1570s when it became evident that he was making unavoidable concessions to the Protestant nobility instead of taking action to ensure the hoped-for return of his subjects to the bosom of the Holy Mother Church. Rome even threatened excommunication if he did not revoke his assurances, and the anxiety this must have produced for Karl and his spouse Maria, who was so loyal to the Church, is easy to imagine.

Maria was just as unshakeably committed to the Catholic Church as her husband, and she backed him up in the political conflicts of his reign. At the same time, she remained especially closely tied to the Jesuit order, and always chose her father confessor from the ranks of its padres. But until 1600, when her eldest son took energetic steps to recatholicise his territories, most of Inner Austria remained Lutheran. Hence, by no means did all of the subjects view the religious commitment of their ruler's consort in positive terms. A Protestant report from Graz in January 1581, for example, accused her of wanting to "govern" the Lutheran confession "only senselessly by the sword".[5]

What Maria cared about here as a conscientious princess was not just her own salvation and that of her family, but also the salvation of her subjects. In this respect, she was no different from the "Reformation princess", Elisabeth of Brunswick. But if many of the residents of Inner Austria staunchly refused to return to the Catholic faith—which was the only conceivable one for Maria—then they rebuffed the archduchess both as a mother of the people and as a Catholic. For her part, Maria's public and aggressively practised Catholic piety in a predominantly Lutheran capital like Graz contributed to the conflicts—for example, when she publicly attended processions and pilgrimages.

Moreover, the archduchess did not see the adherence of the Protestant territorial estates to their confession merely as "heresy". Since it was inseparably tied to the effort to achieve greater independence from the prince, her husband, for her it simultaneously constituted "disobedience in political matters against the princely territorial authority"[6]—hence it was actually an insurrection. Moreover, it was an insurrection that also threatened the salvation of all Inner Austrians, including the Archduke Karl and Maria herself, because it prevented having everyone act in accordance with the decrees of the Church. Maria's position on the matter was therefore clear: particularly given "that this time it is not only and merely about religion and the salvation of many thousands of souls, but also about political obedience",[7] the resistance could not be tolerated under any circumstances. As the ruler's consort, she consequently saw her job as leading the territory and its inhabitants back to the proper faith. She acted on this conviction, doing so with such forcefulness that in 1581 Pope Gregory XIII conferred upon her the Golden Rose of Virtue to acknowledge her dedication.

The fact that her husband drew Archduchess Maria into territorial politics would prove to be useful far sooner than anyone had hoped. In July 1590, Archduke Karl died more or less unexpectedly. He left his wife heavily pregnant, and with 11 children (three had already died) and many unresolved political problems. Even though Maria was sure that she probably knew best as to "what my dearest spouse's blessed will was",[8] Emperor Rudolf II, as head of the Austrian line of the Habsburgs, appointed a regent in Graz who was supposed to guide the fate of the territories. This was necessary because the oldest son and heir, Archduke Ferdinand, was only 12 years old and therefore unable to rule.

The archduchess was deeply affected by the loss of her spouse, but she nonetheless fought energetically to have herself appointed legal guardian of her eldest son, as Karl had stipulated in his will. Despite receiving serious support from her brother, Duke William V of Bavaria, Maria never achieved this. But she remained a politically active princess, both during the regency and after 1595 when power was taken over by her son, with whom she fostered a close and trusting relationship until her death.

Testifying to this relationship are letters from both parties, in which the archduchess appeared as a strict mother who, on the one hand, demanded obedience, but, on the other, promised (and also provided) her support, and who preserved her influence on all of the children even after Ferdinand became the head of the family. Ferdinand, for his part, still regularly wrote letters from the imperial diet in spring 1608, where he appeared as the emperor's deputy, in which he kept his mother up to date on the course of the negotiations and asked her for maternal advice and for support in sensitive political issues.

This relationship at the same time draws our attention to the archduchess's connections to her children in general. Raising the next generation was an important task in all families of the ruling estate and had far-reaching political implications, since rulership was passed along through family affiliations by way of the dynasty. Hence, it was important to firmly establish ties to the family and political principles through education. And this task strongly dominated Maria's time as archduchess for decades, all the more from 1590 when she became a widow with 12 children—from baby Karl to the almost fully grown Archduchess Anna—and bore the main responsibility for their upbringing.

In this respect, Maria expected unconditional obedience from her children—the children had to fully subordinate their will to their parents, always respond to them with obedience and deference, and naturally be eager learners. Maria's letter of 1593 to Emperor Rudolf II, in which she noted that her eldest, Ferdinand, as an obedient son "must rightly respect and fear" her,[9] also shows the strict standards of maternal authority. Of course, this did not prevent the archduchess from being close to her children, whose development she meticulously observed and to whom she often gave presents, for example. In 1598, when Maria travelled to Spain with her daughter Margarethe, she wrote from Italy to her eldest son, who had to look after his younger siblings in her absence: "Nicholas[10] is coming. Would like to know whether you will prepare something for your siblings. He has not come to me yet, but if at some point he travels through Milan, I will see if he will send you a little something: for he cannot carry very much, I'm afraid, because he is very old."[11]

In her understanding, Maria's love and care for her children were inseparably tied to educating them to (Catholic) piety and godliness. From early on, all were accustomed to praying three times a day and getting up early, and to listening to mass twice a day. The result—the religious character of the children and court life in Graz—made a big impression on contemporaries. When Cardinal Enrico Caetani visited Graz in May 1597, he very favourably remarked on the ardour with which the archducal children attended religious service, noting: "I do not believe that another mother in the world could have a more thriving and radiant family of boys and girls."[12]

The Lutheran environment in Graz always made Maria, as a deeply pious Catholic, very anxious about the salvation of her children. Of course, as far as we know, none of the children gave cause for specific apprehensions, but her concern, especially for strengthening Ferdinand's faith, runs through her letters from her early widowhood. The heir apparent had already been sent to Ingolstadt to study with the Jesuits prior to her husband's death. When Archduke Karl died, Maria's biggest worry was that Ferdinand would be forced to return. In this event, the Protestant territorial estates planned to set up a custodial regency for the still underage archduke and thereby achieve greater influence on territorial and religious policy. The archduchess feared that this would jeopardise not only the salvation of her son but also the continued existence of the Catholic confession in Inner Austria as a whole. She repeatedly urged her brother, William of Bavaria, to prevent this from happening and, in particular, to force a corresponding decision by Emperor Rudolf II as head of the dynasty. In September 1590, with regard to Ferdinand's possible return, she wrote, fiercely determined: "I will certainly not do it, [even] if the emperor sits on my head, unless one forces me or does it with violence."[13]

While the children's proper Catholic education was simultaneously a heartfelt concern for the archduchess and a political duty, the responsibility for the further course of their lives was at least equally important to Maria and the House of Habsburg. Since Emperor Rudolf II and his numerous brothers all remained childless, for a long time Maria's children constituted the house's "dynastic reserve"—her daughters were the ones whose marriages would create the politically expedient connections; and her sons were the ones who (like Ferdinand) would have to take over rulership in the Habsburg territories or underpin this rule by way of offices and ecclesiastic titles.

In the 1580s, when, in a report on the confirmation of Archduke Ferdinand, the nuncio of Graz, Germanico Malaspina, noted that the seven beautiful daughters of the archducal couple in Graz could all be wives for the Catholic princes of Christendom, he touched upon an area where Archduchess Maria would later find herself heavily engaged. Arranging marriages for daughters and sons was an area in which princely women could traditionally get involved, and where they frequently established informal contacts and conducted negotiations before such marriage projects were elevated to an official level and became a matter of state. As a widow, Maria naturally took part in all of the marriage brokering involving her daughters, not least because she wanted to see that they were provided for by a marriage appropriate to their status before she died.

Of course, Maria's thoughts on the matter were not the sole deciding factor; rather, every marriage had to be guided by the weal of the House of Habsburg and coordinated with the emperor as the chief custodian and head of the house. Reasons of family could demand sacrifices, both from Maria and from her daughters. Anna, the eldest, who married the king of Poland in

1592, refused her consent for weeks, but the marshalling of all available forces finally moved her to agree. Against the will of her mother, Rudolf II decided that Maria Christina needed to be married off to Transylvania in 1595. Archduchess Maria was basically intent on not having to force her daughters into any marriage, but in both cases she needed to bow to outside pressure, as did the girls themselves.

After years of preparation, which also involved the participation of Empress Widow Maria living in Madrid, Maria's daughter Margarethe was able to marry King Philip III of Spain in 1598. From her new home at the Spanish court, she later supported the brokering of marriages for her sisters: Konstanze was also married off to Poland in 1605, after her sister Anna died in 1598; and in 1608, just a few months after her mother's death, Maria Magdalena married Cosimo de' Medici in Florence and later became the grand duchess of Tuscany. Incidentally, evidently quite eager for adventure, the archduchess used the marriages of her daughters as opportunities to make extended journeys, in that she accompanied all of her girls to their future husbands: to Kraków, Alba Iulia, and Madrid. It should also be noted that Maria deliberately used these travels to cultivate contacts within the spheres of her sons-in-law, to office holders of other courts.

But the archduchess also worked on providing for her younger sons, who, in contrast to Ferdinand as the heir apparent, needed to keep their eyes open for offices and income outside Inner Austria. As early as 1598 (much to the displeasure of her brother in Bavaria) Maria pushed through the election of her son Leopold as bishop of Passau. To do so, she intervened personally with Pope Clement VIII, whom she had met in Ferrara during the marriage of her daughter Margarethe. Various plans were hammered out for her second youngest son, Archduke Maximilian Ernst. Initially, he was supposed to marry the daughter of the Russian czar; then he was supposed to become the Spanish governor of Portugal, for which Maria and her daughter Margarethe tried to win over the emperor. And an ecclesiastic career was launched for her youngest son, Karl—shortly after his mother's death, he became the bishop of Wrocław (Breslau).

Maria of Inner Austria appeared as an anxious wife and mother, as a music lover, and as an enthusiastic traveller and pious Catholic. But above all, she understood her position as a princess to also be an office assigned to her by birth and God's will, an office where one assumed responsibility towards the territory and the subjects, as Maria pointed out to her son: "But remember that you and I and people like us live in the world not for ourselves but rather for others, also with difficulty and work. That is why our Lord also often stands by us so wonderfully."[14]

When Maria died in Graz in spring 1608, her eulogy extensively described the merits that the archduchess had acquired with regard to the Catholic faith. The preacher emphasised that she had always spoken up in favour of Catholics, such that her help for the religion had saved hundreds of thousands of souls. Even if this figure is exaggerated, Maria's resolute and sometimes militant advocacy for the Catholic confession had long-term consequences. This applied to the territories of Inner Austria, where Maria's son Ferdinand implemented a very vigorous recatholicisation policy around 1600. But this also applied to her children, all of whom were formatively influenced by her praxis of piety. It was her son Ferdinand who declared piety and reverence for God to be the ruler's greatest virtue, and thus gave "Pietas Austriaca"—the special piety of the House of Habsburg—a central place in the Habsburg understanding of rulership. After 1619, as Emperor Ferdinand II, he ensured that religion and the praxis of piety were used to represent the special divine grace on which the House of Habsburg based its position in the empire.

Notes

1 As a complex of territories, "Inner Austria" consisted of Styria, Carinthia, Carniola, and Gorizia, and was formed along historical lines in 1564 by Emperor Ferdinand I as a dominion for his youngest son Karl.
2 Quoted in Wehner, J. (1965) "Maria von Bayern, Erzherzogin von Österreich: Ihr Leben bis zum Tode ihres Gemahles (1590)". PhD thesis. University of Graz, p. 45.
3 Quoted in Wehner, "Maria von Bayern", p. 91.

4 "Exotica" referred to objects from distant lands, especially Asia and South America, which were a coveted component of many curiosity cabinets and princely collections during the early modern period.
5 Quoted in Loserth, J. (1898) *Akten und Korrespondenzen zur Geschichte der Gegenreformation in Innerösterreich und Erzherzog Karl II (1578–1590)*. Vienna: Hölder, p. 152.
6 Quoted in Hurter, *Geschichte Ferdinands II*, vol. 2, p. 566.
7 Quoted in Hurter, *Geschichte Ferdinands II*, vol. 3, p. 508.
8 Stieve, F. (1886) "Wittelsbacher Briefe aus den Jahren 1590 bis 1610", in *Abhandlungen der Historische Classe der Königlichen Bayerischen Akademie der Wissenschaften*. Munich, vol. 17 (1886), pp. 385–497, p. 435.
9 Quoted in Hurter, *Geschichte Ferdinands II*, vol. 3, p. 544.
10 St. Nicholas Day was approaching—a day on which one gave gifts to children.
11 Khull, F. (ed.) (1898) *Sechsundvierzig Briefe der Erzherzogin Maria an ihren Sohn Ferdinand*. Graz: Styria, p. 47.
12 Quoted in Betz, S.H. (2008) *Von Innerösterreich in die Toskana: Erzherzogin Maria Magdalena und ihre Heirat mit Cosimo de' Medici*. Frankfurt am Main: Peter Lang, pp. 63–64.
13 Stieve, *Wittelsbacher Briefe*, vol. 17, p. 432.
14 Khull, *Briefe*, p. 92.

Selected bibliography

Hurter, F. (1850–1864) *Geschichte Kaiser Ferdinands II. und seiner Eltern, bis zu dessen Krönung in Frankfurt. Personen-, Haus- und Landesgeschichte; mit vielen eigenhändigen Briefen Kaiser Ferdinands und seiner Mutter, der Erzherzogin Maria* (11 vols). Schaffhausen: Hurtersche Buchhandlung.

Keller, K. (2012) *Erzherzogin Maria von Innerösterreich (1551–1608): Zwischen Habsburg und Wittelsbach*. Vienna: Böhlau.

The Seventeenth Century

Princesses, Businesswomen, and Artists

POLYXENA OF LOBKOWICZ (1566–1642)

Between Bohemia and Spain

When receiving his instructions while still in Rome in 1619, the newly appointed papal nuncio to Vienna, Fabrizio Verospi, was informed as follows: "At the imperial court there are two exceptional women: the Countess of Mansfeld and the high chancelloress.[1] It is necessary to visit them regularly for conversation. These women know all of the news and secrets of the court. You must be wary in discussions with them. Be careful what you say in front of them."[2] The two women—sisters-in-law and of noble origins—were evidently important purveyors of information and had a political clout that was not limited to the offices of their respective husbands. But who was this "high chancelloress" to whom the papal administration ascribed such importance for the success of the nuncio's dealings?

Her name was Polyxena of Lobkowicz, born in 1566 as the ninth child of one of Bohemia's most important families. That same year, her father, Vratislav of Pernštejn, began serving as the kingdom's high chancellor and accordingly held one of Bohemia's most important offices. His marriage in 1555 to María Manrique de Lara, a maid of honour of Queen—later Empress—Maria, not only reflected his proximity to the House of Habsburg and the Catholic confession but also increased it. However, Polyxena's father would die in 1582, leaving her mother to deal with astronomical debts that had been incurred through Vratislav's incumbency and holding of court. With the support of the emperor, as well as aristocratic friends and relatives, she managed with great effort to reorganise and finally secure the family's properties.

DOI: 10.4324/9781003252870-10

María of Pernštejn and her many children (nine were still alive when their father died) lived alternatively in Litomyšl Castle, one of the family's largest domains, and in the palais at the Prague Castle. Little is known about the schooling and youth of Polyxena and her sisters. However, the girls must have had a comprehensive education, since, according to statements by contemporaries, Polyxena's older sister Johanna mastered five languages: Czech, German, Latin, Spanish, and Italian. And the substantial library of Polyxena's mother (consisting of more than 1000 volumes) suggests that she placed just as much value on literature and languages as on the schooling of the girls in fine handicrafts, dancing, music, and religion.

Spanish and Spanish traditions played a major role in the children's education and in the social life of the House of Pernštejn. María of Pernštejn stemmed from an influential Spanish family and saw to it that the contacts with Spain and Southern Italy were never lost. On top of that, Polyxena's brother, Jan, married a Spanish cousin, Anna Maria Manrique de Lara y Mendoza; and two of her sisters lived in Spain. Johanna went to Spain in 1581 with the Empress Dowager Maria, whom her mother had previously served as a maid of honour. She was accompanied by her sister Luisa. Whereas the latter entered the Monastery of Las Descalzas Reales in Madrid, where she lived with the empress dowager, Johanna married Fernando de Aragón, Duke of Villahermosa. In addition, the Prague palace of the Pernštejns was quasi the second home of the Spanish envoy Guillén de San Clemente, who regularly represented the interests of María of Pernštejn both in Spain and to Emperor Rudolf II, who likewise resided in Prague as of the late 1570s.

As a widow, María of Pernštejn was also responsible for making sure that her daughters married in accordance with their social standing, and all the more so after Polyxena's older brother Jan, the head of the family, fell in the war against the Ottomans in 1597. For Polyxena, who was known early on for her beauty, education, and piety, the choice in this respect fell in 1587 on William of Rosenberg, the richest man in Bohemia and, as high burgrave, likewise a high-level officeholder. The wedding—the fourth for William—took place in the presence of Emperor

FIGURE 8.1 Polyxena of Lobkowicz, ca. 1585

The Lobkowicz Collection, Prague, Czech Republic

Roland de Mois (attr.), *Polyxena of Lobkowicz, around 1585*, The Lobkowicz Collections, Lobkowic Palace, Prague Castle, LR5488

Rudolf II. The greatest hope of her substantially older husband was surely that Polyxena would finally give him a longed-for son and heir. Although this never occurred, their marriage seems to have been very amicable, as evidenced by gifts from both sides. Due to her husband's position and her own origin, the young wife of Rosenberg soon became the first lady of court society in Prague.

Before Rosenberg died in 1592, he guaranteed that she would own the Bohemian domain Roudnice nad Labem, which he had previously already ceded to her as a gift. This made Polyxena financially independent, especially since it soon became clear that she was very good at managing her possessions and was able to generate a substantial income. Over the next years she lived either in Roudnice Castle or in the Palais Pernštejn in Prague in close contact with her mother and sisters.

At the same time, the palais was the hub of a broad network that had been elaborated through the marriages of Polyxena's sisters. Apart from the two sisters in Spain, with whom Polyxena maintained mail contact throughout her life, another sister, Elisabeth, married a high-ranking imperial officeholder named Albrecht von Fürstenberg, and their son Vratislav von Fürstenberg would later also hold high offices at the imperial court. Bibiana married Francesco Gonzaga di Castiglione from the high Italian aristocracy, and Franziska married Andrea Matteo Acquaviva d'Aragona Principe di Caserta in 1607. Hedwig was first a maid of honour for Queen Dowager Elisabeth of France in Vienna and then entered the Queen's Monastery (Königinkloster), founded by the latter. There seems to have been steady contact among all of the sisters. They wrote to each other and sent gifts, including above all portraits of themselves, their husbands, and children, who in this way were supposed to remain in the memory of the Bohemian relatives.

Many of these pictures still survive in the gallery of the Lobkowicz family, for after a ten-year period as a widow Polyxena decided to remarry. We do not know her precise motivations for doing so after such a long widowhood, but she no doubt made a good choice. In 1603 she married Zdeněk Vojtěch Popel of Lobkowicz. He had been the Bohemian high chancellor since 1599, and one of the land's leading Catholic politicians. His acceptance into the exclusive Order of the Golden Fleece (like Polyxena's father earlier) and elevation in 1624 to the rank of an imperial prince reflect his prominent position in Bohemia and at the court of Ferdinand II. The couple's only son, Václav Eusebius, was born in 1609.

Polyxena had a harmonious marriage with Zdeněk Vojtěch of Lobkowicz as well, until his death in 1627. This is shown not least by their surviving letters from the period between 1618 and 1627.[3] The couple wrote to each other in Spanish, which indicates again how strongly Polyxena was influenced by her maternal upbringing and connections with Spain. Lobkowicz knew the language because he had been to Spain and Portugal on an educational tour around 1590 and later also served there as a diplomat. The letters written by the two of them before 1618 were probably lost or destroyed. Besides, prior to 1617 they seem rarely to have been apart; Polyxena also accompanied her husband on several journeys, such as to Frankfurt am Main for the imperial coronation in 1612 and to the imperial diets in Regensburg in 1608 and 1613.

Their close relationship was a precondition for Polyxena to also use her political talent and substantial influence as a wife. In doing so, she acted to benefit the interests of the curia and Spain in Bohemia and at the imperial court—after her mother's death in 1608, Polyxena inherited both her position in the Spanish networks and role as the head of Pernštejn family. The latter was reflected in particular by her assumption of the guardianship of her nephew Vratislav Eusebius, the last male member of the Pernštejn family. The former is indicated by the fact that the Lobkowicz couple regularly received the papal nuncio and Spanish envoys in their Prague palais or at Roudnice Castle.

That Polyxena and her husband were and remained Catholic and sided politically with the emperor would, in a very particular way, draw them into a conflict of momentous significance for the history of Bohemia and the empire. In spring 1618, the Bohemian Protestant estates decided to engage in open and violent resistance against Emperor Matthias and King Ferdinand of Bohemia. The symbol for this was the defenestration of Prague in May of that year, which today is considered to have triggered the Thirty Years' War. Polyxena was in Prague at the time, and she was initially detained due to her husband's office and her own political connections. Not until late summer 1618 was she able to travel to her husband in Vienna. After the victory of imperial troops in autumn 1620, she returned to Bohemia. On the other hand, Lobkowicz in the following years mostly stayed in Vienna or accompanied the emperor on his travels to Hungary and into the empire.

The couple made very good use of the propitious moment after the imperial victory to work on expanding their possessions. After the defeat of the Protestant nobility, they bought many confiscated estates so as to create a largely enclosed dominion in the area around Roudnice. Here it was mostly Polyxena who kept an eye out for suitable estates and then, with her husband's approval, arranged for their acquisition, while he looked after securing the support of the emperor or Bohemian officer holders. In June 1625 she made the prince aware of an opportunity to acquire additional estates in the Upper Palatinate as well and thus enlarge the family's holdings outside the borders of Bohemia. In this case, Princess Lobkowicz benefited from the extensive experience she had acquired from managing her estates independently during her widowhood, which she now could draw on during her husband's lengthy absences.[4] And over time, she had become a successful actor in the credit business, through which she also contributed to the family's financial security.

The correspondence of the Lobkowicz couple contains references to Polyxena's political interests and savvy, which were by no means restricted merely to Bohemia and Spain. For example, writing from Sopron in Hungary in June 1622, where he had gone with the emperor for the territorial diet, Zdeněk Vojtěch reported in detail about the situation in the Ottoman Empire after the murder of Sultan Osman II. In March 1625, he wrote to Polyxena about a decision by Ferdinand II that turned out to be exactly what she had already assumed. He was always amazed, Lobkowicz noted, by how accurately his wife could predict the emperor's decisions. And soon thereafter he gave her a letter addressed to the pope so that she could review the style and phrasing.

The ability of Princess Lobkowicz to proceed both energetically and diplomatically in discussions is described, for example, in a detailed entry of the diary of Prince Christian II of Anhalt-Bernburg. The latter had fought on the side of the Bohemian rebels against the emperor and was taken prisoner in 1620. He did not receive an imperial pardon until the end of 1621. A few days later he made a courtesy call to Princess Lobkowicz in Vienna. Polyxena first expressed her gratitude for his father's support during her departure from Prague in 1618, but at the same time also suggested that the young prince, who belonged to the Calvinist faith, should convert. "And when I came to her, she undertook to demonstrate to me, with many polite words, all that which was in her power, because she knows my gracious dear father well, accepted me as a son, and wished that my soul was doing well. And that she wanted to fish me into the net of the Catholic religion, although she was over 60 years old, and [I] could more likely be brought to that by young ladies".[5] She then went on to address the House of Anhalt's participation in the uprisings, asking why the prince refused to kneel before the emperor, and complaining that, in Prague, relics once owned by her father had been destroyed. In short, she subjected the young Prince of Anhalt to a thorough interrogation—albeit in a courtly and gallant manner—in which she did not hesitate to make her own political positions clear.

Princess Lobkowicz continued working on her networks throughout her life. This included, for example, brokering a marriage in 1626 between her niece Giovanna Gonzaga and Georg Adam von Martinic, and looking after the outfit of the bride. The connection with the Martinic family was evidently of a longer nature; already in March 1625, the princess had asked her husband to help Jaroslav Bořita von Martinic acquire the office of the Bohemian Chamber President. She also retained her role as the head of the Pernštejn women—after the death of her only nephew in 1631, she and her niece Frebonia were the last two members of the family still living in Bohemia. Frebonia remained unmarried and lived almost permanently with Polyxena in Prague, as did an unmarried sister of Prince Lobkowicz.

Polyxena's life and her relationship to her second husband were informed by a decidedly Catholic piety. This was reflected, for example, by their joint endowment of the Capuchin monastery in Roudnice in 1615. They specifically supported this order because, on the one hand, it was Lobkowicz's uncle who, as the archbishop of Prague, had brought the order to Bohemia. On the other, the Capuchins were regarded especially highly in Spain, which also surely garnered them esteem with Polyxena. In addition, she passionately collected relics, some of which she had lavishly decorated, and devotional images, many of which she would donate to churches and monasteries during the last years of her life.

Particularly well-known in this respect—and still remembered in Prague today—was Polyxena's gift to the Maria Victoria Carmelite monastery in Prague's Lesser Town in 1628, shortly after her husband's death. It is a wax figure of the Infant Jesus, which Princess Lobkowicz probably inherited from her mother, and the likes of which were widespread in Spain as devotional statues. In the years that followed, the Carmelites successfully endeavoured to present the figure as performing miracles. As the "Infant Jesus of Prague", to this day it remains a goal of pilgrimages and an object of veneration. At the same time, the gift yet again demonstrated the support of Princess Lobkowicz for the Catholic Counter-Reformation, for after the church in Prague had been consecrated as a Lutheran church in 1613, it was subsequently given to the Carmelites in 1624 in gratitude for the victory of the imperial Catholic troops at White Mountain.

Apart from this religious statue, Polyxena of Lobkowicz also left traces that can still be identified in the Roudnice Lobkowicz Library, belonging to the princely family. The Lobkowicz Library holds parts of Polyxena's personal collection of books, which probably consisted of more than 3000 volumes. They include at least 62 Spanish and Portuguese printed works and several Spanish manuscripts that Polyxena, for her part, inherited from her mother and to this day form the heart of the Lobkowicz Library's Hispanica collection.

After the death of her second husband, Princess Lobkowicz did not withdraw, for instance, into the reclusion of a widow's seat. She continued holding court in Prague and Roudnice, surrounded by a princely household of around 70 people, men and women. She remained a key player of Prague's aristocratic society until the end of her life, even though she often struggled with illness in later years. The cardinal and archbishop of Prague, Ernst Adalbert von Harrach, reported on his regular visits to her, where he found her admittedly bed-ridden but in "customarily good conversational form"[6] and surrounded by other guests. Polyxena continued to actively manage the family's extensive properties until 1637, when she also transferred her own estates to her son, Václav Eusebius.

However, it seems that in later years Polyxena, as the only Pernštejn sibling who had remained in Bohemia, deeply missed the contact with her family. Even in the early 1630s, she wrote to her sister Luisa living in a convent in Madrid: "My Señora and sister, you also must recall that we are here on earth as in times past. Of the 20 children that our mother brought into the world, I alone am in the homeland and, I could say, have remained in the world, for you, my Señora, have renounced the world. So I can say that I am all alone and have watched our house fall. I want to say no more of this other than God's will be done. I am at home."[7]

After a long illness, the princess died in May 1642 in Prague, having been given all of the sacraments and clothed in the habit of a Carmelite nun. She is interred in Roudnice in the Wenzel Church—that is, the church of the Capuchin monastery endowed by her and her husband.

The political role that Polyxena of Lobkowicz played in Bohemia and for the relationships between the emperor, curia, and Spain awaits further research. What is certain is that, as a Catholic partisan, she used her influence in accordance with her own religious convictions. The "Infant Jesus of Prague" is not only a sign of her piety but also a symbol of its donor's close connection to Spain. Familial and political contacts with Spain were the basis for cultural transfers that, in Polyxena's case, are clearly identifiable both in her library and in specific pious donations. Thus Princess Lobkowicz exemplifies not only the potential political influence of aristocratic women and their role in spreading Counter-Reformation piety, but also the way familial contact interlinked the empire and Europe.

Notes

1 Anna María Manrique de Lara y Mendoza and Polyxena of Lobkowicz (née Pernstein), respectively.
2 Silvano, G. (ed.) (2003) *Le istruzioni generali di Paolo V. Ai diplomatici pontifici 1605–1621* (Edizione promossa dall'Instituto Storico Germanico di Roma). Tübingen: Niemeyer, p. 1146.
3 Marek, P. (ed.) (2005) *Svědectví o ztrátě starého světa: Manželská korespondence Zdeňka Vojtěcha Popela z Lobkovic a Polyxeny Lobkovické z Pernštejna* [Testimony to the Loss of the Old World: the Conjugal Correspondence of Zdeněk Vojtěch Popel of Lobkowitz and Polyxena Lobkovicka of Pernštejn]. České Budějovice: Jihočeská univerzita v Českých Budějovicích, Historický ústav.

4 The experiences and interests also included collecting recipes, especially for desserts and juices—Polyxena's Czech-language cookbook, with 320 recipes, which often also indicate which aristocratic lady gave it to the collector, survives to this day.
5 Christian II. von Anhalt-Bernburg (2013) *Digitale Edition und Kommentierung der Tagebücher des Fürsten Christian II. von Anhalt-Bernburg (1599–1656)*. Wolfenbüttel: Editiones Electronicae Guelferbytanae, entry for 13 December 1621. Available at http://diglib.hab.de/edoc/ed000228/start.htm.
6 Keller, K., and Catalano, A. (ed.) (2010) *Die Diarien und Tagzettel des Kardinals Ernst Adalbert von Harrach. Edition und Kommentar*, vol. 4. Vienna: Böhlau, p. 469.
7 Quoted in Marek, *Pernštejnské*, p. 442.

Selected bibliography

Marek, P. (ed.) (2018) *Pernštejnské ženy. Marie Manrique de Lara a její dcery ve službách habsburské dynastie* [Pernštejn women. Marie Manrique de Lara and her daughters in the service of the Habsburg dynasty]. Praha: Nakladatelstvì lidové Noviny.

Richterová, A. (2010) *"Polyxena von Lobkowitz, geborene von Pernstein (1566–1642): Sammeln zwischen Politik und Frömmigkeit im katholischen Böhmen"*, in Bepler, J., et al. (ed.), *Sammeln, Lesen, Übersetzen als höfische Praxis der Frühen Neuzeit: Die böhmische Bibliothek der Fürsten Eggenberg im Kontext der Fürsten- und Fürstinnenbibliotheken der Zeit*. Wiesbaden: Harrassowitz, p. 229–224.

ANNA OF BRANDENBURG (1576–1625)

How Prussia came to Brandenburg

The Duchy of Prussia, which in the eighteenth century would become eponymous with a major Central European power, lay just beyond the eastern border of the Holy Roman Empire. Until 1525, it was held as a fiefdom of Poland by the Teutonic Order. The latter's grand master, Albert of Brandenburg-Ansbach from the House of Hohenzollern, then used the Reformation to have himself declared the Duke of Prussia and therefore a secular prince, de facto making the Duchy his property.

However, the line of the Hohenzollern dynasty established by this move would not be afforded a long existence. Albert's son, Albert Frederick, had "only" daughters after his two sons died as small children. Given the lack of male descendants, by the late 1580s it was apparent that his eldest daughter, Anna, born in 1576, would be able to assert a claim to the duchy. Anna's marriage in 1594 in Königsberg to her cousin John Sigismund of Brandenburg from the electoral line of the House of Hohenzollern was consequently at the same time an advance decision on the succession with regard to the Duchy of Prussia.

Anna as an heiress, however, was even more important by way of a different relationship, namely, as a point of intersection through which claims to substantial territories devolved on the House of Hohenzollern. Not only was she the daughter of the Duke of Prussia; through her mother, Marie Eleonore, she was also the niece of the childless Duke Johann Wilhelm of Jülich-Cleves-Berg, who ruled extensive regions along the Lower

DOI: 10.4324/9781003252870-11

Rhine—that is, on the far western side of the empire. The parents of Johann Wilhelm and Marie Eleonore were Duke William V of Jülich-Cleves-Berg and Archduchess Maria, a daughter of Emperor Ferdinand I. Due to the high rank of the bride, upon their wedding in 1546 it was stipulated that female succession would henceforth also apply to the House of Jülich-Cleves-Berg, ensuring that the daughters of the ducal couple would also be entitled to inherit.

Based on this arrangement, Anna of Prussia became a daughter-heir in these Rhenish regions as well—through her hereditary titles as the eldest niece of the duke, territorial possessions and rights could be passed on in whole or in part to her own children[1] and thus to a different dynasty. Anna's mother, Marie Eleonore, was very well aware of this fact and raised her daughter with this in mind, preparing her for this inheritance. This is reflected not least by a journey the duchess of Prussia took together with her daughters to the Rhineland in 1591/92 to the court of Duke William V in Düsseldorf.

In her person, therefore, Anna of Prussia unified entitlements to the Duchy of Prussia and hereditary claims in the Rhineland—both played a key role in setting up Anna's marriage with John Sigismund of Brandenburg. Moreover, Duchess Marie Eleonore was all the more strongly involved in the preliminary negotiations because mental illness had rendered Anna's father incapable of ruling. As a result, he was under the guardianship of male relatives who, with the support of Anna's mother, conducted the affairs of government in Prussia. For many years, this role was filled by George Friedrich of Brandenburg-Ansbach, who ultimately, in consultation with the duchess, brokered the marriage on behalf of the House of Hohenzollern.

Evidently, Marie Eleonore carefully considered which of Anna's sisters should enter into which marriages. Marie later married the margrave of Brandenburg-Bayreuth; Magdalena Sibylle married the elector of Saxony; Eleonore married Anna's father-in-law, the elector of Brandenburg; and Sophie married the duke of Courland. Hence, with the help of Anna's mother, a dense web of dynastic relationships emerged in the northern part of the empire, which, on the one hand, secured Prussia for the House of Hohenzollern, and, on the other, would reinforce existing dynastic relationships with neighbouring princely families.

Meanwhile, negotiations connected to the succession in Prussia had already been under way since 1603, although Anna was less involved in them than her mother in Königsberg. The duchy was not a hereditary fiefdom; rather, its possession had to be confirmed after every change of rulership by the king of Poland as the feudal lord. Thus it was necessary to motivate him to consent to a transfer to the Brandenburg line. Moreover, there was no stipulation regarding female succession. Nonetheless, the marriage with Anna played a decisive role here as an argument, making it possible to obtain this consent in 1611. But the duchy did not pass as a fiefdom to the elector of Brandenburg until Duke Albert Frederick of Prussia died in 1618.

FIGURE 9.1 Electress Anna of Brandenburg, around 1605

Stiftung Preußische Schlösser und Gärten Berlin-Brandenburg

Daniel Rose (attr.), Herzogin Anna von Preußen, around 1605, Stiftung Preußische Schlösser und Gärten Berlin-Brandenburg, G47, GK I 51244, Fotograf: Wolfgang Pfauder

At the same time, Anna's husband and his advisors pursued diplomatic efforts in connection with her inheritance claims to the territories along the Lower Rhine. However, the electress was not about to leave these matters solely to them but rather formulated her own clear ideas and demands. As early as 1608, when Elector John Sigismund travelled to Königsberg after the death of Anna's mother to make new custodial arrangements for her father, she explicitly instructed him to search his mother's papers for documents: "take into your presence ... everything on which there is title to the Jülich matters and abdication and other things ... for [this] concerns Your Beloved alone and does not concern them."[2]

It was not long before these precautions paid off: Anna's uncle Johann Wilhelm died childless in spring 1609—and the fight over the inheritance was on. Apart from Brandenburg (representing Anna's claims), the duke of Palatinate-Neuburg, who was married to Anna's aunt of the same name, could also assert claims by way of female succession. And the elector of Saxony could make such claims based on an imperial privilege. The conflict soon escalated militarily as well and, by 1610, after the emperor got involved as an arbitrator, Protestant and Catholic troops were facing off against each other. Although no major military operations ensued, the confrontation in the inheritance dispute over Jülich-Cleves-Berg revealed the highly charged nature of the political situation in the empire, which would ultimately lead to the Thirty Years' War.

Initially the parties managed to negotiate an agreement in spring 1611, which brought about a settlement with Palatinate-Neuburg and Electoral Saxony. But Anna of Brandenburg rejected this settlement as impermissible because it involved partitioning the territories, and she energetically intervened. Although Elector John Sigismund acted as her matrimonial guardian, based on the regulations of inheritance, the agreements made by the electress's husband still required her consent—which Anna refused due to the division of the territories. Evidently, she was not only very well informed about the legal requirements but also had her own ideas on how to handle her inheritance.

Moreover, she repeatedly stressed in her letters to her husband that the coveted territories constituted *her* inheritance and that of her son. She admonished him, for example, "to give away nothing that belongs to me and mine", and asked him "whether Your Beloved rightly has the power to take what is mine out of my hands from me and my underage children".[3] Even though she often used obliging language to excuse the liberties she took in expressing her opinions, thereby accommodating contemporary norms regarding the subordination of wives, she nonetheless expressed herself very decisively and demanded that her husband protect her rights:

> Your Beloved does not in one way or another want to give cause that I must, against my will, do something that might not be beneficial for us, for, as per an old adage, opportunity makes a thief. I therefore fear that this will happen to me too, when I see that I could not get any condolence or protection from Your Beloved, but rather that Your Beloved deliberately wanted to deprive me of my rights and grant them to others instead of our children ... I ask once more, Your Beloved will probably want to take care and not throw this warning so completely to the wind, but rather, even if it is unveiled in haste and coarsely from my misunderstanding, to kindly consider it good of me, and please pay proper heed to the one who warns Your Beloved of harm, and be my dear faithful lord and husband.[4]

Anna finally consented in 1614 after a different plan for dividing the Rhenish territories[5] had been proposed, although here too with some reluctance, having previously put forth her own ideas about the division between Brandenburg and Palatinate-Neuburg. And her correspondence with her eldest son, George William, acting as governor in Jülich-Cleves-Berg since 1613, clearly shows how the mother influenced or sought to influence his administration, not least with regard to the organisation of finances.

She upheld her extensive claims to all parts of the Jülich inheritance throughout her life, even protesting to the emperor against their restriction. Anna of Brandenburg consequently felt herself duty-bound, as daughter-heir, to secure this particular inheritance for her children, and tried to assert her inherited rights as broadly as possible. Admittedly, in doing so, it was primarily her husband who acted at the level of the empire—but in legal terms, the Brandenburg line of the House of Hohenzollern could only raise these inheritance claims on the basis of the elector's marriage to Anna. To assert her claims, however, she, in turn, was largely dependent on the cooperation of her husband, who needed to demand those rights politically and, if need be, militarily.

However, Anna of Brandenburg also demonstrated her self-confidence and ability to act as a ruler's consort in ways that went beyond the securing of her inheritance. In letters exchanged between the spouses, she routinely made critical assessments of her husband's government leadership. The latter repeatedly travelled to the Duchy of Prussia, staying there for long periods; in addition, he often went hunting for weeks at a time and thus was hardly available. During these times, as Anna explained to him, "disorder" made its way into the electorate because he failed to look after the finances and council proceedings. However, John Sigismund clearly tacitly approved that Anna presumed to personally intervene in government affairs during his absence. She monitored the treasury, for example, and therefore the principality's revenue, and even took part in council meetings. She always kept well abreast of its decisions. In addition, she corresponded with the electorate's office holders about administrative issues—for example, with Adam Gans von Putlitz as the governor of Berlin.

Unfortunately, the letters exchanged between the elector and electress during his travels have not yet been published. Yet they show that Anna clearly had ideas about how the princely regime should be led and strove to implement them. However, she was also aware of the limits of her capacity to act and in letters often gave her advice conditionally: She did "not [want to] prescribe anything" to the elector, "but rather [I] ask for nothing more than that Your Beloved will forgive me if I write too much in this or that matter. My intent is directed at nothing other than to prevent harm to Your Beloved as far as I can foresee."[6] Even so, contemporaries looked askance at the electress's involvement in the administration of the territory and expressed their criticism. However, such critics may well have been among the elector's advisors that Anna repeatedly warned her husband about because she felt they were untrustworthy or insufficiently knowledgeable. In any event, in this respect the electress was well prepared when her husband suffered a stroke in 1616, which greatly reduced his capacity to act. Anna henceforth continued to conduct government affairs quasi in her husband's stead.

Despite occasional differences, the elector and electress pulled together when it came to government. The same was true for the political and military efforts to secure Anna's inheritance in the western part of the empire and at its eastern border. But there was one area where conflict between them grew ever more apparent: her religious confession. Anna of Brandenburg had a strict Lutheran upbringing, shaped by her mother Marie Eleonora's uncompromising commitment to Lutheranism. By 1606 at the latest, John Sigismund, on the other hand, was leaning more towards the Calvinist faith. Ever since the second half of the sixteenth century, the two confessions had opposed each other in a confrontation that emerged from theological differences and became increasingly irreconcilable. So at Christmas 1613, when the elector, together with his brothers and high-ranking court officials, took communion in accordance with the Palatinate—that is, Calvinist—ritual, thereby publicly consummating a change of confessions, he also committed an affront against his wife. Thereafter it became difficult for the Brandenburg Hohenzollerns to demonstrate dynastic unity, especially since Anna's daughters and sisters-in-law likewise cleaved to the Lutheran confession, as did her influential sisters in other German territories.

At the same time, by taking this step the elector also alienated large sections of the Brandenburg and Prussian nobility, who also remained Lutheran, as well as, naturally, the Lutheran clergy of his domain. These groups strove vehemently to reverse the confessional change, finding in this effort a close ally in the electress. Anna developed her own clientelist system among the Lutheran clergy, who gave her support. In the years after 1613, this made the electress an important actor within Brandenburg's fragile confessional structure, who was also supported by the Prussian territorial estates in her resistance in religious matters against Elector John Sigismund.

Amidst this tense situation, in 1615 there was even unrest in Berlin. Shortly before Easter, the elector had all of the pictures and alters removed from the Berlin Cathedral, since, as per Calvinist doctrine, he viewed them as unnecessary, indeed as "papist". Thereupon agitated citizens attacked the homes of the Calvinist court chaplains, joining together and sounding the tocsin in order to defend their preachers and their church. Even though the tumult could be quelled relatively quickly, Calvinist preachers blamed the electress, accusing her of having incited the Lutheran agitators by cheering them on. While this could not be proven, it nonetheless shows that everyone was aware of the electress's position and the conflict in the princely house.

Anna herself emphatically rejected this allegation in a letter to her son; even so, the incident strained their relationship. Although the electress had given much care and attention to the education of her eldest son, George William, he distanced himself from her. He followed his father in changing his confession and repeatedly disengaged from her, especially after he became elector in 1618. The confessional conflict in the House of Hohenzollern came to be publicly perceived as mainly a conflict between mother and son.

Anna was certainly not somebody who compromised on political or religious issues. Instead, she repeatedly acted against the ideas of her son. This probably became most obvious in 1620 when she married off her daughter Eleonore to King Gustav II Adolf of Sweden. In so doing, she sabotaged a marriage plan of her son, who wanted his sister to marry the Polish crown prince to secure his hold on Prussia. Although the Swedish House of Vasa also reigned in Poland, deep-seated animosities prevailed between the Catholic Polish line and the Protestant Swedish line of the house. Anna's decision in favour of Sweden consequently sparked new conflicts with Poland, Calvinist circles at the court, and naturally with her son, the Calvinist elector. Nor were they resolved in the period that followed.

Anna died in Berlin in 1625 but wanted to be interred in Königsberg and not at her husband's side, a choice that was probably meant symbolically in two respects. She decided here on a Lutheran city and a Lutheran church for her final resting place;

and at the same time, she demonstrated her lasting attachment to the Duchy of Prussia, her inheritance.

The older literature—insofar as it found her worth mentioning—often described Electress Anna of Brandenburg as imperious and headstrong. The ideas she repeatedly expressed concerning the succession in Jülich-Cleves-Berg were seen as overblown. But this fails to do justice to her continuous efforts as a daughter-heir to assert her own interests and those of her children. She was obviously deeply influenced by an understanding of the responsibility for this inheritance and ultimately for preserving the memory of the two princely dynasties for which she stood: the House of Hohenzollern and especially the House of Mark. She had an undeniable energy, which she used to defend these rights. At the same time, she also defended her own status as an heir and demonstrated her self-confidence as a woman with her own rights to dominion—which in the long-term she admittedly had to pass on to her husband and, respectively, her son. By virtue of the territorial claims that Anna's marriage into the dynasty brought to the Electoral House of Brandenburg and through her striving to be continuously active in government, the electress laid an important cornerstone for Brandenburg-Prussia's ascendancy as a major European power. Recognition for this dedication, even though it was not always crowned with success, was pithily expressed by Christopher Clark when he described her as "the redoubtable Anna of Prussia".[7]

Notes

1 By 1607, four sons and four daughters had been born, of whom Crown Prince George William, another son, and three daughters reached adulthood.
2 Quoted in Drexl, *Weiberfeinde*, p. 332.
3 Quoted in Drexl, *Weiberfeinde*, pp. 338–339.
4 Quoted in Drexl, *Weiberfeinde*, p. 341.
5 According to which the Duchy of Cleves and the County of Mark passed to Brandenburg, while the Duchies of Jülich and Cleves went to Palatinate Neuburg.
6 Quoted in Drexl, *Weiberfeinde*, p. 330.
7 Clark, C. (2006) *Iron Kingdom: The Rise and Downfall of Prussia*. Cambridge: Harvard University, p. 120.

Selected bibliography

Drexl, M. (2006) *Weiberfeinde – Weiberfreunde? Die Querelle des femmes im Kontext konfessioneller Konflikte um 1600*. Frankfurt am Main: Campus.

Kaiser, M. (2016) "Die Tochter ihrer Mutter: Anna von Preußen und das politische Erbe der Maria Leonora", *Kulturgeschichte Preußens – Colloquien* 2. Available at: https://perspectivia.net/receive/ploneimport_mods_00010412

Puppel, P. (2016) "Die 'Principalin': Herzogin Anna von Preußen (1576–1625), Kurfürstin von Brandenburg und Erbin von Jülich-Kleve-Berg", in Schneikart, M., and Schleinert, D. (eds.), *Zwischen Thronsaal und Frawenzimmer: Handlungsfelder pommerscher Fürstinnen um 1600*. Cologne: Böhlau, pp. 295–333.

MARIA MAGDALENA HAIDENBUCHER (1576–1650)

Abbess in Troubled Times

Maria Salome Haidenbucher was born in Kaufering near Landsberg am Lech, probably in 1576. She stemmed from a family of Bavarian officials; her father was a ducal official and non-noble estate owner. She and her twin sister Maria Cleophe were the youngest of several siblings. Orphaned by the deaths of their parents in 1585, the two girls entered a convent at an early age.

Maria Cleophe joined the Cistercian convent in Niederschönenfeld on the river Lech. Maria Salome, on the other hand, was sent to the Benedictine convent on Frauenchiemsee in Upper Bavaria, where she adopted the monastic name Maria Magdalena and, at age 15, took her final vows, the monastic profession. Her acceptance suggests that she received an education prior to joining the convent, for the Benedictine nuns tested the Latin skills of their girls prior to their monastic profession. Only with such skills could they follow the shared readings and assume liturgical responsibilities. Where Maria Salome and her sister acquired them, however, is unknown.

Frauenchiemsee had undergone difficult times in the sixteenth century, for the Reformation had found supporters even on the convent island in the Chiemsee, the so-called Bavarian Sea. For a long time, the number of convent entrants was extremely low and the economic circumstances were precarious—in 1582, there were only nine conventuals. In the 1570s, Bavaria's Duke Albert V dispatched nuns from the Niederschönenfeld convent to reform Frauenchiemsee. The new abbess, Sabina Preyndorfer, worked hard to reduce the convent's mountain of debts and improve compliance with the order's rules. She also took Maria Magdalena Haidenbucher under her wing and supported her from early on. She entrusted the administration of the convent to Haidenbucher as dean, building her up, so to speak, as her successor. In 1609, Maria Magdalena was then elected as abbess, an office she would hold until her death in 1650.

Even though Frauenchiemsee was one of the larger convents in the southern Holy Roman Empire and looked back on a long history, little would be known about Haidenbucher's work had she not left behind a *Geschicht Buech* (History book). She started writing the book when elected abbess in winter 1609, and it ends with a description of her interment on 31 August 1650 in the convent church. In this book, she recorded, year after year, the construction work performed on the convent and its farm buildings, the sisters who joined, took their vows, or died, the taxes that had to be paid, how much altar wine was bought, the donations the convent received, etc. It constitutes a chronicle of sorts, with which the abbess sought to document the successful administration of her office, but she did not follow the familiar examples of learned chronography from male monasteries. Instead, the book is more reminiscent of housebooks of bourgeois families (Haidenbucher stemmed from such a family, after all), in which one rendered an account of property and family matters for future generations.

This memory book clearly reveals the broadly diversified nature of an abbess's responsibilities and, as becomes apparent in at least a few places, those areas or events that Haidenbucher herself deemed important and worth recording. Very few were related to "big politics"; instead, she kept her focus on her convent and its immediate surroundings. But the notes she made regarding events beyond this regional horizon clearly indicate a contextual framework formed by the Electorate of Bavaria and the Holy Roman Empire, on the one hand, and the Roman Church, on the other. Thus Maria Magdalena noted the election of Emperor Ferdinand II in 1619 and his death in 1637, and likewise the deaths and elections of popes during her time in office, the widowhood and remarriage of the elector of Bavaria in 1634/35, and then the birth of the long-desired electoral prince in 1636.

Although she wrote little about personal matters, deliberations, or impressions, the book nonetheless provides an opportunity to gain a few insights into the life and administrative work of an abbess. In this respect, we can assume that Maria Magdalena Haidenbucher's responsibilities and challenges were typical for many monastic women of southern Germany. In light of the author's long life and tenure, two aspects will be emphasised here because of their major influence on her life and administration: first, the changes to convent life entailed by the Catholic reforms after the Council of Trent; second, the challenges posed by the Thirty Years' War for an abbess who bore responsibility for dozens of nuns, lay sisters, peasants, officials, and staff.

Frauenchiemsee was ecclesiastically subject to the prince-archbishop of Salzburg; hence the spiritual wellbeing and personal good behaviour of the convent women were monitored from here. Secularly, on the other hand, the lord of the convent women was the duke—as of 1623, the elector—of Bavaria; taxes were assessed, the election of the abbess confirmed, and the convent assets supervised from Munich. At the same time, the properties under the administration of Abbess Haidenbucher were widely scattered between Salzburg and Munich and in Lower Bavaria and Tyrol. In many places, such as Gstadt on the Chiemsee or Pfaffenhofen near Rosenheim, the abbess acted as the parish patron, appointing the pastor and drawing revenue from these parishes. In 1636, when the vicar in Rosenheim arrogated these rights for himself, Haidenbucher as a "church woman"[1] successfully intervened, compelling the vicar to leave the parish. In managing these extensive properties, the abbess was supported by officials—but she needed to supervise and monitor them, as well as the judges in the villages belonging to the convent.

As already indicated, in her office Haidenbucher herself was subject to several instances of supervision by the men who constituted the ecclesiastical and secular authorities—a supervision system that increasingly expanded after the Council of Trent. Ducal commissioners kept watch over the abbess's economic conduct, such as when she took out loans; and visitation inspectors of the prince-archbishop of Salzburg exercised ecclesiastic authority. Much space in Haidenbucher's records is dedicated to reports on visitations, for which delegates from Salzburg appeared at the convent almost every year. They always provoked unrest in the convent and were awaited with trepidation—and their departure was welcomed with relief.

Until 1630, the focus of visitations was on modifying and tightening the order's rules in accordance with the stipulations of the Council of Trent. In Frauenchiemsee, this was reflected, on the one hand, by the introduction of a new order for convent life. During the visitation of 1628, after an exact register of all of the sisters was set up and everyone was questioned, the abbess was handed a book with these new rules. When Haidenbucher notes in this regard that objections to individual stipulations could only be raised in writing, one senses a certain scepticism on her part towards this approach. Above all, this order significantly intensified enclosure—that is, the restriction of the life of convent women to the space within the convent walls.

However, when visitation responsibilities were assigned to the provost of the neighbouring monastery of Herrenchiemsee in 1641, Haidenbucher vigorously protested, for she had long been in a dispute with the provost because he was striving to gain dominion over properties of her convent as well as ecclesiastical supervisory authority over Frauenchiemsee's father confessors and chaplains. However, the Salzburg prince-archbishop refused to be persuaded, so Haidenbucher ultimately had to tolerate her competitor's visitations. But in her memory book she recorded, "[I] also do not want to be blamed for this, that I bear witness with God that we strongly defended ourselves not to agree to this, but we were ordered to under pain of losing all grace and the threat of an excommunication. In the end we had to give in to this, but thus only by order, not out of our own will."[2]

The abbess defended herself primarily through writing, for the intensification of the order rules and, concomitantly, enclosure entailed substantial complications for an abbess's administrative work: in the event of problems, she could not appear anywhere in person, for she was no more allowed to leave the convent than were her fellow nuns. Moreover, starting in 1629, no one was allowed to enter the nun's enclosure anymore. As a result, the abbess was compelled to have a new window to the courtyard installed in the wall, for example, so that the mistrustful peasants could monitor the weighing or counting of their tributes. In 1634, a new "letter vault"—a file archive—had to be built because the judges and other office holders who managed the convent's villages needed access to the files but could no longer enter the enclosure. And on a festive occasion two years later, the convent women had to arrange the stations of the cross inside the convent church because they could no longer participate in any processions outside the enclosure.

Haidenbucher did not comment on such obstacles; however, she regularly noted that these reforms occurred at the behest of the authorities. Namely, the directives that were interfering in the life of the convent sisters came not from her but rather from the prince-archbishop and they also curtailed the abbess's own power to act. External monitoring of the convent was further strengthened by the use of permanent father confessors as the nuns' spiritual advisors—previously in her tenure between 1619 and 1622, Maria Magdalena Haidenbucher had engaged in a conflict with the father confessor Martin Feuerstein, who evidently claimed full supervision over her convent and thereby intervened in her official powers. She only prevailed after threatening the Salzburg Consistory with her resignation. Notably, she makes no mention of this conflict in her writings. It was quite certainly not an event from her tenure that she wanted to record for her successors.

However, the next father confessor from the Seeon Abbey, with whom the abbess worked together in trust, also tried to further reduce the liberties of the convent sisters. The intensification of enclosure meant that small pleasures such as boat trips and walks on the island were no longer allowed, the censorship of correspondence was increased, and visiting times were restricted. It even worked towards inhibiting the formation of close friendships among the sisters.

One of Haidenbucher's main concerns was quite clearly the beautification and modernisation of the church. In her first years in office, she mentioned many construction projects for the convent buildings in general, but especially for the church itself. As part of this effort, in 1627 the abbess had a crib[3] set up for the first time, which was fervently venerated by nearby village residents. The figures and the custom itself have been preserved in Frauenchiemsee to this day.

Haidenbucher's baroque predilection for church ornamentation and her effort to safeguard the rights and status of her convent are reflected in a particular event of October 1631, which she described in detail. At the abbess's instigation, the remains of the first abbess of Frauenchiemsee were exhumed and reinterred. The abbess Irmengard stemmed from the Carolingian imperial house and had been a grandchild of Emperor Charlemagne. Maria Magdalena Haidenbucher herself had urged the prince-archbishop for the translation of the relics and arranged for the new interment site. Presumably she wanted her official predecessor to be declared a saint, which would certainly have benefited the convent. But even though Irmengard had long been venerated in the Frauenchiemsee region as an advocate, this did not occur until 1928.

FIGURE 10.1 Maria Magdalena Haidenbucher, Abbess of Frauenchiemsee

Abtei der Benediktinerinnen Frauenwörth im Chiemsee

Maria Magdalena Haidenbucher, Darstellung im Äbtissinnengang des Klosters Frauenchiemsee, Fotografin: Sr. Hanna Fahle OSB

And the convent, its subjects, and its abbess would soon have urgent need for advocacy. A major conflict that would later be known as the Thirty Years' War had been raging in the Holy Roman Empire since 1618. Haidenbucher had barely noticed its start in Prague in 1618. In the 1620s, however, when financial manipulations related to war financing led to a major currency devaluation, it appeared in her writings as "horrendous inflation"[4]. But the war would not really arrive in the Chiemgau until 1632 with the unstoppable advance of Swedish troops under King Gustav II Adolf.

In mid-April that year, the Swedes crossed the Lech and moved towards Munich. Even though they were still a fair distance from Frauenchiemsee, Haidenbucher feared that "the Swedish force may possibly become stronger and come to Wasserburg."[5] This did not in fact occur, because the Swedes turned north again before crossing the Inn. But a few days after their advance, other people were already coming to Frauenchiemsee: the convent women of numerous monasteries in the regions that had fallen into the hands of the Swedes.

The first to arrive were 37 Cistercian sisters of the Niederschönenfeld convent, including Maria Magdalena's sister, Maria Cleophe. The convent lay directly on the Lech, and when the Swedes crossed the river the frightened sisters had only a quarter of an hour to flee. In addition, however, the abbess of Frauenchiemsee also took in 46 Cistercian nuns from Seligenthal, 36 Dominican nuns from Altenhohenau, and 10 Benedictine nuns from Holzen in Swabia. Back in late 1631, the Frauenchiemsee convent itself had counted 24 convent women, two novices, four students, and ten lay sisters. Over the year, the initial group of refugees were joined by individual nuns who, wearing secular garb, had made their way to the safety of Frauenchiemsee. And many of the refugees stayed for months. Consequently having to provide for as many as one hundred and fifty extra people, the abbess faced a daunting task, which made an orderly monastic routine wholly inconceivable.

The fear that prevailed among the convent women is only alluded to in Maria Magdalena's long entry on this difficult year. Just the idea of having to leave the convent would have frightened the abbess and her sisters, for they had not been outside its walls for years or decades. They would certainly have viewed the violence of the Lutheran Swedes, who were the subject of the wildest rumours, as an existential threat. The relief after the Swedes withdrew was expressed in a procession of thanksgiving, during which a reliquary from Herrenchiemsee was brought to Frauenchiemsee for veneration.

Looking back on the "Year of the Swedes", Maria Magdalena Haidenbucher noted: "Not a single Swedish soldier ever came to our dear house of God, God be eternally praised, honoured, and thanked, how much we and our dear convent were in great terror and fear. ... All of the surrounding convents, such as Seeon, Baumburg, Ettal, Altenhohenau, Gars, all proceeded to flee, only Herrenchiemsee and we stayed. God the almighty and the blessed mother Virgin Mary and the blessed founder [Irmengard] protect us mercifully from these miserable times and that we persevere in the convent until the end, amen."[6]

However, at least for her as abbess, the war had by no means vanished into the far distance, even if for now the military engagements took place elsewhere in the Holy Roman Empire. Haidenbucher needed to ensure the supply of her own convent and provide for the fluctuating numbers of refugee nuns who came seeking shelter over the following years. Each year, the convent had to come up with and pay for several horses and grooms to equip the Bavarian troops and repeatedly pay additional taxes. In 1633, soldiers were even supposed to be quartered in Seebruck, Gstadt, and in the convent itself, which terrified the convent's residents. However, by pleading to Munich, Haidenbucher successfully arranged for a monthly payment of 120 gulden instead.

This alone shows that impositions and dangers came not just from the "enemy" but also from one's "own" troops. In late 1633, for example, the abbess once again worried that the convent would be plundered, this time by Spanish and imperial troops, who were actually allied with Bavaria. She therefore sent the precious church ornaments and files to Kufstein for safekeeping, where they remained until late 1634. At this time, the first plague deaths occurred in nearby Wasserburg, and in the following year the epidemic raged in the convent's hinterland—as was often the case, epidemics followed the route of the large military contingents.

After a few quieter years, the war drew closer again to Bavaria and consequently also to Frauenchiemsee. At first the elector demanded pistols, powder flasks, and weapons to equip the troops. Since the convent, obviously, did not have the demanded supplies available, the abbess had to procure them at the convent's expense and, in addition, once again had to provide three horses with grooms. In early March, the court fled from Munich before the advancing Swedes and French to Wasserburg, and convent women fleeing from Bavaria and Swabia arrived again at Frauenchiemsee. This time Maria Magdalen actually had to refuse the request for refuge of her sister, who had since become the abbess of Niederschönenfeld, because so many refugees—including nobles from the convent's hinterland—were already staying at Frauenchiemsee. In this regard, she noted, "There was such distress that, upon one's recollection, there was never such distress as in this adversity. ... this adversity also lasted the entire winter; may our dear Lord and the Queen of Heaven send peace. Amen."[7]

Peace negotiations had already been under way in Münster and Osnabrück since 1645, but the struggle for an agreement among the European powers was tough, and all the while the fighting, plundering, and demands for contributions continued. Frauenchiemsee was directly affected again as late as 1648, the last year of the war, when in early June Swiss and French troops advanced to Wasserburg and besieged it for several days. The bombardment of the town was heard as far away as the convent.

As enemy troops approached, the abbess decided with a heavy heart to send a number of her fellow nuns to other convents as a precaution. Those going to Salzburg took the church ornaments and relics along with them again, bringing them to Salzburg's Saint Peter's Monastery for safety. The abbess herself remained in the convent with seven older nuns and several lay sisters in the hope that they would remain unmolested. In the end, this was indeed the case, but these weeks were difficult. On 9 June 1648, Maria Magdalena wrote to the abbot of Saint Peter's, to whom she had entrusted the convent's treasures: "I don't think I ever had such fear. Would want to gladly suffer everything, if only God and the Heavenly Queen would keep us safe in the dear convent."[8]

When the peace agreement was finally reached in October 1648, Maria Magdelena only mentioned it in passing in her memory book. By now she was over 70 years old and looked back on a decades-long tenure as abbess. In contrast to other convent women (such as her sister Maria Cleophe), she "only" had to experience the war as something that occurred outside her convent's walls. In her memory book, the war mainly appears as a more or less dense sequence of flight and return, in which she and her convent—with one exception—always played the role of providing refuge. The war also appears as a sequence of demands for money from the secular authority in Munich, which had to finance its military. Her writings strongly convey a sense of the pressure of the financial demands and the terror instilled by the transiting troops among the convent women, including Haidenbucher herself.

It remains to be said that Maria Magdalena, as abbess, successfully tried to serve as a role model for the convent's sisters while at the same time standing up against impositions from outside. The approval and confidence of her fellow sisters that she had gained during her long tenure surely helped in this regard. As early as 1628, Salzburg inspectors had noted in their visitation report, "Concerning the person of the abbess, she seems mature, wise, pious, a loving mother of her convent [amatrix sui conventus], and full of good intentions, and none of the nuns made a complaint about her."[9]

Haidenbucher left her mark on the Frauenchiemsee convent through many initiatives to furnish and ornament the church, but also through the ultimately successful confrontation with the provost of Herrenchiemsee and his effort to monitor her convent. Maria Magdalena also successfully consolidated the convent's economic situation, which she managed to do despite the hardships of the Thirty Years' War. Obviously, she achieved all of this not individually but rather by developing and using networks, about which, however, little is yet known.

Undoubtedly important was the good relationship with the Seeon monastery, which also provided Frauenchiemee's father confessors. Haidenbucher had a deep-felt connection with the long-time abbot, Honorat Kolb, one of the most prominent Bavarian prelates of his time, who also attended to her on her deathbed. Their brisk correspondence shows, for example, that Kolb supported her in the conflict with Herrenchiemsee, advised her on tax problems, and gave her tips on dealing with visitations. The abbess was evidently also able to use connections to the Munich court, which arose because many of her fellow sisters stemmed from well-known Bavarian noble families, such as Preysing, Törring, and Haslang, or from families of high-ranking officials, and therefore had contact with advocates at the court.

Haidenbucher accepted the changes to convent life demanded by the highest authorities—by the council, the popes, the prince-archbishop—and substantially participated in their implementation. Naturally, this does not mean that she accepted each and every stipulation without objection. As we have seen, she clearly defended against encroachments on her powers as abbess or against the convent's traditional rights, even if not always successfully. Insofar as the portrait of the long-time abbess in the Frauenchiemsee's "corridor of abbesses" (see Figure 10.1) shows a strict and self-confident convent woman, it conveys—notwithstanding any stylisations—what were probably two of Haidenbucher's most important characteristics.

Notes

1 Stalla, *Geschicht Buech*, p. 120.
2 Stalla, *Geschicht Buech*, p. 138.
3 Heisterkamp, K., and Karger, M. (2005) *Die Barockkrippe der Abtei Frauenwörth im Chiemsee*. Weißenhorn: Anton H. Konrad Verlag.
4 Stalla, *Geschicht Buech*, p. 48.
5 Stalla, *Geschicht Buech*, p. 91.
6 Stalla, *Geschicht Buech*, p. 93.
7 Stalla, *Geschicht Buech*, p. 153.
8 Quoted in Schindler, *Krieg*, p. 442.
9 Stalla, *Geschicht Buech*, p. 214.

Selected bibliography

Schindler, N. (2001) "Krieg und Frieden und die 'Ordnung der Geschlechter': Das Tagebuch der Maria Magdalena Haidenbucherin (1609–1650)", in Garber, K., et al. (eds.), *Erfahrung und Deutung von Krieg und Frieden: Religion – Geschlechter – Natur und Kultur*. Munich: Fink, pp. 393–452.

Stalla, G. (ed.) (1988) *Geschicht Buech de Anno 1609 biß 1650: Das Tagebuch der Maria Magdalena Haidenbucher (1576–1650), Äbtissin von Frauenwörth*. Amsterdam: APA Holland University Press.

CATHARINA REGINA VON GREIFFENBERG (1633–1694)

The Poet in Exile

Catharina Regina von Greiffenberg was one of the most important German-language female authors of the seventeenth century. For a long time, however, she was largely unknown, even in her native Austria. Yet this looked different during her lifetime: Greiffenberg was celebrated in the literary public of the Holy Roman Empire; many of her works were printed and read as poetry and devotional literature.[1] She maintained a brisk exchange of letters with figures of the literary world, most importantly her correspondence with the author and well-known literary manager Sigismund von Birken, who described Greiffenberg as a "miracle of our times" (Birken 2015).

Catharina Regina was born in 1633 in Seisenegg, Lower Austria, into a family of recently ennobled landed aristocracy. Her father, Johann Gottfried von Greiffenberg, had inherited a stately fortune, which included the Seisenegg estate not far from Amstetten, where Catharina and her sister Anna Regina grew up. The family belonged to the relatively small group of Lower Austria's rural nobility that remained loyal to the Lutheran confession. This was not easy, given that in 1625 Emperor Ferdinand II, who was also the archduke of Austria and thus the territorial ruler of Lower Austria, had declared Catholicism as the only permitted confession, even for the aristocracy. Aristocratic persons were admittedly still allowed to practice their Lutheran faith, but only privately. Public religious services were forbidden and the few remaining Lutherans repeatedly faced restrictions.

FIGURE 11.1 Catharina Regina von Greiffenberg

Österreichisches Bundesdenkmalamt Wien

Anonymus, Catharina Regina von Greiffenberg, Österreichisches Bundesdenkmalamt, Fotoarchiv KBD 64.595

The death of Catharina Regina's father in 1641 did not make the family's situation any less challenging. Although his significantly younger half-brother Hans Rudolph looked after Catharina, her sister, and their mother Eva Maria, her father had left behind immense debts, which put their land at risk, and Hans Rudolph only managed to consolidate their finances with some effort. This enabled the Greiffenberg women to live in accordance with their social status. But even so, their social interactions remained very limited, for as Protestants they counted among an ever-decreasing minority within the Austrian nobility.

In this environment marked by financial and above all religious constraints, the two girls received a very modern and unusually comprehensive education. Their mother tended above all to the girls' religious education and thereby lay the basis for Catharina's pronounced piety. On the other hand, her legal guardian, Hans Rudolph, a well-read man who had studied in Siena, personally gave Catharina Regina lessons in Latin, French, Italian, and Spanish. She read ancient authors and received instruction in mathematics, history, natural philosophy, and even law. Moreover, like most aristocratic girls, she was given lessons in singing, dancing, and fine handicrafts, and also learned to ride.

She probably also made her first attempts at poetry as a young girl, inspired by her broadly diversified readings from the manor's library and by the lessons from her step-uncle. However, for her literary creativity, one should also emphasise the role of Johann Wilhelm von Stubenberg. He was Protestant as well, and owned Schallaburg Castle, not far from Seisenegg. Very learned in literature, he stood out as a translator and was friends with numerous important literati in Nuremberg and Regensburg. Through the compliments he paid to several of Catharina Regina's early poems, he promoted her literary endeavours. His critical readings helped her hone her abilities. He was also responsible in 1659 for sending one of her poems to Sigismund von Birken in Nuremberg, who was already a famous poet and translator. Stubenberg therefore not only promoted the perception of Greiffenberg as a poet outside her narrow circle of acquaintances but also established the connection to Birken, which persisted until the latter's death and became one of the most important in Greiffenberg's life, both in literary and in personal terms.

Important to her development were also other Protestant aristocrats of Lower Austria, who in a loose circle—the so-called Ister Society (named after the Latin name for the Danube)—cultivated an aristocratic-literary social life. Within the group, they discussed literature and read devotional texts. The participants also included many women, who called themselves "Ister nymphs" and were continuously interconnected through meetings and correspondence. They included Catharina's closest friend, Susanna Popp, for example, although she immigrated to Nuremberg in early 1660 so she could live her faith without restrictions.

Poetry and faith were inseparable for Greiffenberg right from the outset. When pregnant, her mother had made a vow that induced her to raise her child from early on to a godly life. The early death of her beloved sister in 1651 heavily shook Catharina Regina and led to an experience of spiritual awakening, with the light of faith suddenly revealing to her what she described as her "goddess soul" (Seelen-Göttin). This occurred while attending a religious service in Bratislava (Pressburg); located more than 200 kilometres away, this distant city was the closest place where Lower Austrian Protestants could attend a public Lutheran service, which is why the Greiffenberg family regularly travelled there.

After this experience, Catharina Regina decided to embark on a spiritual life path, dedicate herself to reading and poetry, and remain unmarried. She saw poetry as an option, within the boundaries set for her by her social position and gender, to create a monument to God and to serve Him with the help of her gift of eloquence. To this end, in the following years she continued her theological, philosophical, and historical studies on her own. Of course, at that time in the Lutheran world, celibacy was not a godly life path for women, but Catharina Regina saw it as a precondition for being able to dedicate herself to "Deoglori" without being distracted by a husband and family.

She understood this concept, which featured prominently in her texts and letters, as the spreading of the glory of God in a world that was approaching its final days. At least, that is how Greiffenberg understood her times—a view that seems all the more understandable given that she was born in the middle of the Thirty Years' War, which was followed by many further military conflicts in the second half of the seventeenth century. For Austria and thus for Greiffenberg, one must also bear in mind here, first and foremost, the threat posed by the Ottomans, which in 1663/64 developed in a war.

In 1663, Catharina Regina fled from this threat to Nuremberg with her mother. By then she was no longer unknown in the predominantly Protestant imperial city, for her first printed work had appeared there the year before. *Geistliche Sonnette, Lieder und Gedichte* (Spiritual sonnets, songs, and poems), a collection of poems that established her literary fame, had come about through Stubenberg's contacts and with the support of Sigismund von Birken. Whether the author really knew nothing of the book's printing, as emphasised in the foreword, must remain unresolved. What is certain is that her legal guardian, Hans Rudolph von Greiffenberg, facilitated the printing. The stay in Nuremberg, which lasted with brief interruptions until 1666, now provided the opportunity for Catharina Regina to make additional contacts in the literary world of the city and the empire, and, for example, to deepen her relationship with Birken. And the period in Nuremberg for the first time gave Catharina Regina an idea of what life felt like as a member of a large and strong Lutheran community rather than as part of a hard-pressed Protestant minority within a Catholic environment.

However, around 1660—so almost at the exact same time—Catharina Regina's personal life plan to be a pious poet came into sharp conflict with the realities of aristocratic life. Her uncle and legal guardian, Hans Rudolph, almost three decades older than her, wanted to marry his niece, who at nearly 30 years of age was not a young girl anymore. On the one hand, this desire was presumably associated with financial considerations, which was not unusual in the aristocracy, for such a marriage could consolidate a family's diminishing assets. On the other hand, however, Hans Rudolph probably had actually fallen in love with her when she was an adolescent girl. Catharina Regina was quite shocked at first and rejected the request, not only because they were related but also because of her desire to live a life solely dedicated to God and his praise. Only as her uncle's efforts gradually made him the laughingstock of the region's entire aristocratic community and he threatened suicide did Catharina see her herself forced in 1664 to give her consent. This probably occurred just as much out of concern for her own salvation, should he make good on his threats, as out of affection.

Thus began, however, many years of complications, for a marriage between an uncle and niece was permissible in Lower Austria only with a papal dispensation, which was obviously impossible for Protestants to obtain. Moreover, the pastor in Bratislava (Pressburg), to whom Baron Greiffenberg had turned, refused to perform the marriage. The marriage finally took place anyway in Frauenaurach in the Lutheran Margraviate of Bayreuth, but when the couple returned to Seisenegg the authorities would not recognise it. This led to a protracted conflict over the validity of the marriage, in which Catharina Regina's honour as a noblewoman, which was very important to her, as well the ownership of the Seisenegg estate were always at stake.

Despite these adverse circumstances and, from today's perspective, the seemingly unusual way it came about, the marriage between Catharina Regina and Hans Rudolph was largely amicable. To be sure, the poet was often vexed by her household duties because they reduced her time for reading and writing, but she took her responsibilities as a noblewoman quite seriously. In 1669, for example, she wrote to Birken: "The draft is written, the execution still bogs down a little, simply have not had proper peace or time for it, if my beloved husband is here then there is socialising and excursions, if he is out, then I must govern and there is much to do."[2] Among the key responsibilities of an aristocratic housewife were looking after the management of the estate and entertaining and caring for guests.

However, she also enjoyed the positive aspects of rural noble life, loved to go hunting, wandered about in nature, and was interested in current affairs related to politics, literature, and fashion. She also wrote about this to her "dear friend" Sigismund von Birken: "Meanwhile, I live in my autumn passion for the fields and forests, spending the time left over from household affairs with catching birds, fishing, hunting, during all of which the books provide me with sweet company; have now again a completely new romance called Tharsis and Zelie,[3] with which I am amusing myself until fortune brings me to where I can pursue my project; for the sake of Deoglori, I will risk another visit!"[4]

The "visit" she referred to here was a trip to the imperial capital of Vienna, where Catharina Regina made six longer sojourns between 1666 and 1676. The main reason for these journeys had to do with the disputes related to her marriage, but she also wanted to socialise with aristocrats. At the same, however, Greiffenberg was pursuing a major plan in terms of her idea of Deoglori—namely, her mission to realise a unification of the confessions in light of the approaching end of the world.

For a long time, scholars effectively construed Catharina Regina's efforts solely as an attempt to convert Emperor Leopold I to Lutheranism. However, Barbara Becker-Cantarino has recently presented a quite convincing alternative view of the poet's verifiable attempts to make contacts at the imperial court. She interprets them more as a concrete political undertaking by the poet, who was working towards securing the tolerance of the Protestant faith in the Habsburg hereditary lands and, in the long run, towards overcoming the religious schism as a prerequisite for a Christian victory over the Ottomans.

Catharina Regina herself saw the publication in 1675 of her long consecration poem *Die Sieges-Seule der Buße und Glaubens wider den Erbfeind Christliches Namens* (The victory column of repentance and faith against the archenemy of the Christian name) as a statement in "political matters". In the text, which she had completed much earlier (1663), Greiffenberg advocated the unification of divided Christendom in the fight against the Ottomans and addressed this message both to Emperor Leopold I, who to this end was supposed to conclude peace in the confessional conflict, and to the "dear fatherland", the Holy Roman Empire, and all of Christendom. This political initiative—which Sigismund von Birken viewed and remarked on with mistrust— is easily reconciled with Greiffenberg's striving to announce the Deoglori. And it is also plausible insofar as Greiffenberg's education and her indubitably well-informed interest in current events hardly seem in line with a goal as fantastic as that of "converting" the very piously Catholic Emperor Leopold I. A striving for harmony in the "entire Christian empire", however, would fit well with her theological ideas. That said, these ideas also contained many mystical elements, so, when looking back, the said plan of a conversion cannot be definitively ruled out.

Around 1680, the poet's life took another turn: in 1675, her mother died, and in 1677 her husband, for whom she genuinely grieved. The consequences of her widowhood were especially dramatic, since Catharina Regina could not keep warding off her creditors' demands for money, which had been made repeatedly for decades. Reflected here was not any personal failing on her part but primarily the problem of the weaker legal position of single women. Greiffenberg wrote about this herself in 1693: "The widow ... is the target toward which all the arrows of persecution fly, the mark of all the shots of misfortune. ... If there is a lightning bolt in the sky, it rolls around until it strikes a poor widow."[5]

In 1678 she was forced to surrender her beloved Seisenegg estate to her creditors. She used this rupture to change her living circumstances in other ways as well. Ever since 1663, when she had fled with her mother to Nuremberg before the Ottoman troops advancing on Vienna, she had repeatedly stayed in the Protestant imperial city, both because of her contacts in Nuremberg to the literary world and because she could freely practise her religion. Nuremberg had long been an important place for aristocratic and bourgeois "exulants", religious refugees from the Habsburg hereditary lands. Catharina Regina now followed in their path by finally moving to the imperial city for good in 1680.

This gave her the opportunity in her later years to live in close contact with literary friends and to cultivate her piety without having to deal with long journeys. She met not only with Sigismund von Birken, with whom she had long and intensely discussed her literary work and living circumstances by letters. By way of her edited letters, one can cast a figurative glance into the writer's workshop and also see how Birken supported and advised her. Also living in Nuremberg and its surroundings were the trusted "Ister nymphs" Susanna Popp and Potentiana von Laßberg. But literary acquaintanceships also linked Greiffenberg to Wolf Helmhard von Hohberg in Regensburg, a well-known author and former neighbouring estate owner who had permanently left Lower Austria in 1665, as well as to Duke Anton Ulrich of Brunswick-Wolfenbüttel, who for his part wrote several multi-volume novels that Catharina Regina treasured.

In Nuremberg, she also had contact to Lutheran clerics and male members of the "Pegnesischer Blumenorden" (Pegnitz Flower Society), an important literary society. There were several such societies in the Holy Roman Empire during the seventeenth century, and they followed an Italian model and were dedicated to the cultivation of German language and literature. Many of them were open to men and women. Thus since 1678, Catharina Regina von Greiffenberg, under the name of "The Courageous", served as the senior guild mistress of the Lilienzunft (Lily Guild) of the "Deutschgesinnte Genossenschaft" (German-minded association), a language society in Hamburg.

Even though Frau von Greiffenberg had to accept significant financial setbacks because of the loss of her paternal and marriage-related inheritance after her husband's death, by no means did she live in poverty in Nuremberg. Thanks to the inheritance portion from her mother, which was unencumbered by debt, she enjoyed a livelihood very much in keeping with her social status. However, she lived rather in seclusion—during the late 1680s, for example, in the small Steinbühl Castle near Nuremberg, and later in the city at Egidienplatz, which was indeed one of early modern Nuremberg's upscale residential addresses. She evidently kept up an extensive mail correspondence (of which little survives, however), while pleasure trips and visits connected her with old and new friends and acquaintances.

Above all, she worked tirelessly on additional writings and began studying cabalism, learning Hebrew and Greek specifically for this purpose. She managed to finish her most extensive work just shortly before she died. It consisted of 36 prose reflections on the Gospels, which she had probably been working on since 1668. It was published in three parts: *Des Allerheiligst- und Allerheilsamsten Leidens und Sterbens Jesu Christi, Zwölf andächtige Betrachtungen* (Twelve devout meditations on the supremely holy and supremely salvific suffering and dying of Jesus Christ) in 1672; *Der Allerheiligsten Menschwerdung, Geburt und Jugend Jesu Christi, Zwölf andächtige Betrachtungen* (Twelve devout meditations on the supremely holy incarnation, birth, and youth of Jesus Christ) in 1678; and *Des Allerheiligsten Lebens Jesu Christi* (On the supremely holy life of Jesus Christ) in 1693.[6] Proceeding from Biblical texts, she recorded meditations and contemplations with the goal of fulfilling her self-set goal of remembering and spreading the glory of God. These reflections on the passion were an important element for Greiffenberg's contemporary prominence as a poet.

Catharina Regina was certainly not a "miracle" as described by Birken, nor was she by any means exceptional simply because she was a female writer. But because of her origin, her particularly comprehensive education, and her talent, she managed—unlike many women—to gain the attention of the literary public of her times. Significant in this respect was the support she received from men.

Greiffenberg's creativity was characterised by piety and militant Protestantism, combined with mystical ideas of religious awakening and a highly sophisticated language. All of this made her interesting to educated contemporaries, especially those from the empire's Protestant regions; but it also resulted in her quickly being forgotten after her death because her poetry no longer conformed to the more secular Zeitgeist of the eighteenth century.

In her attempt to live a self-determined life plan that combined poetry and service to God, Catharina Regina von Greiffenberg had to struggle against many obstacles: from the ban of the Protestant faith in Lower Austria, financial constraints, the boundaries imposed on her by the gender order, to the hardships she faced because of her problematic marriage. One can find many of these experiences reflected in her literary texts if they are read against the background of the author's life path. In this respect, they are not merely poetical testimonies to the seventeenth-century world of concepts and beliefs and to the literary talents of their author; rather, they were also shaped by a poetical female subjectivity. In her texts, she often expressed herself decidedly as a woman, thus bringing her gender and associated experiences into her poetry even though (or precisely because) at the beginning of her texts she always justified her refusal to be kept, as a woman, from raising her voice.

Notes

1 The modern edition of her collected works consists of ten volumes: Bircher, M., and Kemp, F. (eds.) (1983) *Catharina Regina von Greiffenberg. Sämtliche Werke in 10 Bänden*. Millwood NY: Kraus Reprint.
2 Birken, S. (2005) *Werke und Korrespondenz*, vol. 12: *Der Briefwechsel zwischen Sigmund von Birken und Catharina Regina von Greiffenberg*, part 1: *Die Texte*, part 2: *Apparate und Kommentare*, edited by Laufhütte, H. Berlin: De Gruyter, part 1, p. 122 [9/08/1669].
3 Le Vayer De Boutigny, R. (1665–1666), *Tarsis et Zélie* (4 vols.). Paris: Luyne.
4 Birken, *Korrespondenz*, part 1, p. 34 [27/09/1666].
5 Quoted in Tatlock, *Empathic Suffering*, p. 17.
6 An English translation of selected texts has been published by Lynne Tatlock: Greiffenberg, C.R. (2009) *Meditations on the Incarnation, Passion, and Death of Jesus Christ*, edited by Tatlock, L. Chicago: University of Chicago Press.

Selected bibliography

Becker-Cantarino, B. (2013) "Frömmigkeit und Bekehrung: Catharina Regina von Greiffenbergs 'Sieges-Seule der Buße und Glaubens', oder: Wollte Greiffenberg wirklich Kaiser Leopold I. zum Luthertum bekehren?" in Dane, G., *Scharfsinn und Frömmigkeit: Zum Werk von Catharina Regina von Greiffenberg (1633–1694)*. Frankfurt am Main: Peter Lang, pp. 13–38.

Birken, S. (2015), *Werke und Korrespondenz*, vol. 10: *Der Briefwechsel zwischen Sigmund von Birken und Johann Michael Dilherr, Daniel Wülfer und Caspar von Lilien*, edited by Laufhütte, A., Laufhütte, H. and Schuster, R. Berlin, Boston: De Gruyter, 129.

Tatlock, L. (2007) "Empathic Suffering: The Inscription and Transmutation of Gender in Catharina Regina von Greiffenberg's *Leiden und Sterben Jesu Christi*", *Wolfenbüttler Barock-Nachrichten* 34 (1), pp. 27–50.

Tatlock, L. (2009) "Introduction", in Tatlock, L. (ed.), *Catharina Regina von Greiffenberg: Meditations on the Incarnation, Passion, ans Death of Jesus Christ*. Chicago: University of Chicago Press, pp. 1–38.

MARIA SIBYLLA MERIAN (1647–1717)

Science and Painting

When working out his taxonomic system in the mid-eighteenth century, the still-famous Swedish naturalist Carl Linnaeus used the pictures and individual plant specimens of a prominent female contemporary: Maria Sibylla Merian, born in 1647 in Frankfurt am Main, who died in 1717 in Amsterdam. During her time, she was esteemed both as an insect researcher and as an artist who produced numerous watercolours, published several books, and sold zoological and plant specimens. Her fame only faded with the emergence of "modern" science around the mid-nineteenth century, for her work and presentation method no longer conformed to the new systematising concepts. Since the mid-twentieth century, however, her person and work have undergone a veritable rediscovery—also and precisely under the auspices of the search for women who left their mark on history.

She was born into a family of printers and copper engravers. Her father, Matthäus Merian the Elder, was among the most well-known publishers in the publishing centre of Frankfurt. He produced the *Theatrum Europaeum*, one of the most important chronicles of the seventeenth century. However, he died while Maria Sibylla was just a little girl. Not long thereafter her mother got married again, this time to the painter and art dealer Jacob Marrel, who travelled back and forth between Utrecht in the Netherlands and Frankfurt. Hence, Maria Sibylla stemmed from an artistic family, which made it possible for her to receive artistic training. She learned drawing, watercolour painting, flower

DOI: 10.4324/9781003252870-14

painting, and copper engraving from her stepfather. However, as a woman, she was barred from the "higher school" of painting, namely, travelling to and working in Italy.

In 1665, Maria Sibylla married the painter Johann Andreas Graff, one of Marrel's students. Three years later, the family (her daughters Johanna Helena and Dorothea Maria were born in 1668 and 1678) moved to Graff's hometown of Nuremberg, where they lived in a prestigious house at the Milchmarkt (Milk Market)—while the Graffs may not have figured among the political elite of the imperial city of Nuremberg, they belonged to its affluent citizenry. In the following years, Maria Sibylla was responsible for her duties as a housewife, helped out in the workshop, looked after the children, and was probably also involved in selling her husband's pictures and engravings. But at the same time, she could still pursue her studies and, as an artist, also gradually developed her own specific field of work. As early as 1675, the important Nuremberg art writer Joachim Sandrart reported that Maria Sibylla painted with watercolours and had specialised in the representation of flowers, fruits, and insects. In addition, she worked on textile painting with waterproof colours and gave female students lessons in drawing and embroidery, for which she also designed her own embroidery patterns for flower and animal motifs. She issued a few of these as prints between 1675 and 1680.

Thus "Frau Graffin", as she called herself while married, had chosen and developed her own field of work. But it was quite clearly influenced by contemporary notions about what was appropriate for women: Merian combined observations of nature in the area around her own house with "womanly arts" such as embroidery and flower painting. At the same time, she used the training that was directly available to her at home as the daughter and wife of painters. This way she could combine the spheres of activity of (house) wives with her scientific interests and artistic talents and consequently develop her own field in the border regions between the house, garden, and handicrafts. We can no longer determine just how deliberate her decision was to use watercolours and specifically to avoid portraits and oil paintings as artistic fields, which were both domains reserved for men. At the very least, however, we can assume that, like many women of her times, Maria Sibylla Merian was very well aware that a woman pursuing her own interests balanced on a tightrope between social acceptance and rejection.

But where did she obtain her naturalist knowledge? Various opportunities were on offer to her in this regard: anthologies and other books, contacts with collectors and naturalists (especially later during her period in Amsterdam), visits to gardens owned by aristocrats or commoners. Above all, however, Maria Sibylla Merian relied on her own observations. She had become interested in insects as a child. In her study book, she noted that she had been conducting studies since 1660, starting with silkworms that were being raised in Frankfurt. As a consequence of her research interests, she dealt with the breeding of caterpillars and did not shy away from transforming her kitchen into a laboratory: "Once in Nuremberg, three young larks were brought to me alive … which I killed; three hours later, when I wanted to pluck them, there were 17 thick maggots … on them, even though I had covered them right away. … On the 26th of August, so many beautiful green and blue flies came out, which I had a lot of trouble catching because they were so swift".[1] These and similar observations and breeding operations were the basis for the first volume of her major work *Der Raupen wunderbare Verwandelung* (The wondrous transformation of caterpillars), which Merian published in 1679.

Here she accurately represented insects in their various stages of life (caterpillar, pupa, butterfly, etc.) in exact detail, usually grouped around a blooming plant that served them as food. Each plant was labelled with its Latin and German names, and each table was accompanied by longer texts that summarised Maria Sibylla's observations. Hence, she continued concentrating her artistic work on flowers and insects but conjoined her virtuosic representation with conscientious observations on specific characteristics and on the development cycle of insects.

FIGURE 12.1 Maria Sibylla Merian, 1679

Kunstmuseum Basel
Jacob Marrel, Bildnis der Maria Sibylla Merian, 1679, Kunstmuseum Basel, Inv. 436

At the same time, her caterpillar book and her biological observations were an expression of an understanding of nature shaped by Protestantism. For Frau Graffin was not just a keen researcher and talented painter but also a faithful Christian who in her observations always searched for the order of God. Her contemplation of God's creation seems to have intensified after 1681, when, after her stepfather's death, she returned to Frankfurt am Main with her husband and daughters. She was soon drawn to the Labadists,[2] an end-times religious group that assumed that one could discern God in all things. Ultimately, in 1685 Maria Sibylla Merian, together with her mother and family, left to join the Labadist community at the Waltha Manor near Wieuwerd in the Netherlands.

The reason for this departure remains obscure, for there is no record of Maria Sibylla's thoughts on the matter.

Overall, unfortunately, we know of very few personal statements on her part, almost all of them coming from her printed works. Perhaps the artist, who indeed had long associated the beauty of nature with God's creative power, experienced a religious awakening in Frankfurt. Maybe her stepbrother, Caspar Merian, played a role, for he was quite close to her and had already been living in a Labadist community for a number of years. This departure could have been an expression of the desire for change after a lengthy but still unexplained conflict between Maria Sibylla and her husband. Andreas Graff travelled to the Netherlands with his wife and children, but left the community soon thereafter, which ultimately led to the couple's final breakup.

Life in the community, which was largely shielded from surrounding secular life, certainly impacted Merian's familial status (her marriage ended in divorce, probably in 1692) and her property situation, for the Labadists largely practised a community of goods to which members contributed their respective worldly possessions. But her research as a naturalist continued. Now the native insects, frogs, etc. were joined for the first time by those from the tropics, because the community in Waltha also included members from the Dutch colony of Suriname who had brought with them collections of animals and plants. Her study book, which Maria Sibylla reorganised during this period, clearly shows how she systematically advanced her research.

When Maria Sibylla's mother died in 1690, this seemed to be the signal for a further "transformation" of the researching artist. She abandoned her Frankfurt citizenship, which had previously guaranteed her the right to return to the city, and in summer 1691 moved to Amsterdam with her daughters. It remains unclear whether an alienation from the Labadist lifestyle or the financial problems of the community in Waltha played a decisive role here. In any case, Maria Sibylla had to look for a way to provide a livelihood for herself and her daughters. She found it in trading dyes, a business she had previously pursued in Nuremberg, and in selling preserved birds and insects, which were eagerly displayed in many naturalist collections of affluent citizens. And she sold watercolour paintings on the finest vellum with detailed depictions of insect metamorphoses.

Through her work and research, she gained access to collectors and scholars in Holland who, like her, were interested in insects, such as Caspar Commelin, the director of the botanical garden in Amsterdam, and the enthusiastic collector Nicolaas Witsen, who was also an East India Company administrator. In the collections of these men, she saw exotic insects again, "but in a way that their origin and reproduction were missing, that is, how they transformed from caterpillars ... into pupae ... and so on. All of this inspired me to undertake a great and expensive journey and to travel to Suriname (a hot and humid land ...) to continue my observations there."[3] In June 1699, at age 52, Maria Sibylla Merian, together with her daughter Dorothea, embarked on a journey to the South American colony that would last just over two years.

This was probably the most unusual step in her life, which was already full of twists and turns, for she undertook this journey without male accompaniment, and without any mandate or financing from an aristocrat or prince, as enjoyed by many male travellers. Instead, she financed the project herself. Perhaps the plan was to emigrate so she could pursue her research interests in Suriname over the long term, or maybe to also earn money, for specimens and pictures sold well in Europe. But Merian could not tolerate the heat. For this reason, as she constantly maintained, she had to return home sooner than she had anticipated—her health, but also the news about the beginning of the War of the Spanish Succession, which would endanger sea travel, forced a sudden departure in summer 1701.

In Suriname she had made at least several short excursions into the jungle. During her research, Maria Sibylla seems to have benefited from enslaved people, whom longer-term European residents used in their plantations and households. A slave dived for clams for her because Merian wanted to know what was in them, and she asked slave women (Africans and indigenous people) about the utility of plants, as alluded to by one of her picture descriptions: "One day I went deep into the wilderness and found, among other things, a tree that the natives call medlar tree ... Here I found this yellow caterpillar .... I took the caterpillar home with me and it very quickly turned into a light-wood-coloured pupa. Fourteen days later, towards the end of January 1700, a wonderfully beautiful butterfly slipped out of it. It looks like polished silver coated with the most beautiful ultramarine, green, and purple colours, indeed indescribably beautiful. Its beauty cannot be reproduced by any brush."[4]

154 Maria Sibylla Merian

FIGURE 12.2 The marvellous butterfly. Maria Sibylla Merian, *Metamorphosis Insectorum Surinamensium*, Amsterdam 1705, Table 53

Alamy

In September 1701, Maria Sibylla and Dorothea arrived in Amsterdam again, not only rich in experiences and newly acquired knowledge but also loaded with pictures on vellum, butterflies preserved in brandy, snakes, lizard eggs, and the bulbs and tubers of many plants. Shortly thereafter Dorothea married the ship's doctor, Philipp Hendriks, who repeatedly sailed between Suriname and the Netherlands. Her older sister, Johanna, had already been married to Jakob Hendrik Herolt since 1692; he had also been in Waltha but then turned his attention to trading with the West Indies and Suriname. His commercial contacts had no doubt helped Merian with her own journey.

By 1711, Johanna was living permanently with her husband in Suriname, where Herolt had taken on an administrative position. But even before that time, she had been supplying her mother with material for animal specimens, which remained an important source of income for Merian. This is shown, for example, by one of her few surviving letters from 1702, written to Johann Georg Volckamer in Nuremberg: Volckamer was supposed to order the animals he wanted from Suriname. She still had some in storage, "and I also have people in America who catch such animals and send them to me to sell, I also hope to get [some] from the Spanish West Indies as soon as the route is opened, so that the ships are allowed to go in there, but God knows how soon this will take place."[5]

In the years after her return, Maria Sibylla also dedicated herself to utilising her collections and studies in Suriname. Not least in order to pay off her considerable debts from her journey, she compiled an extensive work of copper engravings at great expense, which she published in 1705 as *Metamorphosis Insectorum Surinamensium* and also colourised upon request. Although not a commercial success for the author, this work finally won Merian broad recognition as a researcher and was essential for her enduring posthumous reputation. Then, shortly before her death in 1717, she finally managed to complete the third volume of her caterpillar book, which she had been working on since the 1690s. Her daughter Dorothea ensured its publication, including a second edition.

Both daughters, Dorothea and Johanna, sometimes worked with their mother and painted images of animal and plants. As has been clearly shown recently by an analysis of their depictions of herbs, they were trained by their mother. In Amsterdam, all three of them formed an artists' workshop. However, Dorothea and Johanna have remained overshadowed by their mother to this day, which can be explained by the fact that they often signed their works using the name of their mother, who was much more familiar to contemporaries, and because they copied Maria Sibylla's older works for selling. After her mother's death, in 1718 Dorothea went to Russia with her second husband, the painter Georg Gsell, where she worked as a painter and gave drawing lessons at the Academy of Sciences in St. Petersburg.

The innovative aspect of Merian's work consisted of the combination of the depiction of insect metamorphosis with images of plants for the purpose of achieving the most lifelike representation. Even though the plants essentially served as accessories for the caterpillars, pupae, and butterflies, Maria Sibylla Merian mostly used the respective plants on and from which the insects actually lived, although her depictions of tropical insects were not always accurate in this regard. For some European species, she was actually the first person to depict and describe them; above all, however, she was the first person to work on such illustrations and publications for a broad audience. The buyers and owners of Merian's books also included many women, for during the seventeenth and eighteenth centuries there were indeed many female collectors of insects, about whom, however, very little is known today. They included, for example, Agneta Block in Amsterdam, who collected paintings and natural objects and for whom Merian herself had worked, as well as Esther Barbara Sandrart, whom Merian knew in Nuremberg.

But Maria Sibylla Merian was not a researcher in today's sense of the term, that is, someone who took note of the academic knowledge of her times and expanded or deepened it. For her this was far from possible if only because, like most women of her times, she did not know Latin and therefore could not acquaint herself with scholarly publications. She seems to have acquired serious skills in this scholarly language only after moving to Waltha, but she was never able to write well enough in Latin for scholarly publications. Instead, she recorded her observations in her own publications, presenting them in a scientific–aesthetic manner. And her goal was never the mere acquisition of scientific knowledge. It was also (or perhaps primarily) about the observation and representation of the beauty of God's creation.

Her person is and remains fascinating as a researching artist and artistic researcher with very specific interests. Notwithstanding her life's twists and turns, what distinguishes Merian is not necessarily the breaching of conventions. However, she obviously did not hesitate to take full advantage of the socially acceptable fields of activity that were open to her because of her origin, living conditions, and talent. There were many women who did business, participated in religious groups, worked as artists, or supported relatives in scholarly work. But Maria Sibylla Merian used all of her available options to design a life that was ultimately unusual in its twisting path and long-term impact, even though she was by no means successful in every regard.

Notes

1 Beer, W. (ed.) (1976) *Maria Sibylla Merian: Schmetterlinge, Käfer und andere Insekten: Leningrader Studienbuch* (2 vols.). Leipzig, vol. 1, p. 223.
2 Named after Jean de Labadie, who adhered to an eschatological faith and preached on the imminent return of Christ. His supporters sought to prepare for this day by withdrawing from the world and focusing on repentance and penitence.
3 Quoted in Beer, *Maria Sibylla Merian*, vol. 2, p. 85.
4 Merian, M.S., *Metamorphosis Insectorum Surinamensium*, Amsterdam: Valk 1705, table 53.
5 Quoted in Wettengl, *Maria Sibylla Merian*, p. 265; also Schmidt-Loske, K. (ed.) (2020) *Maria Sibylla Merian: Briefe 1682 bis 1712*. Rangsdorf: Basilisken-Presse.

Selected bibliography

Etheridge, A.K. (ed.) (2021) *The Flowering of Ecology: Maria Sibylla Merian's Caterpillar Book*. Translated by Ritterson, M. Leiden: Brill.
Reitsma, E., and Ulenberg, S.A. (2008) *Maria Sibylla Merian & Daughters: Women of Art and Science*. Zwolle: Waanders.
Wettengl, Kurt (ed.) (2013) *Maria Sibylla Merian. 1647–1717: Künstlerin und Naturforscherin*. 2nd edition. Ostfildern: Hatje Cantz.
Zemon Davis, N. (1995) "Metamorphoses: Maria Sibylla Merian", in Zemon Davis, N., *Women on the Margins: Three Seventeenth-Century Lives*. Cambridge, MA: Harvard University Press, pp. 140–202.

GLIKL BAS JUDAH LEIB (1647?–1724)

The Experiences of a Jewish Businesswoman

FIGURE 13.1   City view of Hamburg, ca. 1700

Alamy

Johann Baptist Homann, Prospect und Grundris der Keiserlichen Freyen Reichs und Hanse Stadt Hamburg samt ihrer Gegend, Nürnberg, um 1720

Glikl's life stands in several respects for groups that have generally been poorly researched and rarely considered. She was not only a woman; she was a Jewess who spent large periods of her life in Hamburg. And as the wife and widow of a merchant, she was personally active in major trade centres of the Holy Roman Empire. The reason we are able to write about her today as a person and about her economic activities is due to yet another unusual circumstance: Glikl bas Judah Leib[1] left behind a comprehensive autobiographical account, which she wrote for her children. Since the late nineteenth century, this text has been repeatedly published—in whole or in parts—and translated into several languages. Her "memoirs" must be seen as one of the most well-known sources for seventeenth-century Jewish history in the Holy Roman Empire.

DOI: 10.4324/9781003252870-15

She worked on this description of her life for decades, embellishing it with stories and parables. According to her own words, she did this to cope with her grief for her beloved husband—but at the same time she picked up on a Jewish autobiographical tradition in which the example of one's own life was presented as a lesson to others and as a kind of confession of faith. However, Glikl adapted her account to her needs and situation, for she was not a Jewish scholar, even though she had been educated by her father and read many Jewish books. But here we are not going to examine the literary–theological strategies of Glikl as a writer, a subject that Natalie Zemon Davis, for example, already dealt with years ago. Our interest lies above all in what Glikl recorded about her life as a successful female merchant and about herself.

She was born in late 1646 or early 1647 in Hamburg, where, as merchants, her father, Judah Joseph ben Nathan, and mother, Beila bas Nathan Melrich, were respected members of the Ashkenazi Jewish community. This community existed in the Hanseatic city alongside a community of affluent Portuguese Jews, who as important merchants and money brokers doing business with Spain and the colonies had concluded an acceptance contract with the Hamburg City Council in 1612. The Ashkenazi Jews, on the other hand, were typically grain traders and money lenders, and were accepted more reluctantly. Totalling around 600 people in the 1660s, both groups together formed an unusually large community, the likes of which existed in only a few cities of the seventeenth-century Holy Roman Empire, such as Frankfurt am Main, Prague, and sometimes Vienna.

However, all of the Ashkenazi families were expelled in 1649 because of complaints from the citizenry and Lutheran ecclesiastics; most of them, including Glikl's parents, went to neighbouring Altona. This smaller town was subject to the king of Denmark, who pursued a far more liberal Jewish policy than did the Hamburg City Council, such that Jews were protected in Altona and could establish a community there. Even though Glikl's parents managed to return to Hamburg in 1657, later in her writings she repeatedly referred to the uncertainty of Jewish life. In Hamburg, Jews were not allowed to have any temples but rather had to gather for prayer in private homes, and they often went to Altona.

They were very well aware of their dependence on the benevolence of secular authorities, in this case the Hamburg City Council or the king of Denmark. But political events and wars could also influence the situation. Jewish families always had to expect that, if war and politics unsettled Christian life and secular authorities, their properties could be at risk—for example, through coercive taxation—and their economic activities and even their life and limb endangered. In Hamburg, like in many other Protestant territories of the empire, the pronounced anti-Jewish attitude of Lutheran ecclesiastics was also a factor, repeatedly giving rise to demands for the expulsion of Jewish families and for restrictions on their economic activities. Glikl recorded all of this more or less clearly in her writings.

Initially, however, the political and economic situation only played an indirect role for the girl. Just before the age of 12, she was betrothed to Chajim ben Joseph, who was a few years older and the son of a respected Jewish businessman from the city of Hameln. Such early marriage commitments were quite common in the Jewish community and served to secure property and family networks. In the bourgeois circles of Lutheran merchants in Hamburg and most other cities, on the other hand, betrothals prior to age 18 or 20 were very rare. Glikl, in any event, married in 1660, although the young couple spent the first two years with Chajim's family and only afterwards established their own household in Hamburg.

The happy marriage produced 14 children, 12 of whom (six boys and six girls) reached adulthood and then got married themselves. This was an exceptionally large number, which testifies to Glikl's attentiveness as a mother. That she nursed her children herself was rather unusual for an affluent family and surely helped the children survive the dangerous early months. The births—and later the marriages—of her children were always joyous events for Glikl. But she also spoke about the effort and work that the large household and constantly growing swarm of children meant for her. "I gave birth every two years and worked hard, as one does with such a household full of children, may God protect them. I thought no one had a heavier load or worked harder at raising children than I did."[2]

Chajim worked as a merchant during the entire marriage. He traded in gold, silver, pearls, and jewels and was also active in the lending business. Hence, he was working in a branch of trade that was frequently dominated by Jewish merchants since at least the sixteenth century and which often remained closely linked to credit transactions. At the same time, the trade went hand in hand with jewels—old and new, used and pawned—and many of the precious stones or pearls were procured over large distances and through many intermediate locations.

Chajim's contacts in this respect reached from Moscow via Gdańsk (Danzig) to Copenhagen and thus encompassed large parts of the Baltic region. With Amsterdam and London, however, Chajim also had connections in the traditional trading centres of the North Sea region. The old Hanseatic city of Hamburg was no doubt a good base for such extensive trading contacts. One of his sons-in-law, Mordechai Hamburger, entered the London diamond trade around 1700 and in 1712 travelled first to India. Later he settled in Madras, where he died in 1735.[3] One of Chajim's and Glikl's grandsons continued operating the business there until the middle of the eighteenth century.

Glikl was evidently involved in her husband's business decisions from early on, giving him advice as well as pursuing her own business affairs. Above all, however, her memoirs show that the couple stood by each other in difficult times. When her husband became ill at the Leipzig Trade Fair, he postponed all of his further business until he returned to Hamburg, with the reason that "when we get to my house, God willing, we can discuss the matter; my little Glikl will be there to give her valuable opinion."[4] In 1673/74, as substantial business losses mounted in Szczecin (Stettin), Prague, and Hamburg, she and her husband consoled one another and worked together at protecting the family's good name by overcoming failures and debt. In this way, Chajim ben Joseph gradually advanced to become one of the wealthiest Ashkenazi Jews in Hamburg.

However, in early 1689 he suddenly died while still relatively young as the result of an accident, leaving his wife with eight underage children and a flourishing business. Her lamentations over the loss of her husband run through Glikl's writings, which she started—as she herself wrote—to overcome the pain of his death. She later described her "impatience"—her difficulty in giving herself over to God's will as befitted a devout woman—as her greatest sin. On his death bed, Chajim had entrusted not only their underage children but also the handling of the business to her care with the words: "I don't know what to say. My wife, she knows everything. She could continue just as she was doing before."[5]

Thus it was also Glikl's responsibility to look after her children's marriages. Traditionally, marriage was used to secure trade connections and business networks. The two oldest sons remained in Hamburg, as did a younger sister; the others went to Amsterdam, Metz, Berlin, Copenhagen, or Bamberg. At the same time, this set up a safety net, for one never knew when any given city might reimpose restrictions on Jews and even expel them, such as in Hamburg in 1649 or in Vienna in 1670.

And the status-appropriate marriages, which she described in detail in her writings, were also an expression of the commercial success Glikl managed to achieve as a businesswoman. Her memoirs similarly provide a range of information in this regard. She described how, after the mourning period, she examined the business books and discovered debts amounting to 20,000 thalers. She was not worried about paying them back, she noted, for she knew she would be able to cover everything. Even so, the first onslaught of creditors who wanted to secure their money was a major challenge, which she mastered with the support of her son, Mordechai Hameln Goldschmidt. By auctioning off the inventory of gold and precious stones, they managed to pay off the largest liabilities—the transactions were, of course, largely conducted on credit—and this ensured the firm's liquidity. Even though Glikl successfully began her own independent business activities as a result, she made no effort to conceal her disappointment with the conduct of her business partners, as well as with her relatives, for, apart from her children, none had stood by her after Chajim's death.

In the following years, Glikl traded above all with so-called ounce pearls,[6] but she expanded the business by founding a stocking manufactory. She also imported stockings from Holland and sold them in a store in Hamburg as well as at fairs in Brunswick, Frankfurt am Main, Naumburg, and Leipzig, which she attended herself. On such business trips she was usually accompanied by her son Nathan, for as a woman, not to mention as a Jewish woman, it would have been inappropriate and dangerous to travel on her own. She also used her trips to the betrothals and weddings of her children to establish business connections in the empire's most important trade centres and political capitals, even though she did not like being under way, repeatedly emphasised the risks of travel, and reported on adverse events.

Extensive business activities like hers were not unusual for Ashkenazi women; they frequently assisted in commerce or ran their own businesses. The same applied to female merchants of the Christian faith, who often kept the business running at home while their husbands travelled to exhibitions and fairs. Things would only have functioned differently for large trading houses that maintained agents (factors) in important trading centres throughout Europe—here women were less directly involved. Retail trade in cities was also largely managed by women—namely, by the wives of skilled tradesmen who made clothing and furniture, or by peasant women who attended the town markets. Trading in foodstuffs and other retail items was to a large degree the domain of single women, wives, and widows, many of whom also conducted smaller credit transactions.

As a widow, however, Glikl independently ran an intraregional trade and credit business and often travelled herself, which was rather unusual. In addition, she appeared in person—albeit probably accompanied by one of her sons—at the Hamburg stock market, where she exchanged large sums of money. As a result of the jewel trade, she had contact with many of the wealthiest Jewish merchants, as had earlier been the case for her husband. Many of them were so-called court Jews, who were virtually indispensable for financing the large princely courts of the empire. They included the men of the Gomperz family, who lived in Kleve (one of whom was Glikl's son-in-law), Jost Liebmann in Berlin, as well as Samson Wertheimer and Samuel Oppenheimer in Vienna.

In her memoirs, she described her business activities to her children as follows:

> At that time I was doing a brisk business in the fabric trade, selling five or six hundred reichstalers' worth of goods a month. In addition, I attended the Brunswick fair twice a year,

making several thousand at every fair, ... I imported merchandise from Holland and purchased a large quantity of merchandise in Hamburg too, and I sold it. I had my own fabric store. I did not coddle myself—winter and summer I travelled and in the city I was constantly on the go. In addition, I dealt in ounce pearls which I'd buy from the Jews, then I'd sort them and resell them wherever I knew there was a demand. I had an extended line of credit. If I wanted to make twenty thousand reichstaler banco during a single Bourse session, I could do it.[7]

The pride of the successful businesswoman expressed in these lines can be found elsewhere in her writings—for example, in the repeatedly interspersed principles for business life, which she no doubt wanted to recommend to her progeny. The many examples of commendable human beings that arise in these passages show that Glikl highly appreciated erudition, piety, and wealth as positive attributes for men. With respect to women, on the other hand, she primarily mentioned piety, intelligence, and economic competency—therefore, their ability to independently earn a living, to stand by their children, and to support and even provide for the family as a whole. Wealth, expressed in reichsthalers, was very important to her, but she also valued honesty and integrity in business, when dealing both with Jewish and with Christian business partners.

Even though Glikl did not discuss Christendom in her memoirs, Christians repeatedly appeared as trading partners, creditors, and service staff—and also as authorities, who could be a source of danger. However, she reported on positive and negative experiences in her dealings with Jews as well. Glikl repeatedly described conflicts, mostly in relation to the marriage negotiations for her children, but also with regard to business agreements—for example, with Samuel Oppenheimer, who did not pay his debts to her son Nathan when he himself was arrested, or with Chajim's business partner, Judah Berlin, who refused to pay 1,500 thaler owed to the former.

In the late 1690s, after ten years of successful economic activity, the business seems to have become an increasing burden to Glikl. A contributing factor may have been the commercial failure of her son Löb, whom she had to rescue from his creditors with

25,000 thalers. She brought the young man into her business, probably to re-establish his creditworthiness and keep an eye on him. But concerns about maintaining her far-flung business relationships and fears of economic failure evidently burdened her more and more. This was also probably one reason why she considered remarrying and carefully sounded out several candidates, since one of her greatest worries was that she might become a burden to her children in old age because of business losses. In 1699 she finally accepted the courtship of the respected Jewish financier Hirsch Levy from Metz. Glikl largely liquidated her business and moved from Hamburg to Lorraine, together with her youngest and still unmarried daughter Mirijam.

Metz had belonged to the Holy Roman Empire until the mid-sixteenth century, when it became a possession of the king of France. Although smaller and less economically important than Hamburg, Metz had an old Jewish community that, at 1,200 people, made up a substantial portion of the population of the otherwise Catholic town. Glikl's daughter Esther had already lived there for years with her husband, the grain trader Moses Krumbach. For many Jewish merchants, grain and horses were the most important goods, for the area around Metz produced a lot of grain and the French king's large garrisons in the towns along the border of the Holy Roman Empire had to be supplied with foodstuffs.

Glikl thus came to a town that was decidedly different from the Hamburg she knew, and she also had to accustom herself to the living conditions in Hirsch Levy's extravagant household with its many servants. Four of Hirsch's seven children from his first marriage were still living here, and they likely did not greet Glikl with open arms, given that their mother had just died the year before. At first, however, it looked like Glikl would have a peaceful life—until Levy went bankrupt hardly more than a year after she arrived in Metz. He blamed impatient Christian creditors for his downfall; but Glikl was not convinced that he always maintained the necessary order in his transactions. After long negotiations, a debt settlement was reached in 1702. As a result, they were able to save the family's house, but Glikl and her husband were subsequently dependent on their children for financial support.

Glikl may in fact have resumed her trading in precious stones on a small scale. And she was able to arrange a somewhat socially appropriate marriage for her youngest daughter with a Metz horse trader. But when her second husband died in 1712, she had less than one-third left of the amount from her business that she had previously brought into the marriage. Pressured by her stepchildren, she had to leave the Levy house, which had been rescued with such great effort, and for a few years she lived in a rented room on her own with a maid. Later, as an elderly woman, she moved in with her daughter Esther and her son-in-law Moses Krumbach, who in the meantime had become one of the most affluent Jews in Metz and a community leader. What happened in the end was therefore precisely what Glikl had always sought to avoid: in her old age, she became dependent on support. She still lived to see her daughter Mirijam give birth to a son, whom she named Chajim after her father. In 1724, Glikl died at the age of 74.

As a person, Glikl bas Judah Leib certainly did not change the empire with her business activities. But she can stand in for the many women of various social groups, confessions, and religions who participated in the economic development of various cities and regions as merchants and traders, textile workers and peasants. As a memoir writer, Glikl bore witness to her activities, as well as to her ideas and her worldview. This allows us still today to gain fascinating insights into the Jewish world of the seventeenth century.

Notes

1 On the problem posed by the many possible name variants for Glikl, see Turniansky, *Memoirs*, pp. 1–2.
2 Turninansky, *Memoirs*, p. 193.
3 Siebenhüner, K. (2018) *Die Spur der Juwelen: Materielle Kultur und transnationale Verbindungen zwischen Indien und Europa in der Frühen Neuzeit*. Göttingen: Böhlau Köln, pp. 272–284.
4 Turninansky, *Memoirs*, p. 124.
5 Turninansky, *Memoirs*, p. 200.
6 Small, low-quality pearls used for embroidery.
7 Turninansky, *Memoirs*, pp. 222–223.

Selected bibliography

Richarz, M. (ed.) (2001) *Die Hamburger Kauffrau Glikl: Jüdische Existenz in der Frühen Neuzeit*. Hamburg: Christians.

Turninansky, C. (ed.) (2019) *Glikl: Memoirs 1691–1719*. Translated by S. Friedman. Waltham: Brandeis UP.

Zemon Davis, N. (1995) "Arguing with God—Glikl bas Judah Leib", in Zemon Davis, N. (ed.), *Women on the Margins: Three Seventeenth-Century-Lives*. Cambridge Mass.: CUP, pp. 5–62.

EMPRESS ELEONORA MAGDALENA (1655–1720)

How to Care for Your Siblings

When on 14 December 1676 a marriage took place in Passau under loud chiming bells, many in the Holy Roman Empire watched the bridal couple with hope and concern, for the groom that day was Emperor Leopold I and this was his third marriage. His two earlier wives had died relatively young, and while they had given him many children, only a single daughter, Archduchess Maria Antonia, was still alive. Now 36 years old, the emperor was thus the last male representative of the imperial dynasty, and in the event of his death the succession would be completely uncertain. This gave many in the empire reason for concern. The troops of the French king, Louis XIV, were repeatedly threatening the empire's western regions; quite a few princes were allied with him and opposed the emperor. In the southeast, after a longer period of peace, the Ottomans were threatening again. What would happen to the empire if conflict now also broke out among the princes over the succession?

Therefore, given the political and dynastic constellation, the imperial bride bore the heavy burden of extraordinarily high expectations. To be sure, the primary and noblest task of a dynastic woman was to give her husband and dynasty children—especially, of course, an heir to the throne. But if the continuation of the empire's highest-ranking house, the Habsburgs, was simultaneously at stake, then the pressure on the empress was naturally high. And this aspect had also played a special role in choosing the bride.

Eleonora Magdalena Theresia was the daughter of Philipp Wilhelm of Palatinate-Neuburg and his second wife, Elisabeth

FIGURE 14.1 Empress Eleonora Magdalena of Palatinate-Neuburg, 1690

Private ownership

Leonhard Heckenauer, Kaiserin Eleonora Magdalena, 1690, Kupferstich, Privatbesitz

Amalie of Hessen-Darmstadt. They had married in 1653, and Eleonora, born in 1655, was the eldest child of a tremendously fruitful marriage: by 1679, her mother had given birth to a total of 17 children, 14 of whom reached adulthood—six daughters and, believe it or not, eight sons. According to the state of knowledge at the time, such numerous offspring were a good sign that her daughter would also give birth to many healthy children.

Of course, this had not been the only argument in favour of the emperor's marriage to the princess of Palatinate-Neuburg. Eleonora stemmed from a Catholic house, which was *conditio sine qua non* for an imperial bride. Despite a brief alliance with France, her father had been loyal to the emperor for decades and a regular guest at the Vienna court. In Düsseldorf and Neuburg an der Donau, the two most important residences of the Neuburg House, the princess had received an education in keeping with the ideas of the time. She had learned French and Italian, danced with grace, and enjoyed hunting and music. She shared these two inclinations with her imperial husband, along with a deep sense of piety; supposedly Eleonora Magdalena initially preferred the idea of entering a convent over marriage. But she followed her father's contrary decision without resistance.

After the death of Empress Claudia Felicitas in spring 1676, Duke Philipp Wilhelm began working intensively on positioning his eldest daughter as an imperial bride. In the process, he set various confidants in motion at the Vienna court; importantly, they also enlisted the support of Leopold's stepmother, the Empress Dowager Eleonora Gonzaga-Nevers. However, the marriage plans also definitely had opponents among the emperor's milieu, above all because of Eleonora Magdalena's many siblings. Some in Vienna feared that, in the event of a marriage, the emperor would have them "on his hands"—that is to say, he would need to see that his wife's younger brothers were given offices and honours and that her sisters were married off in accordance with their status.

Notwithstanding the many pros and cons, in autumn 1676 the emperor decided in favour of the Palatinate princess. And this decision would prove right in many respects. Eleonora Magdalena gave birth to a total of ten children, of whom two sons, Joseph I and Charles VI, would follow their father on the imperial throne. The couple developed a very loving and trusting relationship. In their almost 30 years of marriage, Eleonora and Leopold were apart for only a few short weeks—such as when the emperor travelled to Vienna after the Ottoman siege of the city in 1683 had been relieved but the empress lay in childbed and could not take such a dangerous journey. The couple's untroubled relationship was an important basis for Eleonora Magdalena's gradual transformation into an important advisor of her spouse, who took her into his confidence in political matters and involved her in his extensive correspondence.

At the same time, she was and remained closely tied to her family of origin and maintained a brisk correspondence with her father, mother, and several brothers and sisters. After the death of her father, who had inherited the title of elector of the Palatinate in 1685, her most important contact person became her eldest brother, Elector Johann Wilhelm of the Palatinate. Her extensive correspondence kept her in touch with her siblings and with many princesses and princes of the Holy Roman Empire, as well as with Spain and the Roman Curia, but evidently only small fragments of these writings have survived.

However, the correspondence that Eleonora conducted with her father and brother for over 40 years[1] very clearly shows that the empress understood her position as a link and as an opportunity to work proactively in the interests of both her families. To a large degree, as her opponents had expected, this did in fact mean finding offices and income for her younger brothers and good marriages for her sisters. Her position opened up numerous opportunities for the House of Palatinate-Neuburg. However, the selection of offices and marriage partners was not only made in the interests of this House. The involvement of the emperor and empress on behalf of princes and princesses of the house at the same time gave rise to obligations for Eleonora's siblings, which in turn proved advantageous to the political interests of the House of Habsburg in the Holy Roman Empire and in Europe. Thus the emperor did not merely have the siblings of his spouse "on his hands", as was expressed prior to the marriage, but rather he also knew how to use the opportunities this provided.

And it was Eleonora Magdalena who actively mediated between Düsseldorf and Vienna in all of these projects. One such case was the marriage of her eldest brother with Archduchess Maria Anna in 1678, a younger sister of the emperor, a plan she pursued together with her mother-in-law, Eleonora Gonzaga-Nevers. Eleonora Magdalena very intensely sought the election of one of her younger brothers as the bishop of Wrocław (Breslau) in 1682/83, and that of another brother as grand master of the Teutonic Knights. She facilitated the military careers of her brothers Ludwig and Karl Philipp in the service of the empire. Whereas plans to have her brother marry a Portuguese princess were pursued for a long time but ultimately not implemented, the empress was able to substantially promote the marriages of her sister Maria Sophie with the king of Portugal (1687), Maria Anna with the king of Spain (1690), Dorothea Sophie with the duke of Parma (1690), and Hedwig Elisabeth with the Polish Prince Jakub Sobieski (1691).

Together with her father, brother, and husband, she thereby built a network through which both dynasties bundled their strengths and complemented each other. The close ties with the imperial house increased the status of the House of Palatinate-Neuburg in the hierarchy of the empire, and the house could make European connections. The House of Habsburg, on the other hand, could use the Neuburg princes and princesses to strengthen its own position through marriage connections and high-ranking positions in the imperial church. At the same time, of course, the empress was and always remained aware that she could float ideas and express opinions, and that she could also use or expedite connections to courtly office holders, diplomats, or foreign courts, but that, ultimately, decisions were always reserved for the emperor or elector—that is, her husband, father, and eldest brother.

This is reflected, for example, by a statement Eleonora made in 1685 to her father, who urged her to advocate for another military command for one of her brothers:

> But if I am not too bold in giving my naïve opinion, then I indeed believe it is better to let the matter go. His Majesty [Leopold] has already been reminded of my brother [Ludwig] and has shown that he has other ideas. So I am worried it might be annoying to His Majesty were I to mention anything more about it against the same, because from the kindness that he has for me, I very well know that, on the one hand, he would not like to refuse me anything, but, on the other hand, due to other ideas, could do it unwillingly or with difficulty, which would not be nice for him if he had to refuse it.[2]

Of course, the empress's advocacy and partisanship were not limited to her closest family; rather, other unrelated or only distantly related princesses and princes also asked her for support. In November 1699, for example, Elector Georg Ludwig of Brunswick-Hanover thanked Eleonora Magdalena after an agreement had been reached on the recognition of the newly created electoral dignity for Hanover. She would be very pleased about this, he wrote, especially given "the large part that you yourself [had] in bringing about this success, which is so pleasing to me".[3] As early as 1696, he had arranged for her to be offered a substantial monetary payment for the support, which proves that he hoped she would provide considerable influence on his behalf. However, at the time the empress also explicitly pointed out to him that she could not accomplish more than what the emperor himself was willing to affirm.

Eleonora Magdalena was therefore just as aware of her options for action as a ruler's consort as she was about the limits imposed upon her as a woman by contemporary norms. But especially when it came to supporting her siblings, she was willing to use her opportunities as empress—both within and outside the borders of the empire—as intensely and fully as possible. In later years, she would also support her children, even though both of her imperial sons struggled at times with their mother's political ideas and her desire to have a say in matters.

This was also no doubt a reason why, after her husband's death in 1705, Eleonora concentrated all the more strongly on leading a pious life. Previously, together with her husband, she had attended churches and monasteries for prayer, registered herself in brotherhoods,[4] and supported various clerics. But now secluded prayer became more central to her life. Already during her lifetime, she was known for engaging in intensive prayer, attending long religious services, and performing regular penitential exercises, as well as for her generous charity towards the poor. This ascetic and at the same time demonstrative piety was in keeping both with Eleonora's own desires and with what was expected of a ruler's widow.

However, her desired retreat into prayer would not be granted without interruption. Instead, during a dynastic and imperial crisis in 1711, she again had to take on an unforeseen level of responsibility to serve the wellbeing of the House of Habsburg. When her son, Emperor Joseph I, suddenly died in April 1711, the imperial councillors in Vienna decided to assign responsibility for the regency in Austria, Bohemia, and Hungary to Empress

Dowager Eleonora Magdalena. Her younger son, Charles, was in Spain at the time, where he had been fighting for the Spanish inheritance of the Habsburgs. This meant that no male Habsburgs were available to take over as a representative, which is why in Vienna—as had already been the case in the Netherlands during the sixteenth century—it was now up to the women of the house to lead government affairs and secure the rulership of the house.

Empress Eleonora Magdalena was well aware of the complex situation in which she assumed the regency in spring 1711. In Hungary, an uprising had not quite ended; fighting over the Spanish succession was under way in Italy, the Spanish Netherlands, and Spain. Sweden and the Ottomans posed additional threats. Money had to be raised for all of these wars, not to mention the daily affairs that pertained to the administration of the hereditary lands. But above all, the empress dowager saw her task as ensuring the election of her son Charles as emperor of the Holy Roman Empire. To this end, she not only urged him to take the necessary steps and, above all, to leave Spain as soon as possible. She also corresponded with the electors—including her brother Johann Wilhelm of the Palatinate—to set the stage for a quick election. The latter finally occurred in October 1711.

In the hereditary lands, the empress dowager ruled as regent from April 1711 to January 1712, when Charles VI arrived in Vienna. In so doing, she received advice and assistance from experienced imperial office holders, who were surprised and sometimes reluctant to find, however, that they had to accept that Eleonora Magdalena definitely had her own ideas about which of her son's suggestions and directives she should follow and which decisions should be made in her name. That Charles affirmed all of his mother's decrees and decisions after he returned shows his approval, on the one hand. But it also shows that Eleonora Magdalena as regent could only operate because she acted as a representative of her son on his behalf, not because she had been granted any rights of her own to exercise such power.

By way of her successful regency in a politically and dynastically difficult situation, the empress once more confirmed her reputation in the eyes of contemporaries as a strong and intelligent woman. This perspective also informed a large number of commemorative writings and sermons that appeared after her death in 1720 in many cities of the Habsburg lands and the Holy Roman Empire. Many of these sermons were published as well, and together these texts described her exceedingly harmonious marriage with Emperor Leopold I and her profound and heartfelt piety. The Vienna court chaplain delivered his sermons under the motto, "Who will find a strong woman" (Proverbs of Solomon 31)[5]. Many felt that Eleonora's strength also expressed itself in the effect of her prayers, through which she contributed more to her husband's political achievements than had "the princes of war in the field".[6] The emperor's military successes against the Ottomans and the French were consequently attributed not least to her intercessions with God.

But the sermons also emphasised Eleonora's actions for the benefit of the House of Palatinate-Neuburg. She was honoured not only as the daughter of an elector, the wife of one emperor, and mother of two emperors and one queen, but also as the sister of two queens, three electors, and six count palatines and five countess palatines, all of whom greatly profited from Eleonora's "kindness and goodness".[7] This shows at the same time that this important dimension of her political action was valued and honoured and not viewed, for example, as objectionable interference. On the contrary, she thereby served as a role model for other princess consorts of the empire.

In one of these commemorative writings, a cleric who knew her well also gave a brief description of her external appearance, which at the same time hinted at several of her qualities as a person.

> The voice was bright and very distinct; enthusiasm and zeal were joined in all things that she planned; the gait often so fast that the court maidens in pursuit could hardly follow; and in all other affairs and efforts, she was always cheerful, never bored, never morose. Otherwise, her nature itself was upright and jovial, indeed not disinclined to joking and laughing; … she had a good and high intellect, and held firmly in memory that which she brought but once to her ears or eyes; she was a superb mistress in womanly arts, and also had no

aversion in advanced age to learning that what she could not do before. ... To also say something about her external bodily figure, thus her length was average, but at that age bent inward because of constant knee-bending in such frequent prayer and the resulting weakness; the forehead visibly broad; the eyes very prominent; the countenance somewhat sprinkled with so-called freckles; broad shoulders; the nose and mouth average; the entire countenance not just pleasant; instead the entire bodily figure and disposition appeared somewhat masculine; just like she namely inherited from benevolent nature most of the masculine virtues, but hardly any of the feminine weaknesses.[8]

The assessment at the end of this description is interesting for reasons that go far beyond the person of Eleonora Magdalena, for it reveals an oft-noticeable strategy of confining actively engaged women in contemporary normative concepts. This occurred regularly by summarily certifying their "masculine" characteristics, their "masculine" intelligence—one sermon also spoke of how Eleonora Magdalena had the "heart of an emperor".[9] Many felt that these characteristics were what enabled her to act politically. Yet a far more likely conclusion is that the empress was acutely aware of the demands placed on a ruler's consort, as well as of the opportunities and limits that defined her scope of action. But this awareness did not require her to have a man's intellect but rather "just" her own.

At the same time, the empress is a good example of how women could mediate and create connections between both of their families—that from which they came and that into which they married. If these were dynasties with their own territories, often enough these women contributed significantly to developing political alliances and connections. Thus the example of Eleonora Magdalena, who acted for the benefit of her siblings, other princely houses of the empire, and her husband and children, shows that the Holy Roman Empire was not just a matter for men. Even though men had the last word, they did not make their decisions and seize their opportunities for offices and dignities independently from the women of their families.

Notes

1 On this, see https://kaiserin-eleonora.oeaw.ac.at.
2 Bayerisches Hauptstaatsarchiv München, Kasten blau 45–9, fol. 459r/v [6/08/1685].
3 Niedersächsisches Landesarchiv Hannover, Cal. Br. 11, Nr. 1275, fol. 8r-9v [15/11/1699].
4 Brotherhoods or fraternities were religious communities of men and women that were usually dedicated to common prayer or to the support of the sick.
5 Brean, F.X. (1720) *Die starcke Tugend Und Tugendsambe Stärcke Eleonorae Magdalenae Theresiae, Weyland Römischer Kayserin ...* Vienna: Heyinger.
6 Wagner, F. (1721) *Leben und Tugenden Eleonorae Magdalenae Theresiae, Römischen Käyserin / Von einem der Gesellschaft Jesu Priestern zusammen getragen.* Vienna: Schwendimann, p. 88.
7 *Castrum Doloris, das ist: Trauer- und Ehren-Gerüst, Welches Auf Allergnädigstem Befehl Ihrer Regierend-Römisch-Kaiserlichen und Königlich-Catholischen Majestät Der Weiland ... Fürstin und Frauen, Frauen Eleonora Magdalena Theresia, ... In der Kaiserlichen Hof-Kirche derer ... Augustiner Barfüssern prächtigst aufgerichtet ...* (1720). Vienna: Schönwetter [p. 8].
8 Wagner, *Leben und Tugenden*, pp. 70–76.
9 Peickhard, F. (1720) *Zahl, Maaß, Gewicht menschlicher Tugend in Leben und Todt Eleonorae Magdalenae Theresiae, weyland Römischer Kayserin ...* Vienna: Heyinger, p. 15.

Selected bibliography

Entries at https://kaiserin.hypotheses.org.

Ingrao, C.W., and Thomas, A.L. (2002) "Piety and Patronage: The Empress-Consort of the High Baroque", *German History* 20 (1), pp. 20–43.

Keller, K. (2021) *Die Kaiserin: Reich, Ritual und Dynastie.* Vienna: Böhlau.

MARIA AURORA VON KÖNIGSMARCK (1662–1728)

The Mistress in the Imperial Abbey

Maria Aurora came from an aristocratic family in Brandenburg; however, her grandfather, Hans Christoph von Königsmarck, had served in the Swedish military as an officer and had been one of the most successful generals of the Thirty Years' War. At the same time, he amassed a substantial fortune and in 1652 acquired a new family estate, Agathenburg, not far from Stade, in an area that belonged to Sweden at the time. His granddaughter, Aurora, was born there in 1662. Her father, Konrad Christoph, died young, and her uncle, Otto Wilhelm von Königsmarck, who had also enjoyed a successful military career, remained childless. After the latter's death in 1688, Maria Aurora, her sister Amalie Wilhelmine, and her brother Philipp Christoph inherited a substantial fortune, but also extensive debts that resulted from the family's ostentatious and extravagant lifestyle.

Countess Königsmarck essentially grew up in Hamburg, which her widowed mother, Maria Christine, who came from the important Swedish aristocratic family of Wrangel, had moved to in 1673 with her children. In 1680, the mother left the city to deal with an inheritance dispute and returned home to Stockholm, followed shortly thereafter by her daughters. Aurora and her sister continued to receive a sterling education there—the young countesses spoke fluent French and Italian, mastered Latin, and were just as well schooled in fine handiwork as in dancing and painting. Aurora's sister, Amalie, was considered a "dilettante"—a talented non-academically trained artist—and she was known for her paintings.

DOI: 10.4324/9781003252870-17

FIGURE 15.1 Maria Aurora von Königsmarck

Nationalmuseum Stockholm

Martin Mijtens d. Ä. (attr.), Maria Aurora von Königsmarck, undatet, Nationalmuseum Stockholm NMGrh 4455

Aurora, on the other hand, who was already renowned as a young girl for her beauty, exhibited more talent in the literary field, which she also demonstrated at the Swedish royal court. She wrote poems in German and French, several dozen of which have survived,[1] as well as short musical comedies and gallant descriptions of festivals. She was especially fond of French literature throughout her life, as shown by the holdings of her library. In 1684, together with her sister and two cousins, she staged the first production in Stockholm of a tragedy by the famous French dramatist Racine, namely, *Iphigénie*, for which she wrote a new prologue. This made her quite famous at court, where for years she and her sister belonged to the inner circle around the young Queen Ulrika Eleonora.

Amalie Wilhelmine von Königsmarck ultimately married Count Karl Gustav Löwenhaupt in 1689, a Swedish aristocrat with ties to the royal family, and thereby escaped (at least for a while) the ever increasing financial constraints caused by the dwindling family fortune. Maria Aurora, on the other hand, still unmarried at 30 years of age, returned to Hamburg in 1692 after her mother's death. From there she repeatedly visited the princely courts in Wolfenbüttel and Hanover, where she had also been a guest as a child. The "Swedish countess", as she was called, was admittedly the idolised focal point of social life at these courts. But she was by no means searching for a husband, which would actually have been in keeping with her social status and could also have alleviated her recurring anxieties about financing her lifestyle.

However, her sister and her brother, Philipp, who was now in Hanover serving in the military, gradually became concerned. Their worries arose not just because Aurora was living beyond the family's means. Beautiful, educated, and witty as she was, Aurora received numerous marriage offers, but she refused them all. Over time, this damaged not only her reputation but also her family's. Her brother therefore wrote in 1693: "Since everybody who wants to marry you turns to me, I need to tell you that one such person is here with me: he is well educated, has a good position, is thirty years old, has an income of 6000 talers, and wants to dedicate to you a capital of 30,000 talers. Since one does not meet such spouses every day, I believed myself obliged … to do you a service by way of this communication."[2]

But he accomplished nothing. Maria Aurora, whose list of rejected suitors already included several young and not-so-young imperial princes and counts, chose none of the marriage candidates. An important reason was presumably her relationship with the Swedish Count Claes Gustav Horn, who in 1684 had been involved in a duel in Sweden, likely over Aurora's favours. But since the Swedish king had prohibited duelling, Count Horn subsequently needed to flee, and he travelled throughout Europe for years. Even so, the two of them apparently remained in contact by letter until they met again in Hamburg in 1693.

This meeting caused a great flurry of excitement for the Königsmarck siblings: whereas Maria was filled with enthusiasm, Amalie and Philipp, in contrast, were anxious about the family's reputation and their sister's future. Destitute and ostracised, the count was certainly not the match they envisioned for the radiant Aurora, and especially not a marriage candidate who might have been able to bring financial security to Aurora's life. Horn's demanding attitude, however, which even led to rumours of a planned kidnapping, together with his notorious unreliability, was probably too much for Maria Aurora as well. She soon fled and travelled to an old acquaintance: Anna Dorothea of Saxe-Weimar, the abbess of Quedlinburg Abbey.

Staying at the venerable imperial abbey on the edge of the Harz highlands did not mean a withdrawal from the world because it was not a monastery. Although hundreds of years earlier the abbey had been founded as such, ever since the Reformation the women living there were Protestant, all of them from the high aristocracy. And entry as a canoness gave unmarried women an opportunity for long-term financial support, while they also remained free to marry at any time and thus pursue the usual career of a woman of high aristocracy. Maria Aurora von Königsmarck stayed in the small town in the Harz region for several months, no doubt becoming very familiar with the local circumstances, but she then left Quedlinburg and travelled to Wolfenbüttel, where she had long been a gladly welcomed guest at court.[3]

There in summer 1694 she received news of the sudden disappearance of her brother, Philipp Christoph. He was about to transfer, as a military officer, from the service of Brunswick to that of Saxony, when he disappeared from Hanover in early June 1694. As we know now, he was murdered and disposed of after the discovery of his long-time affair with the electoral princess of Hanover, Sophie Dorothea. But his sisters knew nothing about this, at least not about his death, and were deeply unsettled, in part because, as head of the family, Philipp Christoph had controlled the domains near Stade. He had also left behind an extensive household, which the sisters needed to maintain at their expense as long as his whereabouts remained unknown.

Aurora von Königsmarck undertook to solve the case and first turned to the elector of Hanover. People there acted as though they knew nothing about it. A few weeks later, the countess travelled to Dresden, hoping for assistance and equipped with a memorandum written in French addressed to the elector of Saxony. The young elector, Friedrich August, today better known as August the Strong, knew Count Königsmarck from their shared military service and had summoned him to Saxony shortly before his disappearance. Moreover, the elector owed Philipp Christoph a total of 30,000 gulden in gambling debts, and Aurora probably hoped that, even if she could not find her brother, she would at least be able to get hold of the money with the elector's help.

She achieved neither. Not until 1696 would she receive a more or less reliable report of her brother's murder. That said, what she did manage to do was to make a deep impression on the elector, who was eight years younger than her. After a brief period she travelled again to Hanover, but as early as summer 1694 she perhaps envisaged entirely new prospects that offered her both social influence and a way out of her constantly stressful financial situation: the position of a mistress.

With the status of a *Maîtresse en titre*, a declared paramour, which had been created at the French court, the mistress of a prince became a sort of court institution; she more or less had an office at court. On the basis of supreme princely favour, whose value in court society could hardly be overestimated, a mistress participated both in ceremonial receptions and in festivals, and through her connection to the prince could develop substantial political influence, which often persisted longer than the actual romantic relationship. With her beauty, education, courtly manners, and social experience, Aurora von Königsmarck had all of the qualities of a mistress.

By autumn 1694, she had evidently decided to take this path, and returned to Dresden where the elector soon held several large festivals in her honour and wooed her at great expense. At the sensationally extravagant carnival of 1695, Countess Königsmarck appeared in a festive procession at the elector's side as the embodiment of dawn. By this time, her new position in court society had become public. In addition, Friedrich August financed an almost regal lifestyle. At the same time, however, through public restraint and sublime appearances at court, Aurora managed to avoid affronting both the electress (August the Strong had been married since 1693) and the elector's mother.

However, the glamorous liaison did not last very long, ending most likely in spring 1696 when August the Strong set off for war in Hungary. But a visible consequence of the relationship was the birth of a son in autumn 1696: Moritz grew up in Dresden and in the Netherlands; his father, who in 1697 also became the king of Poland, formally recognised him in 1710. Henceforth called the count of Saxony, Moritz lived for a longer period at the court of the elector-king in Saxony and Poland. However, his loose living repeatedly gave cause for concern. In 1720 he entered the French military service, but in 1726 still pursued the high-flying plan to have himself elected as the duke of Courland—a plan in which Countess Königsmarck, too, invested much time and money. After this project failed, Moritz de Saxe returned to France, where he gained great fame and died in 1750 as the Marshall General of France in his Château de Chambord on the Loire.

Even after 1696, Maria Aurora von Königsmarck repeatedly returned to Dresden, but seemed to have no problems coming to an arrangement with the (numerous) women who succeeded her as mistress of the elector-king, and she used Friedrich August as a supporter and promoter of her plans. She bought a house in Dresden and probably considered living there long-term, especially since her sister and her husband in the meantime had also settled there, for Count Löwenhaupt had joined Saxony's military service. But at the same time, Maria Aurora pursued a further goal, one that she had likely had her eye on since 1693: acceptance as a canoness—perhaps even the election as abbess—in the Imperial Abbey of Quedlinburg.

The countess had stayed in Quedlinburg for a longer time in autumn 1696 while awaiting the birth of her son; she had probably secured the consent of August the Strong to enter the abbey back then. As the protector of the abbey, he held far-reaching co-determination rights there. Whereas for him this was a convenient opportunity to secure accommodation for his former mistress, for Aurora von Königsmarck it was much more. Her place in the abbey and the office as coadjutor,[4] which she initially sought, gave her an opportunity, as a single noblewoman, to permanently live in accordance with her social status. And what's more, if she became the abbess of Quedlinburg—a position for which she, as coadjutor, would have optimal chances—she would at the same time be an independently governing ruler in the Holy Roman Empire, even if the abbey's territory encompassed just a few square kilometres.

Thanks to the energetic support of the elector of Saxony, in 1698 Aurora von Königsmarck was in fact officially appointed as coadjutor, the deputy of the abbess. However, as a result of the appointment, she circumvented the certified rights of co-determination of the other canonesses—the capitulars—who were actually supposed to decide on the succession. This triggered a long dispute in which the capitulars strongly aligned themselves against not only the actions of the abbess but also against the countess herself. Strictly speaking, apart from an adherence to the Protestant faith, acceptance to the abbey also required a flawless imperial-princely origin and virtuous moral conduct—and, as everyone involved knew, Aurora could point to neither.

The canonesses also directly made their case to Emperor Leopold I and Empress Eleonora Magdalena in Vienna. As a result, they at least managed to keep Countess Königsmarck from being confirmed as coadjutor by the emperor. But when the position of provost, the abbey's second highest office, became vacant in 1700, the abbess, Anna Dorothea of Saxe-Weimar, used her discretionary power to appoint the countess as such. Consequently, Königsmarck held an office with its own revenues (totalling approximately 4,000 talers a year), which permanently secured her social status and gave her influence on the administration and on the election of any new abbess. At the time, she wrote to her brother-in-law, Count Löwenhaupt: "I say to you a thousand thanks for the congratulations with which you have honoured me. I am now starting to understand that it is my purpose to become abbess."[5]

Nothing actually came of this plan. In 1697, the protector of the abbey had changed because Elector Friedrich August of Saxony sold the lucrative entitlement due to a shortage of money to his neighbour, the elector of Brandenburg, who had long been interested in the position. Although the new protector of the abbey also supported Maria Aurora's appointment as provost, he primarily pursued the plan of extensively integrating the abbey's territory into his territorial dominion. The countess had indeed declared her loyalty to Brandenburg from the outset and also stood by this commitment. But she failed in her aspiration to the office of abbess both because of the opposition of the other capitulars and because of other considerations in Berlin. Nonetheless, as provost she played an important role in the elections of abbesses in 1704 and 1708. In the protracted conflicts that followed between the canonesses and the elector of Brandenburg (who since 1701 had been simultaneously the king in Prussia), the provost steadfastly supported the candidates of the elector.

However, after 1704 Maria Aurora largely withdrew from the governing of the abbey. Her activities there had consequently largely been confined to acquiring an office that could serve as a basis for leading an independent life. By supporting the endeavours of the Prussian protector, she doubtless helped weaken the abbey's legal position in the empire. The background for her actions in the office, however, was primarily the preservation of her own interests, not any desire to participate in imperial politics.

As provost, she instead led a largely independent life. She often stayed in Hamburg, or at the family estate near Stade, while the other canonesses managed the affairs in Quedlinburg. She regularly attended the Leipzig Trade Fair and the spa in Teplice, as well as the princely courts of Wolfenbüttel, Berlin, and Dresden. Additional marriage plans are also documented. Although idolised by men even in her advanced age, the countess ultimately seems to have prioritised her independence, even if this was repeatedly overshadowed by financial straits. Only towards the end of her life did she return to Quedlinburg for good, where she died in March 1728.

Countess Königsmarck drew attention to herself like very few women of her times. One can quote from numerous descriptions of her person, of which Voltaire's assessment is merely the most well-known: Maria Aurora von Königsmarck, he wrote, is "famous in the world for her spirit and her beauty", and her qualities made her one of the "most charming persons in Europe".[6] For the nineteenth century, she initially exemplified what was considered a decadent courtly lifestyle, which led to numerous literary biographical accounts of her life. In the middle of the nineteenth century, when excavations in the Quedlinburg crypt revealed the countess's almost fully intact corpse, shrouded in magnificent clothing,[7] this caused a stir throughout Europe and led to a sensationalist tourism that persisted for decades. To some—including her great-great-granddaughter, the author George Sand—the countess figured as an early example of an independent, virtually emancipated woman who made autonomous decisions for her life.

This view no doubt definitely captures an important aspect of her self-understanding. However, one goes astray if one looks only at Maria Aurora's independence, which she safeguarded throughout her life. At the same time, she was aware of the constraints that resulted from her aristocratic origin and the associated standards of behaviour in accordance with her station, as well as of her position as a woman of her times. This always became apparent when, in the context of legal and financial difficulties, she spoke about the problems that arose for her as a woman without close male relatives.

At the same time, however, she thoroughly exploited the liberties that court society could offer women. This was made easier by her beauty and musical and literary talents, as well by her charismatic presence. She made use of both her public but non-marital liaison with the elector of Saxony and her connections to the courts of Wolfenbüttel, Berlin, and Dresden to realise her desire for an independent life. As provost of the Imperial Abbey of Quedlinburg, she finally succeeded in occupying a stable position in the empire's aristocratic society, which enabled her to live a relatively self-determined life as an unmarried woman.

Notes

1 For a bibliography of her writings that have thus far been identified, see Buning et al., *Maria Aurora von Königsmarck*, pp. 331–349.
2 Cramer, F.M.G. (1836) *Denkwürdigkeiten der Gräfin Maria Aurora Königsmark und der Königsmarkschen Familie* (2 vols.). Leipzig: Brockhaus, vol. 1, p. 26.
3 On the history of the imperial abbey, see most recently Schröder-Stapper, T. (2015) *Fürstäbtissinnen: Frühneuzeitliche Stiftsherrschaften zwischen Verwandtschaft, Lokalgewalten und Reichsverband*. Cologne: Böhlau.

4 In the premodern imperial church, an appointment to the office of coadjutor was understood as the early election of a successor during the lifetime of the ecclesiastical elector, bishop, abbot, or abbess to be succeeded.
5 Cramer *Denkwürdigkeiten*, vol. 1, p. 214.
6 Voltaire (2007) *Les œvres completes de Voltaire*, vol. 4: *Histoire de Charles XII*, edited by Proschwitz, G. Oxford: Voltaire Foundation, p. 240. Voltaire, who here also quotes lines from one of Aurora's poems, mentions her in connection with a diplomatic effort to mediate between Poland and Sweden, but we have not been able to describe it in more detail here.
7 For a photo of the mummified countess, Krauss-Meyl, *Die berühmteste Frau*, p. 132.

Selected bibliography

Buning, R., Fiedler, B., and Roggmann, B. (2015) *Maria Aurora von Königsmarck: Ein adeliges Frauenleben im Europa der Barockzeit.* Cologne: Böhlau Verlag.

Krauss-Meyl, S. (2002) *"Die berühmteste Frau zweier Jahrhunderte": Maria Aurora Gräfin von Königsmarck.* Regensburg: Pustet.

Woods, J.M. (1988) "Nordischer Weyrauch: The religious Lyrics of Aurora von Königsmarck and Her Circle", *Daphnis* 17, pp. 267–326.

The Eighteenth Century

Scientists, Writers, and Social Movers

ERDMUTHE BENIGNA OF REUß-EBERSDORF (1670–1732)

Women and the Pietist Movement

Around 1670, a Protestant movement emerged in Frankfurt whose members sought to revive Christian piety and practise their own forms of Christian communality. The movement, which grew more diverse as it spread throughout the Holy Roman Empire during the following period, is referred to as "Pietism" today. Its members called themselves "Pietists" and viewed themselves as an awakened elite, who searched for new paths to salvation and God through frugality, self-reflection, and focused Bible readings.

As during the first phase of the Reformation in the sixteenth century, women figured prominently among the Pietists. Even more intensely than back then, they played an active role from the very start in the "collegia pietatis"—the meetings for readings and prayer—and consequently also had a visible public presence. The most famous of these women was probably Johanna Eleonora Petersen, née von Merlau, who appeared as an author of theological writings.[1] But there were also many other women who became active in this respect, especially women from important aristocratic families of the empire, such as from the houses of the counts of Waldeck, Isenburg-Büdingen, Stolberg-Gedern, or Solms-Laubach.

Countess Benigna and her husband Count Johann Friedrich of Solms-Laubach, for example, are today considered the founders of courtly Pietism, and they maintained close contact with Philipp Jacob Spener, the leader of the Frankfurt Pietists. Their faith and corresponding lifestyle also strongly influenced their children, including Erdmuthe Benigna, born in 1670. Her biography will be

DOI: 10.4324/9781003252870-19

recounted here as an example of the many aristocratic women who were involved in Pietist circles during the seventeenth and eighteenth centuries and therefore helped shape confessional reform movements in the empire.

Erdmuthe Benigna spent her first years in Wildenfels near Zwickau in Saxony. In 1680, the family moved to Laubach in Hessen, a few dozen kilometres north of Frankfurt am Main, because large parts of the County of Solms-Laubach had devolved to Erdmuthe's father by way of inheritance. Her family already had contact with the Frankfurt Pietists, and in 1683 Philipp Jacob Spener sojourned in Laubach for a longer period. He also arranged a teacher for Erdmuthe's brothers, whose lessons no doubt also benefited the family's girls, Erdmuthe and her two sisters.

Her mother, Benigna of Solms-Laubach, was deeply involved in the children's Pietistic upbringing and in several texts recorded her own educational principles for her daughters. She explained therein that even a young countess owed obedience to her husband. A countess could and should only perform tasks of governance if they were explicitly assigned to her by her husband or if she needed to act as the guardian of children after his death. Concomitantly, however, Benigna of Solms-Laubach also saw the need to prepare her daughters for just such a situation and imparted to them knowledge and experience in household management and aristocratic economics as well as a deep religiosity shaped by Pietistic principles.

The court of the count and countess in Laubach was characterised by religiosity, seclusion, and the rejection of pomp and ostentation. Pietists were critical of hereditary nobility, such that the nobles who adopted the faith of this movement virtually needed to compete with bourgeois members of the Pietistic elite to justify their prominent social position by embodying the virtues defined by Pietistic ideals: modesty, critical self-observation, and intense communication in written and oral form about faith and experiences of faith for the reassurance of the community. Erdmuthe learned all of this from her parents. Her personal religious practices were further shaped by the Laubach court chaplain, Johann Philipp Marquard, with whom she remained in contact even long after she married.

FIGURE 16.1 Erdmuthe Benigna of Reuß-Ebersdorf

Bildarchiv Foto Marburg

Erdmuthe Benigna von Reuß-Ebersdorf, Schloss Ebersdorf, Bildarchiv Foto Marburg fm144956

In 1694 in Laubach, Erdmuthe Benigna of Solms married Count Heinrich X of Reuß-Ebersdorf, who had courted her for several years. Her parents only agreed to the marriage once they were sure that the prospective spouse actually led a good Pietistic life. At the same time, the marriage was instrumental in establishing networks between the empire's various houses at the countship level that adhered to Pietism for a more or less long time.

The very amicable marriage of Erdmuthe and Heinrich X produced eight children, although three of their daughters died in childhood. Their only son, Heinrich XXIX,[2] succeeded his father in 1720 as the regent of the County of Ebersdorf. In the small capital, where Heinrich X of Reuß first needed to have a castle built, Erdmuthe Benigna became a driving force of the court's Pietistic influence. As early as 1696, she created a community—the

"Small Connected Society"—where her family members and office holders and their families met. Most of the inhabitants of the town and the surrounding region, however, remained orthodox Lutherans, so the countess had a private chapel set up—including for the servants, who were Pietists—to obviate the need to attend the town's Lutheran church.

Following a practice that she knew from Laubach, Erdmuthe also supported Pietistic religious refugees in Ebersdorf. Pietists were often expelled or persecuted, especially during the first few decades after 1670, because their views and lifestyle markedly deviated from those of orthodox Lutherans. Often they explicitly criticised the official church. Moreover, some proponents of Pietism advocated theological approaches that differed from those of the official church, which frequently earned them a reputation as "heretics".

Erdmuthe remained devoted to her now widowed mother Benigna, visiting her frequently until she died in 1702. Apart from numerous devotional works, some of which were published after her death, Benigna of Solms had also written a book about marriage for her daughter, which was later published. In turn, Erdmuthe, for her part, passed the spiritual-religious principles recorded in this book on to her daughters, along with the skills to deal with practical economic matters, all of which had also been the focus of her own education. Her daughters were taught religion, naturally by Pietist teachers; but, unlike Erdmuthe herself, they also had lessons in Greek and Latin. Erdmuthe taught them household management and aristocratic economics. Later she called on the girls to do writing work, such as copying letters, which no doubt had an educational impact too.

By way of these activities, the daughters, in turn, supported their mother, for in summer 1711 she had entered a new phase in life: after her husband's death, it was up to Erdmuthe Benigna to lead the county's government, acting as the representative of her son. As many noble and princely women before and after her, she assumed an important role in securing the rulership and administration of the domains. Until 1720, when Heinrich XXIX completed his education and married, she was in charge of government affairs in Ebersdorf. Since, legally, the Countess of Reuß could not exercise the guardianship on her own, her brother Carl Otto of Solms-Laubach and Heinrich XXIV of Reuß-Schleiz of Köstritz, both likewise Pietists, supported her. They backed her up in legal and confessional conflicts with other representatives of the House of Reuß, but rarely stayed in Ebersdorf, which meant that the widowed countess managed affairs largely on her own. This is documented, not least, by her recently published letters from this time.[3]

Her actions as a guardian were characterised, on the one hand, by skilled economic management, which improved the revenue from the county. That said, the fact that the county, which in 1711 encompassed only some 11 villages, almost doubled in size during her regency was because of an inheritance in the House of Reuß, not because of her administrative success. On the other hand, the countess emphatically pursued a Pietistic personnel policy. She closely questioned not only candidates for pastoral and official positions but also prospective servants. In doing so, she verified their Pietistic mindset, which the countess regularly took as a fundamental requirement for an appointment. Thus, she actively pursued church politics, for the appointment of Pietistic pastors naturally also had an influence on the county's residents.

Particularly with regard to the church, Erdmuthe Benigna as regent saw herself as an instrument of God, as a propagator of the new Pietistic teachings, as she wrote to her fellow guardian and Pietist Heinrich XXIV. "God will stand by us, he now needs us as his instruments, through which his honour shall be furthered and the realm of Satan destroyed, for if I had received someone other than Your Illustrious Highness as a co-guardian, my hands would have been bound in all good things, for none [of the Lords of Reuß] are of one mind with me in such matters."[4] The Lutheran confession of the other lines of the House of Reuß, to which Erdmuthe is alluding here, as well as the difficulties arising from their involvement in the consistory administration, repeatedly complicated her actions as the church patron and the ecclesiastical authority of the subjects.

And in much the same way as female princely consorts and regents of the Reformation period, Erdmuthe Benigna felt herself directly responsible to God for the salvation of her subjects. This is evident, for example, from her report on a conversation with the superintendent of Lobenstein, who was responsible for the County of Reuß-Ebersdorf, regarding the controversial appointment of one of her chosen candidates to a pastorate. Directly thereafter she wrote to Heinrich XXIV, "in this respect, I then sufficiently said, that their [the cleric's] office is entrusted by us [the counts as secular authorities], and they were not set over us, nor alongside us, but under us, and that I very well knew that the Ius episcopale[5] is entrusted to the lords themselves. For which they will also at some point need to give account, and it also will not help them if they want to lay the blame, where something was neglected or corrupted, on the consistory officials; therefore, the order must well remain as it is, that the lords were to be first and thereafter those to whom they in turn entrusted some of it."[6]

The quote illustrates both the self-assurance of the Countess of Reuß as a member of the ruling estate and the obligation that this entailed for her. And the clear argumentation demonstrates that Erdmuthe knew quite well how to defend herself against the pretensions and impositions on the part of officials and on the part of men from other lines of the House of Reuß. The latter repeatedly tried to curtail her rights as guardian and gave her to know that she herself actually held no rights of rulership, but rather her son. As a woman, Erdmuthe was not allowed to participate in the regular gatherings of the counts of the many branches of the House of Reuß, where family strategies were discussed and conflicts assuaged. Officials of other Reuß territories repeatedly refused to follow Erdmuthe's written instructions unless her male co-guardian had signed them as well. Yet despite such difficulties, the likes of which were faced by many female guardianship regents, she acted with self-assurance and could consistently enforce or defend her rights or move her co-guardians to act in her interest.

Her letters show that governing as a guardian was a burden—Erdmuthe Benigna was always pressed for time, as is reflected in the handwriting of her letters, which were often written in great haste. And her need to defend herself applied not only to impositions pertaining to the legitimacy of her actions. What no doubt bothered her even more was that radical proponents of Pietism denounced her secular activities as regent as a distraction, as vain actions through which she risked losing God's grace. For a woman who defined herself so strongly as a member of the Pietist movement, this would have been a difficult situation. But the alternative would have meant surrendering the guardianship solely to the two men, and the countess could not reconcile this with her responsibility for her son.

During these years of the guardianship regency, Heinrich XXIX of Reuß-Ebersdorf received his education. First, he attended school in Halle, which had become a new centre of Pietism around August Hermann Francke, and then went on an educational tour of Holland and France. His mother and sisters visited him in Halle in 1713, where Erdmuthe Benigna personally got to know Franke, who, for his part, visited her a few years later in Ebersdorf.

In 1720, a friend of Heinrich from his school and travel days also came for a visit to the small Thuringian capital: Nicolaus von Zinzendorf, who would later found the Herrnhut Unity of Brethren, which is also known as the Moravian Church. The court at Ebersdorf, with its Pietistic sociability, came to serve as a model for the young Count Zinzendorf, and his courting of Erdmuthe Benigna's daughter, Erdmuthe Dorothea, no doubt deepened the relationship. At first, the mother was not very impressed by the mission-conscious young man; but the marriage between him and her daughter nonetheless took place in 1722. Through the Ebersdorf model and the strong connection with Zinzendorf, Erdmuthe Benigna's activities consequently influenced the development of the Moravian Church. In 1745, Zinzendorf himself placed the Herrnhut religious community in a line of tradition with Erdmuthe's "Small Connected Society" at the Ebersdorf castle.

After the end of her regency in 1720, Erdmuthe Benigna of Reuß-Ebersdorf largely withdrew again to a life of religious devotion, but still, of course, following and supervising the developments surrounding Zinzendorf and her daughter. Conflicts about the forms of religiosity at the Ebersdorf court arose in 1721 between Erdmuthe and her daughter-in-law, Sophie Theodora of

Castell-Remlingen, who leaned more strongly towards the Pietism of Halle. Only after the departure of Sophie Theodora's court chaplain in 1726 was the earlier form restored. After a long illness, Erdmuthe Benigna died in 1732 in Ebersdorf, where she was interred in the family crypt.

Even though, apart from the aforementioned letters of the countess, few sources have survived that provide for more precise insights into the nature of Countess Erdmuthe Benigna as a person, she was evidently more than simply the daughter of a mother more famous in the history of Pietism, and more than the mother-in-law of the even more famous founder of the Herrnhut Unity of Brethren. Erdmuthe Benigna was also the successful regent of an imperial territory, however small. For many years, she was a key player in the network of noble and non-noble male and female Pietists that extended from Laubach via Frankfurt and Halle into Upper Lusatia. As a prominent figure of the small court, she left her mark on Ebersdorf: as a place of Pietistic sociability, and as a place of refuge for Pietists of all persuasions. As an educator, she played an important role in developing the personalities of her children, all of whom later joined the Moravian Church. The influences of the Moravian Church on the architecture and culture of Ebersdorf and its environs still remain visible today and in large part can be traced back to the workings of Erdmuthe Benigna of Reuß.

Notes

1 On her person, see Peterson, J.H. (2005) *The Life of Lady Johanna Eleonora Petersen, Written by Herself: Pietism and Autobiography*. Translation, with notes and introduction by Barbara Becker-Cantarino. Chicago and London: University of Chicago Press.
2 The first name of all of the men of the House of Reuß in its various lines is "Heinrich". Hence it is customary to also provide the numerations. The count occurs separately within the individual lines and therefore differs substantially within a single generation.
3 See Prell, M., and Schmidt-Funke, J. (eds.) *Digitale Edition der Briefe Erdmuthe Benignas von Reuß-Ebersdorf (1670–1732)*. Jena 2017 [Work in Progress]. Available at http://erdmuthe.thulb.uni-jena.de.
4 Erdmuthe Benigna of Reuß to Heinrich of Reuß, undated [1712]. Available at https://collections.thulb.uni-jena.de/rsc/viewer/HisBest_derivate_00017902/PK12_1_0001.tif

5 Ius Episcopale: episcopal jurisdiction, which in the Protestant churches was the responsibility of the respective territorial lord—and in this case the countess as the representative of her son.
6 Erdmuthe Benigna of Reuß to Heinrich of Reuß [8/10/1717]. Available at https://collections.thulb.uni-jena.de/rsc/viewer/HisBest_derivate_00017909/PK15_3_0003.tif

Selected bibliography

Langer, R. (2014) "Erdmuthe Benigna von Reuß-Ebersdorf, geb. von Solms-Laubach (1670–1732)", in Meyer, D. (ed.), *Lebensbilder aus der Brüdergemeine*, vol. 2. Herrnhut: Herrnhuter Verlag, pp. 179–193.

Wunder, H. (2013) "Öffentlichkeiten und Geschlechterverhältnisse: Die Regentschaft der Reichsgräfin Erdmuthe Benigna von Reuß-Ebersdorf", in Hochmüller, M. et al. (eds.), *Politik in verflochtenen Räumen*. Berlin: Tranvía Verlag Frey, pp. 242–262.

MARIA MARGARETHA KIRCH (1670–1720)

The Arduous Journey to the Sciences

FIGURE 17.1 Map of the southern starry sky surrounded by the representations of four great observatories: London, Copenhagen, Kassel, and Berlin. The latter is in the lower right corner (1742)

Bayerische Staatsbibliothek München

Doppelmayr, Johann Gabriel: Atlas Nova Coelestis, Tafel 19: Hemisphaerum Coeli Australe, Nürnberg 1742, Bayerische Staatsbibliothek München 2 Mapp. 275 l

DOI: 10.4324/9781003252870-20

Maria Margaretha was born in February 1670 in Panitzsch, a small village not far from the important commercial and trade fair city of Leipzig. Her father, Matthias Winckelmann, who served there as pastor, and her mother, Maria, died in quick succession, so the orphaned 13-year-old girl lived with her older sister a while. The latter was married to Justinus Töllner, a cleric who succeeded her father as pastor in Panitzsch in 1682. Maria Margaretha had already been educated by her father as a child, and she had acquired the basics of not only reading and writing but also mathematics, Latin, and Hebrew. After her father's death, Justinus Töllner continued to teach her. The girl apparently showed an interest early on in a rather unusual field, namely, astronomy.

An important contributing factor here was presumably that, while still a girl, Maria Margaretha established contact with a farmer in the nearby village of Sommerfeld, perhaps through Töllner. The man was Christoph Arnold, who, alongside farming, had been active as an astronomer for many years and was in contact by mail with many other astronomers. In 1682, Christoph Arnold was the first to discover and describe the comet widely known today as Halley's comet. He observed comets and variable stars throughout his life, and in 1690 was one of the first astronomers to describe a passage of Mercury in front of the sun and then publish his results. He consequently became the most well-known of a large number of so-called farmer astronomers who lived in Saxony around 1700.

Arnold was able to work successfully in science even without an academic education because, like most of the natural sciences, astronomy back then was far less academic in nature than would be the case just a few decades later. The collection of knowledge through personal observation still played a greater role than its systemisation. Christoph Arnold took the inquisitive girl under his wing, and, in particular, must have taught her a lot about the practical work of celestial observation. He soon also introduced her to his colleague, Gottfried Kirch, with whom he jointly carried out observations. Both can no doubt be credited with ensuring that Maria Margaretha, too, directed her scientific interest towards the observation of comets, variable stars, and solar activity.

That Maria Margaretha Winckelmann married Kirch, 30 years her senior, in 1692 was perhaps the consequence of their working together. From the very beginning, Kirch viewed his second wife as his "assistant"—and not only with respect to homekeeping and looking after the children but also and especially in carrying out his complex calculations and observations for the production of calendars. But the two also bonded as members of the Protestant reform movement called Pietism. As a married couple, the Kirchs belonged to the Leipzig Pietist community around August Hermann Francke, which, however, grew more and more unwelcome in strictly Lutheran Saxony.[1]

Just a few months after marrying, Gottfried and Maria Margaretha had to leave Leipzig, where Kirch had long made his living as a calendar maker. He was one of many astronomers who calculated and designed calendars, which were then printed in Leipzig, Nuremberg, or Wrocław (Breslau) and brought to market. Such calendars, particularly those compiled by Kirch, were very popular. They contained information on moon phases, sunrise times, and similar astronomical phenomena, as well as on astrological constellations, market dates, weather forecasting, or even on special events of the previous year. Their owners—from the emperor to rural day labourers—often used them as diaries too, with shorter or longer entries.

Having left Leipzig in October 1692 and moved to Guben, where Gottfried Kirch was born, Maria Margaretha and Gottfried were now supporting their growing family with such calendars. Five of the couple's six children were born in Guben, four of whom reached adulthood. Of these, their son Christfried and daughters Christine and Margaretha would later themselves become astronomers and calendar makers, for their parents had them helping with astronomical observations from early on.

As shown by a letter that has recently been discovered, notwithstanding the growing family and many financial worries, Maria Kirch took her scientific work seriously and by no means viewed it merely as a secondary job and a way to support her husband: she tried to enrol at the University of Halle, perhaps in connection with the professional plans of her husband, who sought an appointment there in 1692. This would have been a pioneering move and probably the first such case at a university in the empire. Founded just a few years earlier, the university had the reputation of being keen on reforms, and many professors advocated early Enlightenment positions. The Kirchs also had connections to Halle by way of the important Pietist August Hermann Francke, and he also evidently supported Maria Kirch's desires and tried to see them realised. However, the endeavour failed because of resistance from other professors.

Her husband, on the other hand, succeeded in the struggle for financial security and the recognition of his scientific work. In early summer 1700, he was appointed as an astronomer at the Royal Academy of Science in Berlin, where King Frederick I of Prussia had just had an observatory planned for the newly founded academy. However, the facility was not very lavishly funded, and the Kirchs now had to produce and sell calendars under a royal privilege in order to help finance the entire academy at the same time. Meanwhile, ever since their days in Guben, and in parallel with their astronomical research, Maria Margaretha and her husband had continuously been making weather observations and recording them in writing, presumably not least so that they could be used for their calendar forecasts. The notes Maria Margaretha regularly made for this purpose are known for the years 1697 and 1700 to 1720.[2]

Berlin offered better opportunities for scientific work, including the facility with various instruments such as telescopes, clocks, quadrants, and measuring devices. The actual observatory, however, was not completed until 1709, which is why for a long time their observations were still made from the family's private residence and the building's attic. From at least the age of ten, the couple's children took part in the observations too and were therefore introduced to the methods and fundamentals of observation and calculation. In the same way that Herr and Frau Kirch worked together on an equal footing, substituting for one another in the case of illness or when otherwise prevented from making observations, the older children were soon doing so as well.

The observation logs kept by Gottfried Kirch still survive, and they reflect the joint nature of the couple's work and reveal some of the routine problems they encountered. The observatory itself was too bright for the precise mapping of sun spots. At their home, their attempt to follow the trajectory of a star was thwarted by a roof gutter, while other observations were blocked by laundry hanging in the attic. Instruments often had to be transported from one window to the next, and Maria Margaretha or one of the children often had to run to another storey to look at the clock, and so on.[3]

Despite many complications, Maria Margaretha was thus able to continue her scientific work, which led to an important discovery in 1702. In the night of 21 to 22 April 1702, Maria discovered a comet, as she noted in her observation diary, "between the arrow and the head of the swan",[4] that is, between the constellations Sagitta and Cygnus. Her husband then published this discovery, which no doubt solidified her reputation as an astronomer. And she herself published several small texts on astronomical-astrological questions—around 1700, the divorce of astronomy as a science from astrology was by no means finalised; instead, the latter was still considered a necessary and legitimate part of astronomy. Later astronomers would often criticise Maria Margaretha because she continually dealt with astrological questions, but this part of her work was actually still highly valued by her contemporaries.

However, Maria Margaretha Kirch's work was more generally thrown into question in 1710 when her husband died. She now faced substantial economic difficulties, for this meant the loss of her husband's salary as the family's livelihood. At the same time, his death also endangered her scientific work, for the academy quickly began searching for a successor for his office, and this raised doubts about her access to instruments and observation opportunities.

Maria Margaretha reacted to this with pronounced self-confidence by submitting a "Memorial" to the academy of sciences in which she explained her aptitude, above all as a calendar maker, but she also pointed out her need, as a widow, to provide for her children. The high regard contemporaries had for her as an astronomer and calendar maker is demonstrated, for example, by the assessment of Gottfried Wilhelm Leibniz, probably the Holy Roman Empire's most famous scholar. Apart from being the president of the Berlin academy, he knew Maria Margaretha personally. Not only did he firmly take Maria Margaretha's side in the negotiations over the filling of the position, he had also previously written to the queen in Prussia: "There [in Berlin] is a most learned woman who could pass as a rarity. Her achievement is not in literature or rhetoric but in the most profound doctrines of astronomy .... I do not believe that this woman easily finds her equal in the science in which she excels .... And it is a pleasure to hear her defend that [Copernican] system through the Holy Scripture in which she is also very learned. She observes with the best observers, she knows how to handle marvellously the quadrant and the telescope."[5]

Admittedly, his support was to no avail. The commission tasked with filling the position consulted at length and never seriously questioned the female applicant's technical knowledge, but in 1712 it decided in favour of a man, Johann Heinrich Hoffmann. It was never explained whether this occurred because the commission generally did not believe that a woman could do the work, or because Maria Kirch, as a woman, could not demonstrate an academic education, or because the commission did not want to employ a woman at a public institution like the academy. What is certain, however, is that the rejection was based on the fact that she was a woman, and that the academy was afraid of exposing itself to ridicule if it allowed a woman to produce its calendars. On this point, Johann Theodor Jablonski, the secretary of the academy, had already told Leibniz accordingly: "that she be kept on in an official capacity to work on the calendar or to continue with observations simply will not do. Already during her husband's lifetime, the academy was burdened with ridicule because its calendar was prepared by a woman. If she were now to be kept on in such a capacity, mouths would gape even wider."[6]

However, it soon became apparent that Hoffmann's work, especially his calendar calculations, left much to be desired. But since the calendars were sufficiently important as a source of the academy's revenue, for a while Maria Margaretha was enlisted to support him. This may seem like an insult from today's perspective, but it nonetheless gave her the chance to earn some income from her scientific work. She herself, however, evidently also saw the work as an impertinence, for, despite her financial need, she gradually withdrew and concentrated on her own observations. For a long time, she was able to carry them out in the private observatory of Bernhard Friedrich von Krosigk in Berlin-Neu-Cölln, where her husband had often worked before.

Maria Margaretha's options changed again when her son, Christfried, who had since completed his studies, was appointed "observator" at the Berlin observatory in 1716. Maria Margaretha Kirch and her daughters, who had been staying in Gdańsk (Danzig) since 1715, moved in with him on the academy grounds and shared his scientific work through joint observations and calculations. For a long time, this was controversial: for one, this meant that Christfried Kirch was performing some of his observations from home; for another, the women were often present at the academy's observatory, which disgruntled the academic employers. Above all, it was the presence of Maria Margaretha Kirch herself that met with obvious displeasure, and she was finally forced to give up the apartment at the academy. In late December 1720, Maria Margaretha Kirch died in Berlin.

One can hardly overlook the fact that Maria Margaretha Kirch had great difficulty continuing her scientific work after her husband's death, even though she was able to find supporters such as Baron von Krosigk and her son's appointment eased the situation. Even so, the refusal to appoint her to a scientific position as her husband's successor marked neither the end of her work nor the end of the work of women in astronomy. In Berlin, her daughters Christine and Margaretha were still working as astronomers into the 1770s, and Caroline Lucretia Herschel, who came from Hanover, provides a notable example in London. In the public eye and according to the worldview of the men of the Berlin academy, however, women only really had a right to work on scientific subjects as the helpers and assistants of men.

Beyond her individual scientific merits, Maria Margaretha Kirch therefore serves in many respects as a typical example of the difficulties women had to overcome to work in science. They were denied the opportunity to study at universities until well into the nineteenth century—they could only get educated within their family milieu. As long as their education and scientific work took place basically within the household, guided by the male head of the household, they were largely accepted. This constellation was no doubt also socially legitimised by the fact that such joint work by married couples large corresponded to what could be observed in artisanal households. Here too, wives and daughters often worked as "assistants", without whom the everyday work would hardly have been possible.

As a result, men played an instrumental role also and especially in facilitating opportunities for women to work in science. The approval of a father, husband, or brother, or better still their involvement in education, was central; the developmental options of women remained substantially dependent on male support. And to this day, even our memory of the scientific achievements of women often remains hidden behind the men who took centre stage. This also applies to Maria Margaretha Kirch, even though an asteroid was named after her in 2000 and she is therefore permanently present in the heavens.[7]

Maria Margaretha Kirch herself took note of the difficulties women faced in gaining recognition for their scientific work, and commented on this in the beginning of one of her texts:

> To be sure, the womanly name may draw some contemptuousness to the matter [i.e., her writings]. But if one considers that, in the prophesies of Joel, both the female sex and the male are included under the promise of the gifts of the mind and spirit ... then it is not difficult to take from this that female persons can be just as skilled .... And because now I, according to my humble self, have practised the art of stars for many years, and have many times delighted in the orderly structure of the heavens and movement of the great heavenly bodies, I thus have been emboldened to write something about the starry heaven ...[8]

Her use of Biblical examples to justify her position was in keeping not just with the ideas of her time but also with Maria Margaretha's own piety. One generation after Maria Margaretha Kirch, there would be a woman in the Holy Roman Empire who unequivocally raised her voice in writing against the customary approach towards women's educational aspirations and interests in science: Dorothea Erxleben, who in 1754 became the first woman to receive her doctorate at the University of Halle. But her life's journey is another story.

Notes

1 See also the biography of Benigna of Reuß and the introduction, p. 20–21, 196–97.
2 Her observations for 1700 and 1701, which often include small notes on the life of her family, have been published: Hellmann, G. (1893) "Das älteste Berliner Wetter-Buch 1700–1701", *Jahresbericht des Berliner Zweigvereins der Deutschen Meteorologischen Gesellschaft* 10, pp. 11–19. See also Herbst, *Gottfried Kirch*, pp. 439–441.
3 On the survival of the papers of Gottfried and Maria Margaretha Kirch, see https://archiv.bbaw.de/nachlaesse/nachlaesse/familiennachlass-kirch and Kirch, G. (2006) *Die Korrespondenz des Astronomen und Kalendermachers Gottfried Kirch (1639–1710)*. Edited by Herbst, K., with Knobloch, E., and Simon, M. (3 vols.). Jena: IKS Garamond.
4 Quoted in Herbst, *Gottfried Kirch*, p. 510.
5 Klopp, O. (ed.) (1873) *Die Werke von Leibniz, 1. Reihe: Historisch-politische und staatswissenschaftliche Schriften*, vol. 9. Hannover: Klindworth, p. 295 [January 1709].
6 Harnack, A. (1897) *Berichte des Secretars der Brandenburgischen Societät der Wissenschaften J. Th. Jablonski an den Präsidenten G. W. Leibniz (1700–1715) nebst einigen Antworten von Leibniz*. Berlin: Akademie-Verlag, pp. 79–80 [1/11/1710].
7 https://newton.spacedys.com/astdys/index.php?pc=1.1.0&n=9815.
8 Winckelmannin, M. (1711) *Vorbereitung zur grossen Opposition, oder merckwürdige Himmels-Gestalt im 1712 Jahre* ... Cölln an der Spree: Liebpert, pp. 3–4.

Selected bibliography

Hargittai, Magdolna (2023) *Meeting the Challenge. Top Women in Science*. New York, NY: Oxford University Press.

Herbst, K. (2022) *Gottfried Kirch (1639–1710): Astronom, Kalendermacher, Pietist, Frühaufklärer*. Jena: HKD.

Kühn, S. (2020) "Scholarly Households", in Eibach, J., and Lanzinger, M. (eds.) *The Routledge History of the Domestic Sphere in Europe, 16th to 19th Century*. Abingdon: Routledge, pp. 134–154.

Schiebinger, L. (1982) *The Mind has No Sex? Women in the Origins of Modern Science*. Cambridge Mass. and London: Harvard University Press.

LUISE ADELGUNDE GOTTSCHED (1713–1762)

More than the Woman at his Side

FIGURE 18.1   Luise Adelgunde Gottsched, 1757

Alamy

Johann Martin Bernigeroth, Portrait der Ludovica [!] Adelgunde Gottsched, Kupferstich, Leipzig 1757

DOI: 10.4324/9781003252870-21

When Luise Adelgunde Victorie Gottsched, née Kulmus, died in Leipzig on 17 June 1762, she was a prominent figure in the literary life of Saxony's book and trade fair city and of the entire Holy Roman Empire. The fact that, contrary to so many other women of the early modern empire, neither she as a person nor her literary work were forgotten had much to do with her husband: Johann Christoph Gottsched had been one the German Enlightenment's leading literary theorists and commentators for decades. His dedication of an extensive commemorative volume to his deceased wife, in which he laid out her biography as the success story of an educated woman, for a long time played a vital role in the literary remembrance of "the Gottschedin".[1] His expositions in this respect are still an important source, especially for his wife's youth, without which many aspects of her biography would hardly be available.

Luise Adelgunde was born in April 1713 in the large Hanseatic city of Gdańsk (Danzig) on the Baltic as the daughter of a successful physician, Johann Georg Kulmus, and his wife, Katharina Dorothea. The city was under the dominion of the king of Poland and had long been a centre in the Russian and Polish grain trade. Ever since the medieval Hanseatic era, Gdańsk had maintained diverse contacts with Scandinavia, the Netherlands, and England, as well as with the empire's large commercial cities such as Nuremberg, Augsburg, Frankfurt, and Leipzig.

Both of the girl's parents were educated and interested in science; her father was also a member of the "Academia Imperialis Leopoldina Naturae Curiosorum" (Imperial Leopoldina Carolina German Academy of Natural Scientists, today: Leopoldina). Her mother was initially in charge of the schooling for Luise and her two younger sisters; in particular, she ensured that Luise learned French, while it was her older stepbrother who taught her English. Luise was already very keen on poetry and literature, and she wrote her first texts and poems and translations from French as a young girl. She was also interested in history, geography, and music—she played piano and lute.

In 1729, Johann Christoph Gottsched, who came from Prussia, got to know the young Luise Kulmus during a visit to Gdańsk and evidently was immediately impressed, for she seemed to be the manifestation of the educational goals for women that he had propagated a few years earlier in his journal *Die vernünftigen Tadlerinnen* (The reasonable female tatlers). He had already vigorously advocated the enlightened education of women prior to meeting Luise Kulmus. In his effort to spread new Enlightenment ideas about reforming the German language, he had also worked with women who supported and implemented his proposals. One, for example, was Christiana Mariana von Ziegler, a poet living in Leipzig with whom he had collaborated between 1725 and 1730, including on the *Vernünftigen Tadlerinnen*. Another would later be the Leipzig theatre director Friederike Caroline Neuber, whom he won over around 1730 for his efforts to reform the German-language theatre.

After his visit, Gottsched maintained a correspondence with Luise Adelgunde Kalmus, which in 1734 led to a promise of marriage and to the marriage itself in 1735 in Gdańsk. The surviving letters of Luise Adelgunde from these years reveal that Gottsched viewed his exchange with her as a teacher–student relationship. He wanted to show his bride the path to be the educated and adaptable wife of a successful scholar, building, of course, on what the young woman had taken from her upbringing and education in her parental home. Luise Adelgunde seems to have gladly accommodated this desire, for the contact with Johann Christoph was intellectually stimulating and encouraged her to pursue further studies, such as deepening her linguistic skills through Latin and Greek.

After their marriage in 1735, Luise Adelgunde lived with her husband in Leipzig, where he served as a professor at the university. As a university town and centre of trade, Leipzig played a key role in the empire's bourgeois Enlightenment. Later her husband would never get tired of pointing out that Luise Adelgunde was a stalwart "helpmate" in the years and decades that followed, a "constant companion" in his various enterprises. The Gottscheds were a successful literary working couple for many years: she translated and edited texts, prepared excerpts from books and reviews for his journals, catalogued his library, and discussed translation and literary issues with him.

The marriage remained childless, which was no doubt part of the reason Gottschedin had the time for her "scholarly lifestyle", even though she also had to supervise the household of a tenured university professor, which surely was not small. The couple lived in the house Zum Goldenen Bären near the university. Johann Christoph's position as a professor, as well as his renown as a journalistic critic and commentator, led to wide-ranging contacts with professors and scholars, merchants and jurists, as well as students and travellers who visited his house. As was common for professors, there were also boarding students who took part in meals and were taught at the professor's home.[2]

As a result, Luise Adelgunde assumed many duties and, as the lady of the house, she had to make sure that visitors and guests were provided for and accommodated. However, this aspect of her work by no means figured among her favorite activities, as she complained to a friend:

> Here I need to fill my head each day with veritable trivialities, with house-related and economic concerns, which ever since childhood I have considered the most miserable activities of a thinking being; and of which I would gladly like to be spared. Just one essential part of the exquisite bliss of the male sex must be in the relief from these meaningless things.[3]

Many of her letters, only some of which have been published,[4] also document social contacts with nobles who lived in or near Leipzig or visited the city, such as Friedrich Heinrich von Seckendorff and his wife, Clara Dorothea, or Count Ernst Christoph von Manteuffel. The Gottsched couple was also linked with them through a social association called the Society of Alethophiles. In this group, people played music and participated in theatrical events and festivals—albeit all in the service of enlightened truth as defined by Gottlieb Wilhelm Leibniz and Christian Wolff. Luise Adelgunde positioned herself in this circle through her extremely sharp-tongued satirical pamphlets against the adversaries of this truth, which above all included representatives of Saxony's official Lutheran Church. Personal acquaintance and long-standing correspondence also linked Luise Adelgunde Gottsched with Johanna Elisabeth of Anhalt-Zerbst,[5] who as a widow spent much of her time in Leipzig, and with Dorothea Henriette von Runckel, a dear friend during her later years. Luise's letters have long been known and appreciated as examples of the Enlightenment's culture of letters; Dorothea Henriette published many of them ten years after Luise's death.[6] Although there are only a few modern editions so far, they clearly reveal Luise Adelgunde's stylistic skill and eloquence as a correspondent.

However, social life and domestic obligations by no means kept Luise Adelgunde Gottsched from her creative literary work. She made her own independent contributions to the German-language theatre of her times, above all with her comedies and translations of English and French plays. Most of them were directly associated with the *Deutsche Schaubühne* (German theatre), a collection of dramas published by her husband from 1740 to 1745. In her works, Luise Adelgunde systematically implemented her husband's ideas on literary reform—but with much more literary talent than he had himself. Her pieces always centred on female figures who represented Enlightenment virtues: they critically analysed their surroundings, exhibited an independent capacity for judgement, and distanced themselves from stupidity and vice. But any search for rebellious women or men in Luise Adelgunde Gottsched's works would be in vain.

Even though Luise Adelgunde's comedies and letters have long been part of the literary-historical canon, the image of her as a woman of letters has substantially changed in recent years. On the one hand, this change arose in part through the investigations into the particularities of female authorship and gender discourses in eighteenth-century literature. On the other hand, special emphasis has been placed on the monumental scope of Luise Adelgunde's translation work, which made her an important mediator of Enlightenment thought—for example, from French and English philosophy—in the German-speaking realm.

Luise Adelgunde Gottsched translated philosophical, theological, and scholarly texts, as well as dramas, poems, prose, and journalistic articles.[7] Thus she was responsible for more than half of the texts of the German translation of Pierre Bayle's *Dictionnaire Historique et Critique*, which came out between 1741 and 1744. She translated the ten-volume *Histoire de l'Academie Royale des Inscriptions et de belles Lettres* (*Geschichte der königlichen*

Akademie der schönen Wissenschaften zu Paris, Leipzig: 1750 to 1756), as well as *The Rape of the Locke* by Alexander Pope, published by Breitkopf in Leipzig in 1774 as *Herrn Alexander Popens Lockenraub, ein scherzhaftes Heldengedicht*.

It is striking that Luise seems to have associated her name most prominently with her translations, in that her name appeared on the title pages and she wrote forewords for the actual texts. If one also keeps in mind the distinctive literary status that contemporaries assigned to translations and the generally close overlap between literary production and translation work in the seventeenth and eighteenth century, the relative importance of this aspect of Luise Adelgunde's literary creativity increases even more. Translation was obviously associated with an analysis of content and the appropriation of knowledge. Hence it should come as no surprise that contemporaries valued Luise Gottsched both as a woman of letters and as a scholar. This is clearly reflected by the remarks with which Empress Maria Theresa showed Gottsched her appreciation during an audience in Vienna in 1749: she described the professor's spouse from Leipzig as the "most erudite woman of Germany".[8]

Luise Adelgunde's library, whose catalogue was likewise published by her husband in 1763, further testified to her erudition. She had already owned a collection of books when she married, but also continued to maintain it as her own collection until her death. With more than 1000 volumes and additional manuscripts, it reached almost unbelievable proportions for a bourgeois woman of the eighteenth century. It contained volumes from a wide range of scientific and scholarly disciplines, including philosophy and theology, but above all an extensive collection of contemporary dramas.

Despite the extraordinary scope of her work, Luise Adelgunde Gottsched is still today discussed and contemplated primarily in connection with her husband. The reason for this lies both in the couple's intensive collaborative endeavours and in how they were retrospectively described by Johann Christoph Gottsched after his wife's death. In his commemorative text, he in fact described the course of Luise Adelgunde's development as the education to the ideal wife of a scholar, and for a long time this is how she primarily appeared in literary history. However, in doing so he described a model that conformed to his own ideals and those of the times—we have very few direct statements of her own that illuminate her attitude.

When she was young, Luise Adelgunde clearly wanted the guidance and teaching of her future husband, and as his wife she also benefited from his academic position. This is the only reason, for example, that she was able to follow his lectures on rhetoric— albeit only from the door, for as a woman even *Frau Professor* remained excluded from academic life. But still, as a professor's wife she was able to use the Leipzig University library, located a few steps from the house. And she accompanied her husband on several journeys, including to Vienna in 1749.

Because of her scholarly and literary activities, however, Luise Adelgunde increasingly developed her own positions, also and especially on the literature of her times, which her strident and decidedly vain husband did not share. This created a tension that overshadowed the couple's concord and collaboration, since her husband demanded Luise Adelgunde's unconditional loyalty in his battle against new trends in German-language literature. Luise Adelgunde could therefore only voice her conviction that poetry could actually be written outside her husband's strict system of rules through subtle literary criticism or privately, such as in letters. Externally, she stood by her husband's side, even though, for example, his rejection of "wild" literature that did not conform to the rules—which for him also meant the works of Shakespeare!— increasingly irritated her.

The last ten years of her life were overshadowed by illness and health problems, which she herself traced back to her intensive literary work, and by her husband's dubious moral conduct and his vehemently argued conflicts about the "pure doctrine" of his poetics. One can discern anxieties and melancholy in many of her letters. In addition, the suffering and destruction visited upon Saxony as a result of the Prussian invasion in 1756 and the occupation of Leipzig throughout the Seven Years' War left her very depressed. At one point, King Frederick II of Prussia visited the Gottsched home, where he requested samples of Luise Adelgunde's translation work from Johann Christoph, and he later sent her a commendatory note, but the encounter and special recognition left her cold: "I would not be so indifferent here if the general misery did not almost lay me low in the dust. My eye can behold the victor only full of tears."[9]

At the same time, Luise Adelgunde felt increasingly overburdened by the wide range of tasks demanded by the joint work with her husband—in a letter to Frau von Runckel she sarcastically likened her work to that of a galley slave.[10] Of course, the clearly manifested conflicts and tensions were not just personal in nature but also show Luise Adelgunde in a structural conflict. On the one hand, she had internalised contemporary norms and Enlightenment positions regarding the role of women. Women were now "permitted" to acquire a certain education, but they were only supposed to use it to further their own development and to support their husbands; consequently they were not meant to aspire to their own careers or to appear independently in public. Personal erudition was allowed, but public exhibition of the same was not.

In a foreword to a translated play published in 1735, Luise herself had observed that if a woman wanted to avoid being exposed to criticism and hostility, then it was "hardly advisable to publish one line". To be sure, this did not keep her from publishing: "For my justification, I consider it unnecessary to refute those grounds that to me never seem to be strong enough that they should ever prevent me from devoting my leisure hours to the beautiful arts and sciences."[11] As she put it here, women were supposed to use their leisure hours to dedicate themselves to scholarship and literature; but they were not supposed to view such activity as a vocation.

The latter, however, is in fact what Luise Adelgunde managed to do: she pursued literary activities for decades, ever since her marriage to Johann Christoph Gottsched. And she did so publicly, in a manner that, by virtue of her publications, was visible far beyond Leipzig and to a degree that clearly exceeded the permissible scope of a "hobby". But this only seemingly contradicted her own image of womanhood, for the basis on which the literary world and Leipzig's urban public could accept and indeed positively value her work, on which she herself could reconcile her work with her self-understanding, was her marriage with Professor Gottsched. On the one hand, he admittedly used her work for his purposes and prompted his wife to bolster his positions in literary debates. But on the other hand, it was precisely by presenting her to the public as his assistant, which was also how she defined herself, that he strongly supported her own publishing activities.

This construct of the collaborative couple, which in a certain sense also played a role in the work opportunities of the astronomer Maria Kirch, created the basis on which a contemporary public was prepared to accept an educated woman. However, as the constellation of the "assistant" became a problem, as working together became more difficult and sometimes exceeded her strength, Luise Adelgunde saw no possibility of a solution. She remained true to her moral and educational aspirations as an enlightened woman. In this respect, Johann Christoph Gottsched's portrayal of her in 1763 in fact probably corresponded with his wife's own self-image. The changing conception in the nineteenth century of the artist as a genius and the man working on his own, however, cast the image of the "assistant" in an unfavourable light that did not exist during Luise Adelgunde's lifetime. But for a long time, this also unjustly obscured her own particular importance for the development of German-language literature, which made her one of the most well-known German authors and translators of her lifetime.

Notes

1 Contemporaries (including her husband) usually referred to her in print as "Gottschedin". This corresponds to a common practice in German at the time of giving family names a feminine form. German-language literary historiography usually refers to her this way as well. Gottsched, J.C. (1763) *Der Frau Luise Adelgunde Victoria Gottschedinn, geb. Kulmus, sämmtliche Gedichte, nebst dem, von vielen vornehmen Standespersonen, Gönnern und Freunden beyderley Geschlechtes, Ihr gestifteten Ehrenmaale, und ihrem Leben, herausgegeben von Ihrem hinterbliebenen Ehegatten.* Leipzig: Breitkopf. Also includes the catalogue of her library on pages 487–532. Available at https://mdz-nbn-resolving.de/urn:nbn:de:bvb:12-bsb10109581-0.

2 Goodman, "Gehülfin", p. 105.
3 Luise Gottschedin to Dorothea Henriette von Runckel [19/09/1753], in Kording, I. (ed.) (1999) *Louise Gottsched— "mit der Feder in der Hand": Briefe aus den Jahren 1730–1762*. Darmstadt: Wissenschaftliche Buchgesellschaft, p. 196.
4 See Kording, *Louise Gottsched*, and Gottsched, J.C. (currently up to 1750) *Briefwechsel: Unter Einschluß des Briefwechsels von Luise Adelgunde Victorie Gottsched. Historisch-kritische Ausgabe*. Available at https://www.saw-leipzig.de/de/publikationen/digitale-publikationen/Gottsched.
5 Widowed in 1747, the princess was the mother of Catherine the Great, born Sophie Auguste of Anhalt-Zerbst and to whom Gottsched dedicated the commemorative volume on his wife in 1763.
6 Runckel, H.D. (ed.) (1771–1772) *Briefe der Frau Louise Adelgunde Victoria Gottsched gebohrne Kulmus* (3 vols.). Dresden: Harpeterische Schriften.
7 A list is found in Brown, *Translator*, pp. 206–214.
8 Luise Gottschedin to Maria Regina Thomasius [28/09/1749], in Gottsched, *Briefwechsel Gottsched*, vol. 14, 610.
9 Luise Gottschedin to Dorothea Henriette von Runckel [19/10/1759], in Kording, *Louise Gottsched*, p. 273.
10 Goodman, "Gehülfin", p. 105.
11 Gottsched, L. (1735) Foreword to *Der Sieg der Beredsamkeit. Aus dem Französischen der Frau von Gomez übersetzt durch Luise Adelg[unde] Victoria Kulmus*. Leipzig: Breitkopf, unpaginated.

Selected bibliography

Ball, G., Brandes, H., and Goodman, K. (eds.) (2006) *Diskurse der Aufklärung: Luise Adelgunde Victorie und Johann Christoph Gottsched*. Wiesbaden: Harrassowitz.

Brown, H. (2012) *Luise Gottsched the Translator*. Woodbridge: Boydell & Brewer.

Döring, D. (2003) "Luise Adelgunde Victorie Gottsched (1713–1762)", in Weimers, G. (ed.), *Sächsische Lebensbilder*, vol. 5. Stuttgart: Steiner, pp. 213–246.

Goodman, K. (2004) "Learning and Guildwork: Luise Gottsched as 'Gehülfin'", in Hohkamp, M., and Jancke, G. (eds.), *Nonne, Königin und Kurtisane: Wissen, Bildung und Gelehrsamkeit von Frauen in der Frühen Neuzeit*. Königstein/Taunus, pp. 83–108.

Kerth, T., and Russell, J.R. (eds.) (1994) *Pietism in Petticoats and Other Comedies*. Columbia: Camden House.

Kord, S. (2000) *Little Detours: The Letters and Plays of Luise Gottsched (1713–1762)*. Rochester, NY: Camden House.

DOROTHEA ERXLEBEN (1715–1762)

A Medical Doctor Prevails

"This is why I say that if both sexes were permitted to develop this use, exercising, and application [of reason], then it would have to be obvious that the reason of women reaches precisely the same degree and measure that is reached by the reason of men."[1] These energetic words—no less timely today—were written by a woman in 1738 and printed in 1742. The author further maintained, "If it were introduced through practice that men and women enjoy the same education, then those people who cling so much to once-introduced custom would not find it nearly as dangerous as it seems to them right now because one is not accustomed to it."[2]

This fervent plea for women's access to higher education was made by Dorothea Christiane Leporin, born in 1715 in the town of Quedlinburg in the Harz region. She was the daughter of the physician Christian Polycarp Leporin and his wife, Anna Sophia, whose father was a highly regarded cleric in the city. The girl was sickly as a child and often bed-ridden, but this may be precisely why she developed a passion for reading and learning at a young age. Fortunately, her father counted among the men of his time who openly welcomed women's desire for education. So he had nothing against the fact that Dorothea was taught alongside her brother Christian Polycarp Junior and therefore got a comprehensive education. The other two siblings, Marie Elisabeth and Johann Christian, on the other hand, evidently had no such ambitions and thus their education never advanced beyond a primary level.

DOI: 10.4324/9781003252870-22

FIGURE 19.1 Dorothea Erxleben

Alamy

But Dorothea both wanted and could do more. So, when her brother entered the city's academic secondary school, Christian Polycarp Leporin employed private tutors to continue his daughter's schooling. This applied above all to Latin, but also to science lessons, both of which were indispensable for attaining an advanced academic education. Girls, however, could only learn these fields from private tutors, for they were not permitted to attend the city's academic secondary school. After her brother Christian finished school in 1735, he and Dorothea were again taught in tandem, once more by their father, who introduced them to academic medicine with text books and practical exercises.

These lessons did not go unnoticed in Quedlinburg and elicited derision and hostility towards the "erudite wench" Dorothea. In response, she wrote a detailed exposition that followed the rules of academic argument and sought to refute such prejudices and reproaches both in general and with regard to her person. Her father felt the text was "well done" and had it published in 1742 under the title *Gründliche Untersuchung der Ursachen, die das Weibliche Geschlecht vom Studiren abhalten* (Thorough investigation into the causes that prevent women from studying).

Dorothea Christiane highlighted this support from her father in her foreword to the book (to which he also added an introduction), knowing full well that publishing it on her own could provoke further recriminations, for it was improper for a woman—and a young, unmarried woman at that—to publicise her knowledge and argumentative capabilities. Yet Leporin was not the only woman dealing with precisely this question at this time. The poet Mariana Ziegler in Leipzig, among others, was doing so too in *Abhandlung, ob es dem Frauenzimmer erlaubt sey, sich nach Wissenschaften zu bestreben* (1739) (Treatise on whether it is permitted for women to pursue sciences). But the question about women's suitability for education and how much education was appropriate for them repeatedly occupied male scholars as well. And Dorothea Leporin had a clear opinion about the naysayers:

> Supposing a few men have a loathing for erudite women, what harm would that cause us? Or why should we be obliged for this reason to despise erudition? As if we heard that a few men believed it would be good for them if they had a wife who could not see, would we therefore talk the woman into gouging out her eyes so that she might appeal to these crazy people?[3]

Yet this debate, which began intensifying around 1700, was far from changing anything about women's lack of access to academic secondary schools or universities. Even the much-vaunted figures of the eighteenth-century Enlightenment by no means saw equality of education opportunities as a goal. Education and access to learning opportunities were supposed to stay tiered according to one's estate, and not open equally to men and women. To be sure, "educated" women were fully expected to be interested in scholarship and literature, but this education was in any case more on offer to bourgeois and aristocratic groups. Although it was true that broad sections of the population, men and women, were allowed school lessons, many people—including the women of the "higher" or "educated" estates—were denied access to higher learning, which into the nineteenth century also meant Latin.

Yet the background for the publication of Dorothea Christiane's exposition in 1742 was not just the Enlightenment debate about the education of women but also a concrete problem that arose regarding Dorothea's further education as a physician. In spring 1740, her brother was called up to enlist in the Prussian military. Christian Polycarp Junior, however, actually wanted to study medicine in Halle and had already enrolled. Dorothea Leporin turned to the king with an appeal for clemency, asking for an exemption from service for her brother and referring, in particular, to her hopes of being able to start a course of study together with Christian Polycarp Junior at the University of Halle. For if she had really planned to study, back then it was inconceivable for a woman—unmarried, no less—to move to a different city on her own without the support of a male relative. And any woman in Brandenburg-Prussia who wanted to study at university needed the highest royal permission.

Dorothea's plea was, in fact, heard by King Frederick II; in 1741 he actually allowed her to start the study programme with her brother. However, by then the latter had left Prussian territory for fear of being forced into military service. He was consequently considered a deserter, which ultimately also compelled his father to flee, because he faced a prison term just like his son. Thus, even though Dorothea had supreme royal permission to study, she could not make use of it. Instead, she seems to have tried to maintain her father's medical practice in his absence, for it was the source of the family's livelihood, including that of her mother and sisters. After her father returned in April 1741, however, Dorothea could not immediately use the granted permission because her brother was still prevented from coming back, which is why he abruptly enrolled to study medicine in Göttingen, which belonged to the sovereign territory of the elector of Hanover. The royal Prussian permission was no good to Dorothea for this university, and so for the time being she did not make use of it, since, as mentioned above, going to Halle alone was not an option.

On 14 August 1742, Dorothea Christiane Leporin married Johann Christian Erxleben, who was 18 years her senior, a deacon of the St. Nikolai Church in Quedlinburg, and previously the husband of her recently deceased cousin. Writing about her marriage, she noted that she "became convinced through experience that matrimony [need not end] the woman's studying"; "rather, that studying can be more enjoyable in the company of a reasonable husband".[4] Thus her husband, too, supported her desire for advanced education, which she then pursued on her own. As the mother of five stepchildren, which by 1753 had been joined by four of her own, her time budget was admittedly tight. But as she had indicated in her earlier book, she felt that managing a household was no more of an obstacle to further study than the growing horde of children. She taught the children herself and, no doubt with the help of maids, looked after the extensive household, including the orchard and small farm.

At the same time, as a pastor's wife[5] she took on responsibilities in the congregation in Quedlinburg, which in her case prominently included caring for the health of its members. During the following years, her marriage, her husband's ecclesiastical office, and the existing tradition of women's healing lore allowed her to publicly apply her medical knowledge and put it into practice. She continued to do so even after her father's death in 1747.

In 1753, however, the Quedlinburg abbey governor, the direct representative of the Prussian regime, received a complaint against Erxleben for *Pfuscherei* from three Quedlinburg doctors. *Pfuscherei* in this case did not mean "acting negligently" but was used more in the sense of "working beyond the limits of what is permitted". To be sure, female healers were quite socially acceptable. But the application of remedies with internal effects as practised by Dorothea Erxleben was actually a privilege reserved for the medical profession. Academically educated medical practitioners also felt their privileges were threatened because she practised publicly, going to patients like a doctor instead of waiting for them to come to her more or less surreptitiously.

Dorothea Erxleben reacted promptly. Making reference to her royal permission to study from 1741, she declared her desire to submit a doctoral dissertation in medicine as proof of her competency.

Her plea was again conveyed to the king of Prussia for a decision. The king granted her request, including an extension of the original deadline since Erxleben was advanced in pregnancy. On 6 January 1754, Dorothea Christiane finally handed over her dissertation, written in Latin, to the abbey governor. He forwarded it to Berlin, from where it finally arrived at the medical faculty of the University of Halle. The public examination took place in May (also in Latin), and on 12 June 1754 Dorothea Erxleben became the first woman to be awarded a doctorate from a university of the Holy Roman Empire. She revised her Latin dissertation herself for a German edition, which was published in 1755.

In her dissertation, Doctor Erxleben came across as a comprehensively educated woman with clever and precise arguments. As a doctor, she searched for pragmatic solutions and drew on a range of healing methods, whereby she acted professionally as per the state of the art. Her father had familiarised her with the works of Georg Ernst Stahl, Michael Alberti, and Johann Juncker, who chaired her doctoral committee. Her expositions contain aspects from older humoral pathological medicine, which dominated European medicine until well into the early modern period. According to its doctrines, diseases and ailments were triggered primarily by an imbalance of the body's fluids. However, Dorothea Erxleben argued explicitly against many errors associated therewith, such as the tendency to prescribe more or less arbitrarily combined medications with very expensive components. This no doubt also reflected her decades of experience as a practising physician.

Did the fact that she could appear in 1754 as a seasoned housewife and mother with nine children help her gain her doctorate? However that may be, in his report on her doctoral graduation, the deacon of the medical faculty in Halle emphasised that the candidate had answered all of the questions eloquently, accurately, and with the serenity that comes with age—Erxleben was 39 at the time. He certified that she had a "thorough understanding of the art".[6] But the fact that he felt compelled to give quite a detailed account on the subject of erudite women in the printed programme of the graduation ceremony suggests that, despite royal approval, Erxleben's success was not achieved without controversy.

Women had already achieved doctorates in France and Italy (e.g., Laura Bassi in 1732). And back in 1740, when the abbey governor had forwarded Dorothea's plea for admission to studies to Berlin, he had pointed out that he supported the plea because it was high time for Germany to have examples of such educated women. As crucial as comprehensive knowledge and professional standing were to Dorothea Erxleben for her doctorate, equally important for her success was clearly the support from her milieu.

This included the fact that King Frederick II of Prussia granted the permissions that were needed for Erxleben's every academic step, which surely had something to do with his Enlightenment sympathies. He allowed "reasonable arguments" to apply to women as well and thereby made her graduation possible. At an earlier stage, however, there were other men[7] who created the conditions for her unusual undertaking: her father; the tutors, who were instructors at the local academic secondary school; the abbey governor; her husband; and the deacon of the medical faculty. These men were all willing to accept that Frau Erxleben was practising as a physician and thereby expanding her knowledge or to recognise that she had this knowledge.

Another crucial factor for the doctor's acceptance in the city was her integration—as the pastor's wife and the granddaughter of the previous pastor—into the congregation of Saint Nikolai, although she also treated patients from the surrounding region. This included, not least, the noblewomen of Quedlinburg Abbey[8]—Dorothea Erxleben dedicated her doctoral dissertation to Abbess Maria Elisabeth of Holstein-Gottorf. Although by the early eighteenth century the abbess as a ruler had very restricted powers of control, the parish of Saint Nikolai, where Dorothea was active as the pastor's wife, was under her jurisdiction—the abbess was the church patron. Whether Doctor Erxleben's scope of action increased after her graduation must remain unresolved. But the fact that her patients addressed her as *Frau Doktor*—and that they had done so long before she received her doctorate—suggests that she exhibited the professionalism usually attributed to academically educated medical practitioners.

Dorothea Erxleben died on 13 June 1762, three years after her husband, at the age of only 47, "from a cancer-like ulcer in the breast" in her parental home, to which she had returned after the deaths of one of her sons and her husband. In Germany, no other woman would receive a doctorate in medicine until 1901.

Notes

1 Leporin, D.C. (1742) *Gründliche Untersuchung der Ursachen, die das Weibliche Geschlecht vom Studiren abhalten* ... Berlin: Rüdiger, §42, p. 28–29. Available at https://mdz-nbn-resolving.de/urn:nbn:de:bvb:12-bsb10731980-7.
2 Leporin, *Gründliche Untersuchung*, §128, p. 82.
3 Leporin, *Gründliche Untersuchung*, §174, p. 108.
4 Erxleben, *Akademische Abhandlung*, p. 130.
5 On this, see also the chapter on Katharina Zell in the sixteenth century.
6 Erxleben, D.C. (1754) *Academische Abhandlung von der gar zu geschwinden und angenehmen, aber deswegen öfters unsichern Heilung der Krankheiten* ... Halle: Gebauer, p. 137. Available at https://gdz.sub.uni-goettingen.de/id/PPN858610884; includes her curriculum vitae, pp. 121–134.
7 On this constellation, see also the life paths of Maria Margaretha Kirch and Maria Sibylla Merian.
8 On the imperial abbey, see also the biography Maria Aurora von Königsmarck.

Selected bibliography

Brinkschulte, E., and Labouvie, E. (eds.) (2006) *Dorothea Christiana Erxleben: Weibliche Gelehrsamkeit und medizinische Profession seit dem 18. Jahrhundert*. Halle (Saale): Mitteldeutscher Verlag.

Fulda, A. (2004) "'Da dergleichen Exempel bey dem weiblichen Geschlechte insonderheit in Deutschland etwas rar sind': Gelehrtes Wissen, ärztliche Praxis und akademische Promotion Dorothea Christiana Erxlebens (1715–1762)", in Hohkamp, M., and Jancke, G. (eds.), *Nonne, Königin und Kurtisane: Wissen, Bildung und Gelehrsamkeit von Frauen in der Frühen Neuzeit*. Königstein/Taunus: Ulrike Helmer Verlag, pp. 60–82.

Nielsen, A.-S. (2021) "Were there any radical women in the German Enlightenment? On feminist history of philosophy and Dorothea Erxleben's Rigorous Investigation (1742)", *Intellectual History Review* 31 (1), pp. 143–163.

Poeter, E. (2008) "Gender, Religion, and Medicine in Enlightenment Germany: Dorothea Christiane Leporin's Treatise on the Education of Women", *National Women's Studies Association Journal* 20 (1), pp. 99–119.

EMPRESS MARIA THERESA (1717–1780)

The Heiress

"Now she appeared, the greatest woman in Europe, who through her rule not only makes many nations happy now but shall also make them happy in her children. … [I was] confounded, moved, full of awe and joy at the presence of this great woman …. This all leaves me completely powerless."[1] With these euphoric words, Luise Adelgunde Gottsched, the woman of letters from Leipzig, described her meeting with Empress Maria Theresa during a visit to Vienna in 1749.

We can set aside the question of whether Maria Theresa of Habsburg was really the "greatest woman" of her time. But today she is certainly the most famous woman in the history of the early modern Holy Roman Empire, and her governance between 1740 and her death in 1780 undoubtedly had a major influence on the empire and European politics. It is hardly possible to provide a systematic account of her diverse political activities in a brief biography of just a few pages. In past decades, scholars—at least outside Austria—paid scarce attention to the empress and her reign, and she has often been overshadowed by her great political and military rival, King Frederick II of Prussia, but this has since changed. In honour of the 300th anniversary of her birth, several comprehensive biographies have been published that examine her person in the light of recent research, and we can reference them here.[2]

Maria Theresa was born in spring 1717 in Vienna as the second child and eldest daughter of Emperor Charles VI and his wife, Elisabeth Christine of Brunswick-Wolfenbüttel. Her older

DOI: 10.4324/9781003252870-23

brother Leopold Joseph had died as an infant just a few months earlier, and the imperial couple's two later children were "just" daughters, Maria Anna and Maria Amalia, the latter of whom also died young at age six. As the vivacious and beautiful Maria Theresa grew older, it became increasingly clear that there would not be another brother, which posed a serious problem for the House of Habsburg and the entire empire. Who would inherit the Habsburg lands, as well as Bohemia and Hungary—that is, the Habsburg's extensive territorial possessions? And who would become the emperor of the Holy Roman Empire, where a Habsburg had always been elected emperor for more than 250 years?

These questions also deeply preoccupied Maria Theresa's parents. Her mother, Elisabeth Christine, described by her contemporaries as one of the most beautiful women of her times, deeply mourned her inability to give birth to an heir—that is, a son. Prayers, pilgrimages, and various medicinal treatments not only to failed help, but in fact ultimately harmed the empress's health. Although Emperor Charles VI never gave up hoping for a son, he began making political arrangements for the succession early on.

When he issued an edict on the succession of the House of Habsburg in 1713, he took recourse to agreements that had been made during the lifetime of his father, Leopold I, between himself, who back then was supposed to become the king of Spain, and his older brother Joseph I. Since Emperor Joseph I, too, left behind "only" two girls when he died in 1711, Charles VI promulgated the so-called Pragmatic Sanction even before his own children were born. This edict stipulated that the daughters of the house would now also be entitled to inherit the Habsburg hereditary lands, and it gave the daughters of Charles precedence over those of Joseph. This arrangement was gradually accepted by the representatives of the various lands held by the Habsburgs, and many European powers also pledged to acknowledge it.

None of this probably affected Maria Theresa at first. She received an education similar to that of most princesses: reading and writing, religion, dancing, and music. But she was also educated by Jesuits in Latin and history, in arithmetic and geography, as well as in Italian and French. When she wrote, upon taking the throne in 1740, that she felt fully unprepared, this no doubt pertained to the fact that, unlike what would have been the case for a young man, she had not been introduced to the council bodies and had very little instruction in legal matters. In all likelihood, her father had not felt either of these things were necessary because he expected that, after his death, Maria Theresa would deal with her immense inheritance as was "proper" for a woman.

To be sure, from a legal perspective according to the Pragmatic Sanction, she was the heiress to all of the territories and dominion rights of the House of Habsburg. But she was actually expected to leave the practicalities of governance to her husband, who in turn was supposed to preserve and rule the territorial inheritance for his anticipated son. This was the usual mechanism whenever a princely or noble house, large or small, "died out"—that is, had no male heirs. This was also exemplified by Anna of Brandenburg a few decades earlier. Even though the heiress retained all of the dominion rights during this precarious transitional phase, whether and to what extent she exercised and used them herself differed widely from case to case and depended on many factors.

This made the decision about the princess's future husband all the more critical. After long deliberations by the emperor, the choice finally fell on Franz Stephan of Lorraine, who for his part was the heir of a princely house that already had relational ties to the Habsburgs. The question of whether Maria Theresa had a say in this decision must remain unresolved. In any event, she was enthusiastic about her husband, whom she had already come to know as a young girl because he had been raised in part at the Vienna court. Despite various tensions, the couple was very close from when they were married in 1736 until Franz Stephan's death in 1765, as attested to by the statements of many third parties about the ruling couple and by the couple's 16 children, who were born between 1737 and 1756. Testifying to this most strongly, however, are the comments of Maria Theresa herself, such as her note just after her husband's death: "My happy matrimony was twenty-nine years, six months, six days; at the specific hour when I gave him my hand, also on a Sunday, he was suddenly torn from me. Which thus makes 29 years, 335 months, 1540 weeks, 10781 days, 258744 hours."[3]

The complicated arrangements leading up to the marriage of Europe's wealthiest heiress also stipulated that the husband had to give up his inheritance of the Duchy of Lorraine. As compensation, a settlement between France and the emperor granted him the Grand Duchy of Tuscany, where Franz Stephan took power in summer 1737. Maria Theresa consequently became the grand duchess of Tuscany, and the young couple stayed in Florence from January to April 1739. As it happened, they would never return to Tuscany, for Emperor Charles VI died in October 1740, triggering the long-anticipated succession in the House of Habsburg. Larger responsibilities were now awaiting the young woman, who in autumn 1740 was pregnant for the fourth time.

Maria Theresa immediately made it clear that she intended to look after her inheritance herself. At the same time, she was likely well aware of the difficult situation facing her as a regent. To be sure, there were no internal conflicts in the hereditary lands concerning her accession to power. But in the Holy Roman Empire, notwithstanding previous assurances, a number of princes had been waiting to get a piece of the Habsburg pie. How dangerous could a young woman at the head of a large and cumbersome conglomeration of territories with an old-fashioned army even be? The quickest to react was Frederick II of Prussia, who himself had been king and elector for just a few months. As a reward for acknowledging Maria Theresa's rule in her Hereditary Lands, he demanded the cession of Silesia, a large and economically important region within the Holy Roman Empire.

A letter from the young queen in November 1740 to her grandmother, Christine Luise of Brunswick-Wolfenbüttel, reveals Maria Theresa's anxieties:

[I] also cannot silently keep from Your Beloved that the statement of the Prussian Court is causing quite a lot of sensation and trouble, for God has punished me twice, first with the great loss, and second, to have succeeded to such a government where everything is in the worst condition, no troops and no money are available, no experience, tender age,[4] and just a few ministers who tend to make matters more difficult rather than easier. Your Beloved can imagine my situation.[5]

The grandmother could very well understand how the young woman must have felt, given that she had played an important role in the government of the small Duchy of Blankenburg and so knew how important good advisors and financial resources were for successful princely politics.

The feared invasion of Silesia by Prussian troops occurred on 16 December 1740; thus, less than eight weeks after the death of Emperor Charles VI, the young regent was at war with one of the empire's strongest military powers, a war that heavily influenced the history of the empire and Europe. Peace treaties were signed twice; and twice the conflict with Prussia re-erupted. Finally in 1763, at the end of one of the largest international conflicts there had ever been, Maria Theresa was forced to agree to the permanent cession of Silesia.

Meanwhile, in 1740 Elector Charles Albert of Bavaria—allied with Prussia but in his own interest—raised a claim to the imperial throne. He derived this claim from his marriage to one of Maria Theresa's cousins, Maria Amalia, a daughter of Emperor Joseph I. The elector ultimately managed not only to have himself crowned as king in Bohemia but also to secure his election as emperor. But by early 1742, when Charles VII was being crowned in Frankfurt am Main, the fortunes of war had already turned, and Habsburg troops were advancing. After the death of Charles VII in 1745, Franz Stephan of Lorraine became the next candidate, and his election and coronation as Emperor Francis I can be seen as an expression of the restoration of Habsburg power in the empire.

As a result, Maria Theresa became empress of the Holy Roman Empire at the same time. This was and remained her highest rank, but it was not her favourite title because she had become empress like every other empress before and after her: as the wife of a man who had been chosen by the electors. Rumours had been circulating among contemporaries that Maria Theresa might herself be elected, for the gender of the imperial dignity was not explicitly stipulated in the empire's laws. However, one only became emperor in one's own right by being chosen by the electors. And as one contemporary noted: "We have an electoral empire; who wants to put a woman on it."[6] The electors would never have chosen a women as their superior no matter how many countries she ruled.

In contrast, in the hereditary lands, as well as in Bohemia and Hungary, Maria Theresa was the ruler "in her own right", as was said back then, because of her inherited rights. In both countries she was crowned with the ceremonial of a king, that is, actually like a man,[7] which expressed her entitlement to all of the dominion rights, even though she was "just" a woman. And she would also exercise these rights until the end of her life. Admittedly, Franz Stephan took on various governmental functions, above all the responsibilities of an emperor. But particularly in matters pertaining to the Hereditary Lands, Maria Theresa reserved the decision-making for herself. This also remained the case when her son Joseph II acceded to the imperial throne in 1765. This divided rulership was not without conflict, but Maria Theresa's self-understanding and self-confidence as the guardian of the inheritance of one of Europe's most important dynasties ensured that she insisted on her rights. Consequently, she herself preferred using her titles as the Queen of Bohemia and Hungary rather than that of an empress. For as queen, she had the powers of a king, including therefore the right to decide on war and peace, on reforms in the administration and schools, and so on.

After her time in Tuscany, Empress Maria Theresa travelled only once "into the empire", as the saying went, meaning that she left her Hereditary Lands. This was for the coronation of her husband in Frankfurt am Main in 1745. Franz Stephan and the electors would have liked to see Maria Theresa allow herself to be crowned as empress, as her cousin and precursor, Maria Amalia, had done before. But she tersely told all of the men who were urging and haranguing her: "I will not let myself be crowned".[8]

For she was an empress even without being crowned because she held this title automatically as the emperor's wife. The ritual of the coronation as empress would have presented her to a broad public throughout the empire and Europe in a situation where her husband needed to ask the elector of Mainz for her coronation, which the electors needed to approve. The coronation itself would accordingly have publicly subordinated her to the rule of men, whereas the previous coronations in Hungary (1741) and Bohemia (1743) had affirmed her as an independent holder of power. Hence she unflatteringly described the empress coronation as a "comedy" and rejected it. That she was even able to reject this highly honourable ritual shows not only that she was aware of its subordinating symbolism with regard to the gender relations. It also demonstrates above all her agency as a ruler in her own right, whose decisions ultimately also had to be accepted by men.

However, Maria Theresa could not change the fact that, as of 1745, her husband was elevated above her in the ceremonials of the empire, and thus in part also in the ceremonials of the Vienna court. On the one hand, for Franz Stephan this was a relief, for between 1740 and 1745 there had repeatedly been uncertainties about how he should appear. According to the norms of the time, as a man Franz Stephan remained superior to his wife, Maria Theresa; but in court ceremonies, prior to being elected emperor, he had to cede precedence to his wife as queen because he was "just" a grand duke.[9] And the public impact of this constellation, in which the wife took ceremonial precedence over the husband, should not be underestimated, for this ceremonial visually manifested and displayed the social order to contemporaries.

Of course, one cannot conclude from Maria Theresa's self-confident and—in the long run—politically very successful actions that she was an emancipated woman in modern terms. Rather, in her appearances she subordinated herself to her husband in every aspect where he might have expected her to do so according to the eighteenth-century image of the family. The imperial couple, of course, was always supposed to be staged as an ideal married couple and thereby influence the conceptions of the social and political order. Hence, in the aforementioned audience with Luise Gottsched in 1749, the empress introduced her husband with the words: "this is the lord".[10] On the other hand, Maria Theresa expected his support in her many government tasks, which she allowed him to share as co-ruler.

234 Empress Maria Theresa

FIGURE 20.1 Maria Theresa and her family, 1764/65

Alamy

Martin van Meytens, Franz I. Stephan und Maria Theresia mit elf Kindern, 1764/65, Kunsthistorisches Museum Wien, Gemäldegalerie 3149

Her self-understanding as the heiress of the old House of Habsburg was also part of her brilliant portrayal of her role as mother. The imperial couple repeatedly had themselves depicted within the circle of their growing swarm of children, with the pictorial arrangement clearly emphasising Maria Theresa's role as the mother of a new dynasty, the House of Habsburg-Lorraine, and as the link to the old imperial house. She was surrounded by her sons, who as heirs would determine the future fate of the house, while the daughters assembled around their father Franz Stephan. Maria Theresa enjoyed giving audiences in the presence of several of the children and in this way placed the family in the proper light. Her self-representation as a strict and devoted mother of a new dynasty was admittedly just one facet in the broad spectrum of the representations of Habsburg power in Maria Theresa's time. But this narrative about the empress, which especially in Austria is more than present in the popular view of history, has certainly had one of the longest lasting impacts.

Maria Theresa exerted influence over her children's marriages much as she had previously done with respect to their status-appropriate education. All of the children had to accept the marriage partners that their mother selected for them, and she naturally made choices for the benefit of the House of Habsburg-Lorraine and its political networks. The most well-known is probably the marriage of her youngest daughter, Maria Antonia (Marie Antoinette), who at 15 married the heir to the French throne and through her marriage ratified a new order of political alliances in Europe. But the other children—sons and daughters—also had to follow their mother's plans. Maria Theresa's active influence on and governance of her children even after they were married is reflected in many of her letters through which she maintained contact with her children in Italy and France.

All things considered, Maria Theresa had substantially fewer direct dominion rights with regard to the empire than she did in the Habsburg lands, but this did not mean that she had no influence on imperial politics. Far more so than any of the other women we have dealt with in this book, she was actually able to make a substantial impact on the empire's fate, namely, as a largely independent ruler who for decades invested immense energy into the preservation and organisation of her large and politically important territories—for example, in administrative reforms and economic policy.

As the heiress of rulership and territories who could govern in her own right and did so for decades, Maria Theresa was exceptional as a woman in the House of Habsburg. There had admittedly been women from time to time who exercised rights of dominion as representatives of men, such as the governesses of the Netherlands—for example, Maria of Hungary. But Maria

Theresa was unique in that she could act as the heiress of rights of dominion because fortuitous dynastic developments had left her generation without any Habsburg men. Ultimately, with regard to the territorial possessions and the dynasty's name, Maria Theresa inheritance remained decisive: that is, her children were not simply attributed to the House of Lorraine; instead, the name of Maria Theresa's dynasty of origin—the House of Habsburg—was preserved. This testifies to Maria Theresa's unusual position as an heiress and resulted from the rank of the imperial house both in the empire and in Europe.

Maria Theresa's dynastic position more generally as an agent in the transfer of power and territorial possessions, however, was hardly exceptional; rather, it was a role that repeatedly fell to women of various aristocratic and princely houses. Maria of Burgundy had brought her rich inheritances into the House of Habsburg towards the late fifteenth century, as had Joanna of Spain and Anna of Bohemia in the sixteenth century. As an heiress, Anna of Prussia held dominion rights and claims that brought the Duchy of Prussia and substantial possessions in the Lower Rhine to the Brandenburg Hohenzollerns. An aunt of Maria Theresa, also as an heiress, ensured through her marriage with Ferdinand Albrecht of Brunswick-Bevern that the Duchy of Wolfenbüttel was transferred to the Brunswick-Bevern line. But very few of these women could also actively exercise their dominion rights in practice as Maria Theresa did.

Notes

1 Kording, I. (ed.) (1999) *Louise Gottsched – "mit der Feder in der Hand". Briefe aus den Jahren 1730–1762*. Darmstadt: Wissenschaftliche Buchgesellschaft, p. 149.
2 See the selected bibliography.
3 Quoted in Braun, *Eine Kaiserin*, p. 19.
4 Maria Theresia was referring here to her youth, for at the time she was only 23 years old.
5 Niedersächsisches Landesarchiv, Staatsarchiv Wolfenbüttel, 1 Alt 23 Nr. 376, fol. 39v–40r [November 1740].
6 Gundling, N.H. (1735) *Gründlicher Discours über Henrici de Cocceii Iuris publici prudentiam* ... Frankfurt am Main, pp. 280–281.
7 On the coronations, see Stollberg-Rilinger, *Maria Theresa*, 99–102, 114–118, 146–160.

8 Österreichisches Staatsarchiv, Haus-, Hof- und Staatsarchiv Wien, Zeremonialprotokoll 20 (1745–1746), fol. 181v–182r [21/08/1745].
9 Discussions of this, for example, in Braun, *Eine Kaiserin*, pp. 185–204.
10 Kording, *Gottsched*, p. 149.
11 There are several extensive editions of her collected letters, most of them quite old. But a separate list of sources will not be provided here because these editions can easily be found in the referenced biographies.

Selected bibliography[11]

Badinter, E. (2016) *Le pouvoir au féminin: Marie-Thérèse d'Autriche (1717–1780): L'impératrice-reine*. Paris: Flammarion.

Braun B. (2018) *Eine Kaiserin und zwei Kaiser: Maria Theresia und ihre Mitregenten Franz Stephan und Joseph II*. Bielefeld: Transcript.

Lau, T. (2016) *Die Kaiserin: Maria Theresia*. Vienna: Böhlau.

Stollberg-Rilinger, B. (2021) *Maria Theresa: The Habsburg Empress in her Time*. Translated by Savage, R. Princeton: Princeton University Press. (German: *Maria Theresia: Die Kaiserin in ihrer Zeit: Eine Biographie*. Munich: Beck, 2017.)

Telesko, W., et al. (eds.) (2020) *Die Repräsentation Maria Theresias: Herrschaft und Bildpolitik im Zeitalter der Aufklärung*. Vienna: Böhlau 2020.

ANNA DOROTHEA THERBUSCH (1721–1782)

From Innkeeper to Court Painter

Anna Dorothea Lisiewski was born in 1721 as the seventh child of the Prussia court painter Georg Lisiewski and his wife, Elisabeth. By the time she died in 1782 in Berlin, the city of her birth, she had created several hundred oil paintings, drawings, and pastels, and was one of the most famous female painters of her times. She was also one of the first women of the Holy Roman Empire who managed to earn a living from her work as an artist and who was honoured and recognised for her craft through her acceptance into several art academies. Even so, little is known about her life—she hardly left behind any letters and rarely finds mention in other archival sources.[1] Nonetheless, it is still possible to trace the contours of her life.

Anna Dorothea received her initial artistic training from her father, who educated his daughters Anna Rosina and Anna Dorothea to be painters, just as he did his son, Christian Friedrich. Thus, we have come upon a typical constellation for professionally working female artists of the early modern period, as clearly emerged in the case of Maria Sibylla Merian as well. Since women could not receive an academic education, they usually learned their basic skills from their male relatives. Along with Anna Dorothea and her brother Christian Friedrich, her older sister Anna Rosina, too, would later work as a painter. She became a court painter of the prince of Anhalt-Zerbst in 1757 under her married name, Anna Rosina Matthieu, and she also worked as an artist during her second marriage with the jurist and man of letters Ludwig de Gasc.

DOI: 10.4324/9781003252870-24

The first known paintings of Anna Dorothea Lisiewski are from the early 1740s, and they are still strongly influenced by her role models, above all by the style of her father, but also by that of the Prussian court painter Antoine Pesne. Although neither formally nor artistically original, these early pictures nonetheless show that the young woman had mastered various painting techniques. Other aspects of her education are largely obscure, for Anna Dorothea's life seemed at first to be heading in a very different direction.

In February 1742, she married the Berlin innkeeper and amateur painter Ernst Friedrich Therbusch. As the owner of the Weiße Taube, an inn on Heiliggeiststraße in Berlin, not far from the post office and the stock exchange, he was no doubt economically well-off. That he at least started a degree in law suggests that he had quite varied interests. His young wife, however, first needed to conform to social expectations and look after the household, inn, and children. Anna Dorothea and Ernst Friedrich Therbusch had quite a few children, three of whom, a daughter and two sons, reached adulthood.

There is not much to be said about Anna Dorothea's artistic work prior to around 1760, and very few of her early pictures survive. She probably never abandoned her studies, but much of her time was spoken for by her duties as a mother and housewife. At the same, she apparently produced few of her own artistic creations. Instead, she seems to have refined her technique by copying. But after that Anna Dorothea Therbusch took to the stage (again) as an artist, and, with vehemence and considerable skill, plunged into a life as a painter. Why this occurred particularly at the end of the 1750s has not yet been explained. Johann Georg Meusel, who dedicated a brief biography to her immediately after she died,[2] felt that the death of her mother-in-law had opened up new opportunities for Anna after some 20 years of marriage.

In any case, Anna Dorothea now uncompromisingly devoted herself to her artistic work, evidently with the approval of her husband, who always financially supported her in the period that followed. As early as 1761, she left on her own—without her children or husband—to go to Stuttgart to undertake several large commissions as a painter for Duke Karl Eugen of Württemberg. Evidently, she purposefully arranged this opportunity through acquaintances in Berlin, much as male painters also had to do in order to make contact with wealthy patrons and obtain lucrative, prestigious commissions.

Naturally, this not only required personal recommendations to the duke but also presupposed that her pictures must have been familiar to people in Stuttgart. And there in the south German capital they considered the paintings of this woman who had just stepped out onto the artistic stage so remarkable that they were copied by others and people talked about a "Terbuschisch gôut" (Therbusch style). The overdoors[3] she painted for the palace's newly constructed hall of mirrors were highly regarded in Stuttgart, but unfortunately they no longer survive. She was also very popular as a portrait artist, who painted portraits not only of the duke but also of members of court society and other artists. This testifies to her special talent in this genre, which would be an important field of work for her until she died. Back then, portraits were also above all a good source of income for painters, which Anna Dorothea would have needed, for she had to finance her stays outside Berlin at least in part on her own.

It is especially worth mentioning, however, that by at least the 1760s she also routinely focused on historical painting. Quite a few of her paintings have mythological themes and depict ancient legendary figures. This was unusual because historical painting was actually a male domain,[4] for to do such work one needed to complete studies on the representation of the naked human body. Although such studies were offered at the art academies of the times, they were not accessible to women. And even privately, working at nude drawing was risky for any female artist, even for a long-married wife and mother, for, as per contemporary mores, she thereby called into question her modesty and honour. The fact that Anna Dorothea Therbusch evidently dared to enter this dangerous terrain attests to her openness and seriousness as an artist, for she could only advance her art at the risk of her social reputation.

FIGURE 21.1 One of Therbusch's history paintings, entitled "Anacreon"

Stiftung Preußische Schlösser und Gärten Berlin-Brandenburg

Anna Dorothea Therbusch, Anakreon, undat., Staatliche Schlösser und Gärten Berlin-Potsdam, GK I 5566, Fotograf: Wolfgang Pfauder

Therbusch's work in Stuttgart enhanced her renown as an artist, and her pictures brought her more and more recognition. In March 1762, she was accepted into the Stuttgart *Académie des Arts* as a sign of her acknowledgement by male artist colleagues as well. In late 1763, Anna Dorothea then travelled further from Stuttgart to Mannheim where, just a few weeks later, on 7 January 1764, she was appointed as a court painter of Elector Karl Theodor of the Palatinate. No doubt emboldened by this now formally documented recognition, Frau Therbusch developed an even more ambitious plan, which attests to her self-confidence as an artist. She wanted to become a member of the arts academy in Paris, the most distinguished academy of the times, but which rarely gave women the honour of acceptance.[5] Thus, after returning briefly to Berlin, in 1765 Anna Dorothea travelled to France, again via Stuttgart.

Madame "Terbouche", as newspapers and reports soon referred to her, probably arrived in Paris in summer 1766. Here she first had to search for advocates and protection so that she could have some success in presenting her works to the academy. Even though she was known as a painter in Berlin, Stuttgart, and Mannheim, this was not yet the case in Paris. For this reason it was helpful that Anna Dorothea had brought recommendations with her. The Stuttgart court architect Pierre de La Guêpière, for example, endorsed her to the extremely influential Abel François Poisson de Vandières, marquis de Marigny, the "directeur général des bâtiments du roi" (director general of the king's buildings). As a result, the marquis de Marigny had his advisor, Charles Nicolas Cochin, inform him about the paintings of the German artist.

Cochin's response was positive:

> I have seen the works of this woman, painter of the king of Prussia; she does in fact have a talent that goes beyond what one expects to find in a person of her sex, and that is all the more peculiar because she paints history and nudity as a man could do. She has the courage to paint according to nature and put herself above the discourse.[6]

He not only highlighted Therbusch's talent, which, as he tellingly pointed out, was equivalent to that of men. He also referred to the fact that, as a woman, she painted "according to nature"— that is, did nude studies, which exposed her to malicious gossip and defamatory suspicions. But without such studies, her historical paintings, which he emphasised as a distinctive aspect of her work, would have been impossible.

In the end, his assessment must have significantly contributed to Anna Dorothea Therbusch's success in finally gaining acceptance to the *Académie Royale de Peinture et de Sculpture* in February 1767. Key information on the story of her acceptance, as well as a few highlights about her sojourn in Paris, comes from her highly prominent contemporary, the philosopher and art critic Denis Diderot. We have his brief account of the acceptance meeting, in which he claims that the academy rejected the picture[7] put forward by Therbusch as proof of her abilities because of doubts that she had painted it herself. Whether this is accurate cannot be addressed here. In any case, however, the journal *Mercure de France* reported on her acceptance without referring to any such scandal. And *Correspondance littéraire* emphasised in its report that it was not the youth or beauty of the painter, who after all was 45 years old, but rather the quality of her paintings that formed the grounds for her acceptance.

As a result of this membership, Anna Dorothea Therbusch now counted among an extremely exclusive circle of painters who were entitled to call themselves "peintre du roi", a title that she would later routinely use. As a woman, she could not teach at the academy, and she never participated in the meetings during her time in Paris. But in 1767 she made use of her right to exhibit her work in the academy's annual salon, which too was the subject of a brief report by Diderot.

This particular text, however, maintains a somewhat cooler tone and shows that Diderot, who for a time had evidently promoted Therbusch and even had her paint a portrait of him, had soon distanced himself from her again. This finally peaked with the philosopher's sigh of relief, expressed by letter, after the painter left Paris. The reason Diderot turned away from her is not clear from his texts, and, as previously mentioned, we have no statements on the matter by Anna Dorothea. Perhaps she did not respond as per his expectations to his critiques of several of her pictures or did not unconditionally accept him as her mentor. When Diderot implies that Anna Dorothea ultimately failed to succeed in Paris because she was not young and flirtatious enough, this casts a telling light on the attitudes of the times and Diderot himself towards the work of female artists.

But the painter's debts could also have been the reason behind Diderot's relief at her departure, which was more of an escape from creditors. Madame Therbusch had fervently continued to paint both portraits and historical pictures while in Paris. In so doing, she had deliberately selected subject matter that was typical for the Parisian milieu, and she also took advice from Diderot. However, lucrative commissions from the royal court never materialised, even though she presumably tried for them, and so her income always remained low, which brought her into increasing financial straits. Another patron of Therbusch in Paris, the Russian ambassador Prince Dmitri Alexeievich Gallitzin, finally purchased several of her paintings for the Russian court and saved her from the worst of her financial distress. She ultimately accompanied Gallitzin to Brussels in autumn 1768 and then travelled via the Netherlands and Hamburg back to Berlin.

When she arrived back in her hometown in 1769, Anna Dorothea Therbusch had yet another honour in her luggage: in December 1768, the art academy in Vienna had accepted her as a

FIGURE 21.2   Anna Dorothea Therbusch, self-portrait 1782, signed "A.D. Therbusch née de Lisziewska par elle même / peintre du Roi 1782"

Germanisches Nationalmuseum Nürnberg

Anna Dorothea Therbusch, Selbstporträt im Fenster, 1782, Germanisches Nationalmuseum Nürnberg, Inv. Nr. Gm1277, Fotograf: Dirk Meßberger

member as well. The acceptance pieces that Therbusch had sent to the imperial capital were a portrait of her friend, the painter Jakob Philipp Hackert (which still survives), and a historical picture with a depiction of Artemisia in mourning for her husband Mausolos (which has been lost). Anna Dorothea Therbusch had therefore received the academic recognition she had so actively pursued. Now it was time to turn it into economic success as an artist.

As of 1769, she worked permanently in Berlin. Here she managed to achieve what had escaped her in Paris: the king of Prussia bought several of her pictures, which further enhanced her reputation and ultimately her income. This was all the more important when Anna Dorothea's husband died in 1773. From then on she had to maintain her livelihood solely from her artistic work, for the family's inn no longer existed, her two sons, Karl August and Georg Friedrich, having chosen different careers as royal officials.

In the following years, she fulfilled one of her biggest commissions together with her brother Christian Friedrich, who had likewise returned to Berlin. Empress Catherine II of Russia had earlier commissioned seven life-size portraits of the Prussian royal family from Therbusch in 1768, presumably arranged by Gallitzin. From 1773 to 1779, Therbusch and her brother worked together in a studio on Unter den Linden, where they also completed this major Russian commission. As in many artists' workshops, they divided the work, with Christian Friedrich Lisiewski painting the head in some of the portraits while Anna Dorothea dealt with the clothing, no doubt because the true-to-life representation of textures had always been one of her particular strengths.

At the same time, Madame Therbusch continued to paint many portraits, which exhibit the artist's own—and back then very modern—style. Most of them were bust and half-length portraits with a decidedly realistic depiction of the subject. Very much in keeping with the Enlightenment, they dispensed with elaborate motifs that primarily served to represent the subject's social and political status, such as pillars, baldachins, etc. In her later years, she also made several self-portraits, some of which show her with optical aids (Figure 21.2). Despite increasing age and many limitations, such aids enabled the painter to continue her artistic work.

When Anna Dorothea Therbusch died of tuberculosis in early November 1782 in Berlin, several larger commissions still waited to be fulfilled. She was one of the first women in the Holy Roman Empire—other examples were her sister Anna Rosina de Gasc or Ludovike Simanowiz—to gain recognition as an artist from the public and patrons, as well as from academic artists. In the epitaph on her tombstone, her student Johann Christian Gohl commemorated her person: "Whoever you may be, remember on this monument a woman who surpassed many men, whom few men surpassed, in the art of accurately depicting the visual expression of humanity".[8]

After her death, several exhibits held in Berlin still included Therbusch's works. But by the end of the eighteenth century, she fell increasingly into obscurity. The first comprehensive exhibit of her works would not take place until the early 1970s in Potsdam, and a second such exhibit was recently held in Berlin to commemorate the 300th anniversary of her birth.[9] With respect to this long phase of oblivion, as well as to her journey through life, Anna Dorothea Therbusch is typical of many female artists. There were quite a few women who, as daughters or sisters of painters, received training and support in their youth. But in contrast to men, they could not finalise this process with a qualified education at an academy, with a master, or through travel, but rather remained dependent on autodidactic studies. This can be observed in the case of Anna Dorothea, as can the fact that she did not experience her most productive period and develop her own style until she was older. These too are aspects she shares with many other female painters.

Despite such obstacles, Anna Dorothea Therbusch had the desire and strength to not merely dedicate herself to her art within narrow confines but rather to also obtain recognition beyond her home city. This is shown by her efforts to gain memberships in art academies, the most prestigious of which was clearly the academy in Paris. However, Therbusch's stay in Paris and her hasty departure from the city also reveal further difficulties faced by women who worked independently as artists: they were exposed to the enmity of male colleagues and defamatory suspicions; because of their gender, they were subject to limitations not only in terms of their education but also with regard to the subject matter of their work. And, if they wanted to work permanently as artists, they were almost always dependent not only on the protection of patrons of the arts but also on the support of husbands, fathers, and brothers. The fact that the art history of the German-speaking world has long "forgotten" so many female painters—with very few exceptions, such as Angelica Kauffmann—distorts to this day our view of artistic creativity in the early modern period.

Notes

1 A compilation of the previously known sources and a list of the artist's more than 200 previously identified oil paintings is provided in Küster, K. (2008) "Anna Dorothea Therbusch, eine Malerin der Aufklärung. Leben und Werk". PhD thesis, University of Heidelberg.
2 An English translation of this biography is published in Dabbs, J.K. (2016) *Life Stories of Women Artists, 1500–1800: An Anthology*. 2nd edition. Farnham: Ashgate, pp. 430–440. The German version of the text on Therbusch in this volume is available at https://digi.ub.uni-heidelberg.de/diglit/mai1782_1783/0272.
3 Overdoors are the decorative panels above doors or windows.
4 The exception most well known today was Angelica Kauffmann, who, like Therbusch, also painted historical pictures.
5 Prior to Therbusch, only one non-French woman had become a member there: the famous Italian portrait painter Rosalba Carriera.
6 Quoted in Bajou, *Künstlerin*, p. 250.
7 Diderot, D. (1990) "Salon de 1767", in Diderot, D. *Œuvres completes*, vol. 16. Edited by Diekmann, H., and Varloot, J. Paris: Hermann, pp. 370–371. Therbusch's acceptance painting has survived in Paris: "Un homme, le verre à la main, éclairé d'une bougie", oil on canvas, 108 x 92 cm, École Nationale Supérieure des Beaux-Arts, Paris, 1767 MRA.
8 Quoted in Fix and Küster, *Der freie Blick*, p. 25.
9 https://www.smb.museum/ausstellungen/detail/anna-dorothea-therbusch/.

Selected bibliography

Bajou, T. (2000) "Eine deutsche Künstlerin im Paris des 18. Jahrhunderts: Anna Dorothea Therbusch", in Fleckner, U., et al. (eds.), *Jenseits der Grenzen: Französische und deutsche Kunst vom Ancien Régime bis zur Gegenwart*, vol. 1: *Inszenierung der Dynastien*. Cologne: DuMont, pp. 249–268.

Fix, A., and Küster, K. (eds.) (2002) *Der freie Blick: Anna Dorothea Therbusch und Ludovike Simanowiz: Zwei Porträtmalerinnen des 18. Jahrhunderts*. Heidelberg: Kehrer.

ANNA BARBARA GIGNOUX (1725–1796)

How to Defend a Calico Manufactory

FIGURE 22.1   Anna Barbara Gignoux

Kunstsammlungen und Museen Augsburg

Johann Georg Edlinger, Anna Barbara Gignoux, Kunstsammlungen und Museen Augsburg, Inv. Nr. 6203

DOI: 10.4324/9781003252870-25

Still found today in Augsburg's Lech district is a stately bourgeois house that features a commemorative plaque invoking the memory of Anna Barbara Gignoux. Built in 1764/65 at the behest of Georg Christoph Gleich, the second husband of widow Gignoux, the house was meant to be a residence as well as the premises for a calico factory—but the entire venture went bankrupt a few years later because Gleich had overestimated his financial resources, and not just for the construction of the house.

Anna Barbara was born in 1725 as the eldest of seven children of the Augsburg goldbeater Andreas Koppmair, a skilled craftsman in the very specialised trade of goldleaf manufacturing. Hardly anything is known about her youth. However, one may assume that she helped out from an early age in her father's workshop, as was common in the skilled-trade sector and all the more so for Augsburg goldbeaters. Then in 1748, the young woman married Johann Friedrich Gignoux, whose father had immigrated from Geneva.

Since around 1719, the elder Gignoux had run a manufactory in Augsburg that printed calico. His two sons worked as printers in the manufactory, which in the late 1740s counted among the most modern in Augsburg. The printing of cotton textiles as a skilled trade in Augsburg demonstrably dates back to the end of the seventeenth century. In what was a new process back then, wooden blocks were used to print patterns on the textiles with a covering liquid. Then the textiles were dyed, producing patterns that were far more precise and durable than those made with older processes. The number of licensed positions in the city remained restricted to eight Protestant and eight Catholic printers because, since the Thirty Years' War, Augsburg had been a "paritätische Reichsstadt"—a parity imperial city—which meant that the two confessions had to be given exactly the same rights. This rule also applied to the allocation of privileged skilled-trade positions.

Even though calico printing was under the supervision of the weavers' guild, unlike most guild craftsmen, the elder Gignoux by no means did all of his production solely with his sons. The operation employed many other people, each of whom performed a specific step in the work process. Thus there was a division of labour (people did not individually make an entire product), machines were used for printing, and production was not made to order but rather for distribution. The raw materials were bought on the open market, and the products were sold the same way. Augsburg's calico printers were leaders in the German-speaking world and exported their products to England, Holland, France, and Italy, as well as to the American and African colonies. Even though the enterprise remained tied to a privileged skilled-trade position, the operation was already far more akin to a modern factory and its principles than to a traditional skilled-trade workshop; hence the term "manufactory".

Shortly after the wedding, Johann Friedrich Gignoux established his independence with his own enterprise, which remained only loosely tied to that of his father. Anna Barbara's role in the enterprise remains obscure at first, which can be considered typical: while the collaboration of women in the commercial skilled-trades sector in early modern cities was generally quite common, its dimensions are often difficult to assess. But in the case of Anna Barbara, however, after her husband's early death in 1760 she made it clear that he had introduced her to the trade and involved her in the business operation. In particular, this is how she learned to manufacture the dyes, which was considered a trade secret. Her work for the enterprise therefore quickly became too important for her to be able to dedicate her time solely to the family household. The household, which soon included two children, was managed by Anna Barbara's unmarried sister Sabina, at least until the death of Johann Friedrich Gignoux.

Gignoux's early death, which occurred moreover during a phase of entrepreneurial difficulty, confronted Anna Barbara with new challenges. She promptly requested the authorisation to continue the operation from the Weaver's Guild House, which represented Augsburg's textile artisans and also had authority over the calico printers. Her qualifications were reviewed and found to be adequate, and the widow was granted permission to continue running the manufactory for her two children, a son and a daughter.

In doing so, the Weaver's Guild House followed widely acknowledged widow rights that served to protect a master craftsman's family after his death. As a woman, Anna Barbara Gignoux did not receive the skilled-trade entitlement herself, a privilege that was needed to operate the enterprise; rather she held it only as a "proxy" for her son. This allowance was meant to safeguard his inheritance, ensure his training, and enable the livelihood of the surviving family.

It is not quite clear why Anna Barbara Gignoux decided to enter into a second marriage just a few months after her first husband's death. She herself later said that she was urged to do so by her male relatives—by her father, father-in-law, or brother-in-law. In any case, in autumn 1760 she agreed to the marriage proposal of Georg Christoph Gleich, an Augsburg merchant with whom her husband had previously maintained business contacts. However, she seems to have soon regretted this decision, for she quickly gained the impression that she had been "married by him in his mind primarily because of my cotton factory and just secondarily because of my person".[1] And this was not a deceptive impression, as soon became clear.

Even after the marriage, Anna Barbara, who now bore the surname Gleich, insisted on keeping the manufactory's reigns in her own hands until her son came of age—in accordance with the testament of her first husband and probably with her own plans. Georg Christoph Gleich, however, demanded control of the enterprise for himself, denied his wife access to the account books, and transferred money into his commercial operations.

This also gave rise to marital conflicts, which ultimately climaxed in violence on the part of Gleich against Anna Barbara. Consequently, in November 1761 only around one year after they were married, she applied to the Augsburg City Council for a divorce from her husband. In the course of the subsequent proceedings, the entrepreneurial activities of the insubordinate wife were naturally discussed as well. Thus, business friends of Georg Christoph Gleich accused Anna Barbara of being unable to ensure deliveries from the manufactory, which, they argued, clearly proved what people already knew, namely, "how poorly women are able to lead such broad and exacting as well as difficult activities, even if their female circumstances do not at the same time in and of themselves already entail many obstacles and corruptions."[2]

Anna Barbara Gignoux countered as follows:

> In the end, Herr Schwarz [one of Gleich's business partners] is under the delusion as if women were unable to lead a cotton factory, since in my last six months as a widow I actually directed the entire cotton factory with much acclaim, as is known in the city, and in my current state of marriage, have each time set all of the dyes myself, whereas my husband [Gleich] ... was so lazy that he did not even enter anything from the note book of my bookkeeper into the two said [business] books, let alone that he would have been able to take on the directorate of the entire cotton factory.[3]

Despite Georg Christoph Gleich's obvious lack of qualifications, the Augsburg City Council ruled in his favour and awarded control of the manufactory to him. Nonetheless, in the divorce proceedings an effort was also made to reach a settlement that saved the marriage, which eventually occurred in summer 1762. The settlement again stipulated that Gleich was to direct the manufactory, but at the same time he was obliged to ensure the inheritance of his stepchildren and allow his wife to monitor the business affairs. She, in turn, was supposed to give him a hand in the household "economy", as was usual at the time. This no doubt meant organising the household as well as providing for the household employees and "helping" in the manufactory. The latter was absolutely indispensable for Gleich, since the person who knew how to make the dyes and create and utilise the patterns for printing was indeed his wife, not him.

It may seem surprising that Anna Barbara agreed to this settlement, by which the council actually ignored the legal testament of her first husband. But this was her only chance to secure rights of inspection with regard to the manufactory after the Augsburg City Council had granted her second husband ownership and control on the basis of the legal principle of gender guardianship—and this without an opportunity for Anna Barbara to appeal. The settlement at least secured the rights of her children and allowed Anna Barbara to monitor the business activities.

As of 1762, Georg Christoph Gleich was therefore in charge of the manufactory, and he was the one who ordered the construction of the stately house on the Lech—much to the displeasure of his wife, who called it a "pile of stones" and continued to worry about the inherited enterprise. And developments would prove her right. In October 1770, Gleich was forced to file for bankruptcy, and shortly thereafter he fled from Augsburg to avoid debtors' prison, leaving his wife with a pile of debts totalling more than 200,000 gulden. It was in this undoubtedly difficult predicament that Anna Barbara's business acumen proved itself, contrary to the derogatory comments cited above. She managed, albeit with great effort, to settle with her creditors so that she could continue operating the calico manufactory. And within a few years, she expanded the manufactory as "Johann Friedrich Gignoux seel. Erben" into the third largest in the city.

The manufactory's name already suggests that Anna Barbara continued operating the business de jure as the widow of her first husband. This allowed her to continue to exploit guild regulations with their provisions on widows' rights. She soon re-adopted the name Gignoux, but not before seeking a divorce again in 1778. This time, however, the proceedings clearly went in her favour. Gleich had not shown his face in Augsburg since his escape and hence had wilfully abandoned his family. Through business contacts, Anna Barbara learned that he was now living in Großenhain, Saxony, as the manager of a calico manufactory, and had repeatedly committed adultery. In light of this situation, the Augsburg City Council approved the divorce without much ado.

After her son died in 1777, Anna Barbara Gignoux continued running the business just as energetically as when she had earlier fought for her manufactory and ultimately saved it from bankruptcy. Production volumes probably peaked in the 1780s, when the manufactory achieved annual sales of around 300,000 gulden from the printing operation and another 20,000 to 30,000 gulden from the associated cotton business. The prosperous business situation meant that Anna Barbara could build additional operating facilities (a fulling mill and a bleachery), outside the city gates, purchase several houses, and eventually also lay out a magnificent garden.

A contemporary description of the Augsburg economy noted:

> Frau Barbara Gignoux, an insightful, tirelessly active woman, who undisputedly deserves a place in the temple of fame among the noteworthy persons of her sex of the old and new centuries, has for around thirty years, through spirit and courage, raised her factory so high that it may count among the most preeminent commercial houses of this city. This woman leads a business that has already bested many skilled men; with five hundred workers, she daily assigns them their proper task, oversees everything with a sharp gaze, [and] in her trade office provided with many people, reads and signs all of the bills of exchange and invoices herself, notwithstanding her increasing age.[4]

Her tireless activities changed little until Anna Barbara Gignoux died in 1796 as the result of a stroke. Her daughter Felicitas Barbara then continued to run the manufactory before she finally leased it to another Augsburg calico manufacturer in 1805.

The management of a large calico manufactory required technical skills as well as artistic and entrepreneurial capabilities, all of which Anna Barbara Gignoux undoubtedly possessed. But were it not for her first husband's early death and the later conflicts with her second husband, one would know very little about her story today. In fact, the two divorce proceedings were what drew attention to and left a record of her entrepreneurial importance, although in the latter respect she was not unique.

Older economic historiography generally assumed that the fervent and shrewd entrepreneurs who paved the way for the rise of capitalism were men. Women such as Anna Barbara Gignoux, however, prove that whether a person could prevail in the world of entrepreneurial commerce was never a question of gender. At most, it must be noted that women had a far more difficult time acquiring and using technical skills because guilds refused to accept them and restricted their role to that of the "assisting wife", only allowing girls to get proper training in exceptional cases.

Legal regulations, such as gender guardianship[5] and the regionally variegated forms of family and inheritance law complicated entrepreneurial activity—but they did not prohibit it. However, it takes considerable effort to find these entrepreneurial women in the files related to the urban and rural economies of the early modern period. These women often remained overshadowed by men because they managed operations in conjunction with their husbands, as Anna Barbara Gignoux did in her first marriage, or because men forced them into the background, which was initially the case for her after 1761.

The more exacting gaze of recent research, however, has brought to light that, in many economic sectors, there were women who "assisted" in the workshop of their husband or father and therefore were directly involved in the production of goods. There are many indications to this effect across the board in textile production and refinement. But in very isolated cases, in specialised trades such as silk production in Cologne, women themselves could openly appear as master tradeswomen under skilled-trade law. Usually this was only possible for men who had gone through the prescribed qualification process from apprentice to journeyman to master. But there were other sectors, too, such as the production of lace, for example, which was widespread in the towns and countryside of the Ore Mountains, in which women were the qualified workers and designers of new products and also played a major role as merchants.

However, there were also female entrepreneurs who organised and directed operations in mining, the iron processing industry, and glass manufacturing, such as in the Saar region or along the Ruhr. In the sources, one relatively often also finds women—usually widows such as Magdalena Morhart in Tübingen or Susanna Cosmerovius in Vienna—who ran book printing enterprises and were thus simultaneously involved in publishing and the book trade, for there was no clear separation between these sectors until the nineteenth century. Glikl bas Judah Leib was discussed in an earlier chapter as an example of the many women who were involved in intraregional trade, which they often combined with entrepreneurial activity; along with trading in jewels and pearls and making her money market transactions, she also operated a stocking manufactory in Hamburg. For the Hanseatic town of Stralsund, it has even been discovered that, in the second half of the eighteenth century, women controlled 11 percent of the enterprises engaged in long-distance trade.

But as also shown by the example of Gignoux, women rarely founded enterprises themselves; instead, they tended to inherit them (from fathers or husbands) and then continued operating them successfully, whether until the enterprise was taken over by male heirs or permanently, as in the case of Anna Barbara Gignoux. Widowhood also provided for broader legal manoeuvring room, which many female entrepreneurs used to their advantage. In any event, the independent dealings of women played a much larger role in shaping the early modern economy than has long been assumed. Only from the start of the nineteenth century, with the emergence of new ideas about family life and new structures in the world of work and the gradual establishment of large-scale industry, did women recede into the background—yet without fully disappearing.

Notes

1 Quoted in Werkstetter, C. (1996) "Anna Barbara Gignoux (1725–1796), Kattunfabrikantin oder Mäzenin? Zur Entstehung einer Augsburger Legende", in Burkhardt, J., Giering, T., and Werkstetter, C. (eds.), *Augsburger Handelshäuser im Wandel des historischen Urteils.* Berlin: Akademie-Verlag, pp. 381–399 (quote on p. 383).
2 Quoted in Werkstetter, "Kattunfabrikantin", p. 384.
3 Quoted in Werkstetter, *Frauen im Handwerk*, p. 492.
4 *Beleuchtung der in dem Ulmer geographischen Lexikon von Schwaben enthaltenen sehr anzüglichen Stellen die löbliche Reichsstadt Augsburg betreffend* (1791). Augsburg: Lotter, pp. 41–42.
5 See the Introduction, p. 4.

Selected bibliography

Fassl P. (1985) "Die Augsburger Kattunfabrikantin Anna Barbara Gignoux (1725–1796)", in Müller, R.A. (ed.), *Unternehmer – Arbeitnehmer: Lebensbilder aus der Frühzeit der Industrialisierung in Bayern.* Munich: Oldenbourg, pp. 153–159.

Werkstetter, C. (2001) *Frauen im Augsburger Zunfthandwerk: Arbeit, Arbeitsbeziehungen und Geschlechterverhältnisse im 18. Jahrhundert.* Berlin: Akademie-Verlag.

Werkstetter, C. (2008) "'… vorzüglichen meiner Cotton-Fabrique und nur secundario meiner Persohn geheurathet worden': Die gescheiterte Ehe der Augsburger Unternehmerin Anna Barbara Gignoux (1725–1796) im Spiegel der Scheidungsakten", in Weber, W., and Dauser, R. (eds.), *Faszinierende Frühneuzeit: Reich, Frieden, Kultur und Kommunikation 1500–1800.* Berlin: Akademie-Verlag, pp. 185–217.

SOPHIE VON LA ROCHE (1730–1807)

A Life as a Female Author

The future author was born as Sophie von Gutermann in 1730 in Kaufbeuren in the Allgäu, in the far south of the empire. Her father, Georg Friedrich von Gutermann, was a doctor. After a temporary position in Lindau on Lake Constance, he obtained the office of city physician in the large imperial city of Augsburg, where Sophie grew up, raised by her parents as a good Pietist. At the end of her life, she wrote about this retrospectively:

> Every day in the paternal household, along with the work at the side of my mother [Regina Barbara], one meditation in Arndt's *True Christianity* had to be read and one listened to, on Sundays a sermon by Frank in Halle[1].... But apart from that, I also became the best dancer, learned French, drawing, and flower painting, embroidery, piano playing, and how to manage the kitchen and household. On Tuesdays my father had a circle of scholars, where sometimes books had to be fetched from his collection. For this reason, as a joke, he made me his librarian at age twelve because my good memory allowed me to remember all of the titles and all of the places, which I then also used to select books for myself.[2]

As the quotation shows, Sophie received a status-appropriate education a young girl, which, along with homemaking skills, also included languages and lessons in dancing and music, which were important for social life. And she no doubt expanded her horizons on her own by reading from her father's library. Important

DOI: 10.4324/9781003252870-26

not only for her education but above all for the development of her personality was her encounter with Giovanni Ludovico Bianconi, who worked as the personal physician of the prince-bishop of Augsburg. Thirteen years her senior, he asked for Sophie's hand in 1747.

Her parents were wary about this engagement, not least because Bianconi was Catholic. But the meetings it made possible offered Sophie a glimpse into a new world. Bianconi gave her an understanding of Italian literature and language, as well as of antiquity, and he encouraged her to train her singing voice and concentrate on piano playing. After her mother's death in 1748, Sophie's father was more open to the idea of their marriage and even travelled to Italy to get to know the Bianconi family. But since no agreement could be reached as to the denominational upbringing of the children, in 1749 Sophie's father forced the dissolution of the engagement and the destruction of all of her keepsakes from Bianconi.

This plunged the 19-year-old into a deep crisis, and in 1750, probably at least in part to gain some distance from the events, she travelled to relatives in Biberach. There she got to know her cousin Christoph Martin Wieland, who was three years older, and felt attracted to him. They promptly became engaged in August 1750, shortly before Wieland left to study in Tübingen, from where he sent Sophie effusive poetry. But opposition from his mother and her father led to the failure of this engagement, too, and it was dissolved in late 1753. Christoph Martin Wieland would later make a name for himself as a poet and man of letters. After 1772, when he was called to Weimar, he figured, along with Goethe, Schiller, and Herder, as one of the so-called four stars of Weimar classicism. They dominated the circle around Duke Karl August of Saxe-Weimar and were inestimably important for German literary history. He and Sophie remained connected throughout their lives.

The foreseeable failure of this second engagement moved Sophie to make a rash decision: just a few days after the breakup, she married Georg Michael Frank, called La Roche, in Biberach. He was probably an illegitimate son of Count Anton Heinrich von Stadion, a minister in Electoral Mainz, who supported him from a very young age and for whom he worked as a secretary in

Mainz. For Sophie, La Roche was at first probably an expedient way to escape the grip of her father and his decisions over her life. La Roche, for his part, was looking for an educated woman who was capable of exercising the representative functions he needed to fulfil at the court of the elector of Mainz.

In Mainz, Sophie quickly gained a reputation as an intelligent socialiser and lettered woman; she also acted as a reader for Count Stadion and thereby expanded her literary education. The marriage of convenience with La Roche developed into quite a loving and intimate relationship, and by the end of the 1760s the couple had eight children, five of whom reached adulthood. After Count Stadion quit his service in Mainz in 1761, Sophie La Roche lived with her family in a wing of Stadion's castle in Warthausen near Biberach, until her husband became a privy councillor of the elector of Trier in 1770 after Stadion's death.

Sophie La Roche had been making her own attempts at writing since her engagement to Wieland, with the latter advising her and drawing her attention to important contemporary authors such as Jean-Jacques Rousseau and Samuel Richardson. However, hardly any of her early texts survive. Sophie La Roche first stepped into the limelight of the literary world in 1771 with the publication of her first novel *Die Geschichte des Fräuleins von Sternheim* (*The History of Lady Sophia Sternheim*). Looking back, La Roche explained that the conceptualisation and writing of the novel was precipitated by her separation from her daughters, who at Count Stadion's request were sent to a Catholic boarding school in Strasbourg. Personal feelings therefore played a fundamental role in the intensification of her writing and the planning of the work, which started taking shape in 1766.

When the voluminous novel appeared, it quickly became a bestseller, striking a nerve of the times like few others. It went through eight printings within just a few years and was translated into French, English, Dutch, and Russian. In salons, reading societies, and social circles, the era of sentimentalism had begun: people read each other heartfelt letters (or texts formulated as such) to share their personal feelings with kindred souls. The rationalism of the Enlightenment's heyday was consequently superseded. *The History of Lady Sophia Sternheim* now described the life story of a sensitive human being, a woman—and for

FIGURE 23.1 Sophie von La Roche, ca. 1774

Freies Deutsches Hochstift / Frankfurter Goethe-Museum

Anonymous, Sophie von La Roche, um 1774, Freies Deutsches Hochstift / Frankfurter Goethe-Museum, Inv. Nr. IV-00477, Fotografin: Ursula Edelmann

the first time in the history of German literature, such a novel was also written by a woman. Admittedly, at first the novel appeared anonymously, with Christoph Martin Wieland acting as the publisher. But the name of the actual author soon became known.

Contemporaries were enthusiastic: some viewed the work as an Enlightenment coming-of-age novel; others particularly appreciated its sentimental and emotional presentation. One such person who then came to Ehrenbreitstein near Koblenz, where the La Roche couple had been living since 1770, was a young man with literary ambitions of his own: Johann Wolfgang von Goethe. In 1772, he was just working through the aftermath of an unfortunate love affair when he immediately fell in love again, this time with Sophie's eldest daughter, Maximiliane. Sophie was vigilant, however, and protected her daughter, barely 16, from the tempestuous admirer. In 1774, she paved the way for Maximiliane's marriage to the wealthy Frankfurt merchant Pietro Antonio Brentano; afterwards, Goethe would frequently be a guest at his house. Two of Sophie's grandchildren, Clemens Brentano and Bettina von Arnim (her later married name) would become famous themselves as poets.

Goethe took no offence at the gentle rejection by his colleague, plunging instead into his own novel project, which was inspired not least by La Roche's book and his conversations with her. In 1774 he wrote a bestseller himself in just a few weeks, whose style and form of presentation was heavily influenced by *Sternheim*. Goethe's *The Sorrows of Young Werther* would, for its part, substantially influence a young generation and still remains part of the German bourgeois educational canon.

While this book established Goethe's fame, that of Sophie La Roche quickly faded, even though she published another novel in 1775. She had little sympathy to the literary *Sturm und Drang* movement, which paid homage to emotional freedom and genius. Friedrich Schiller's *The Robbers*, for example, which she saw performed on stage in 1785, pretty much repulsed her. And family matters were demanding all of her attention. In 1780, her husband, who had fully supported her literary work, lost his post as the chancellor of the elector of Trier because the latter suspected him of anticlerical tendencies. As a result, the family stood on the financial brink, for his earnings had previously been their only source of livelihood.

Christoph Philipp von Hohenfeld, a former colleague of Georg Michael von La Roche who had likewise resigned because of the latter's dismissal, took in the family at his place in Speyer. But how were they supposed to finance their daily life and the education of their sons? Sophie von La Roche (her husband was ennobled in 1775, entitling him to use 'von') confronted this challenge by deliberately making writing her profession. Of course, this did not occur overnight, but Wieland supported her—for example, with assignments for his journal, *Teutscher Merkur*. In addition, La Roche herself began planning a journal, which she hoped would simultaneously provide her with income.

The first issue of *Pomona für Teutschlands Töchter* (Pomona for Germany's daughters)[3] appeared in January 1783, with La Roche, as editor, describing herself as Pomona, the Greek goddess of autumn. The journal's goal was to convey the kind of parenting and education principles that Sophie had earlier slipped into *Sternheim* to a larger audience of educated women and girls. It dealt with history, mythology, and the natural sciences, as well as with fashion, contemporary schooling, gardening, housekeeping, and memory training. The journal appeared monthly in a run of 1,000 to 1,500 copies. Along with La Roche herself, other female authors, such as Elisa von der Recke and Friederike Jerusalem, also contributed to the various issues.

Sophia von La Roche was not the first woman in the Holy Roman Empire to publish a journal. Between 1779 and 1796, women launched at least 17 different journals, although most were quite short-lived. This also held true for *Pomona*, which had to shut down just two years after appearing. However, the short phase at the end of the eighteenth century catches one's eye, because female publishers of journals would not reappear until during the revolutions of 1848/49 and then again in the late nineteenth century. With her journal, La Roche by no means pursued a feminist programme in terms of demands for equality. Even though, in her foreword to *Pomona*, she explicitly referred to men as publishers of journals for women[4] and distanced herself from them, the journal was not substantively very different from those with male publishers. Instead, it was similarly aimed at the education and enlightenment of women.

Despite being relatively short-lived, *Pomona* was a major step towards establishing La Roche as a professional writer with a very diverse body of work.[5] Even though she herself described the origin of the project—as well as that of most of her other works—as "fortuitous", she had been working with intense focus on her professional future since 1780. This also meant that she herself went travelling and wrote about it in several travel reports, for travel literature was very popular.

In summer 1784, Sophie travelled to Switzerland together with her son Franz and an acquaintance; in spring and summer 1785, she journeyed to France with a friend, Elise von Bethmann.

Next came a trip to Holland and England in summer and autumn 1787, accompanied by her son Carl and another female friend. After her husband's death in 1788, this was followed by another trip, this time to Switzerland from autumn 1791 to spring 1792, and finally in summer 1799 by a trip to Weimar, where La Roche reunited with Wieland and many people in the circle around Duke Karl August of Saxe-Weimar, and then all the way to her son, Carl von La Roche, in Schönebeck on the Elbe.

With each of these journeys, the now elderly Sophie von La Roche evidently also fulfilled long-held desires, and she described them in detail, deftly linking her experiences and encounters to historical and cultural information about the countries she visited. She conveyed her vivid impressions in an eloquent and picturesque language, which made the books very widely read.

The 1790s—the seventh decade of her life—were marked by numerous losses for Sophie von La Roche. In 1791, her son Franz died on their trip to Switzerland, followed by her daughter Maximiliane in 1793 and her son-in-law Brentano in 1797—three of her four children were then taken in by their grandmother, at least for a while. At the time, she was living in Offenbach near Frankfurt am Main, where her husband had bought a small house in 1786 (probably with the help of Pietro Brentano). Then when the elector of Trier had to flee before French troops during the revolutionary wars, Sophie von La Roche stopped receiving her widow's pension, which made her financial situation even more difficult.

But this did not keep her from writing: *Erscheinungen am See Oneida* (Phenomena at Lake Oneida) appeared in 1798, a novel about the American Revolutionary War; it was an unusual subject, through which La Roche no doubt surrendered to her wanderlust again, at least literarily. Her late works, *Mein Schreibtisch* (My desk) of 1799 and *Melusinens Sommer-Abende* (Melusine's summer evenings) of 1806, moved between storytelling and autobiography, admonition and reflection. However, she was unable to build on the success of *Sternheim* with any of her later works—prevailing tastes had passed her by. After La Roche's visit to Weimar in 1799, Goethe, once so impressed, mocked her in a letter to Schiller: "She belongs to those of a levelling nature; she elevates the commonplace and pulls the excellent down, and then serves the entirety with her sauce for any desired taste; for the rest, one would like to say that her conversation is interesting in places."[6]

To be sure, she still received literary recognition even in her final years, in that she was accepted as a corresponding member into the Société littéraire du Musée de Bordeaux. Her acceptance in 1790 into Arcadia, a literary society in Rome, also reflects the international regard for her works. Sophie von La Roche died in February 1807 in Offenbach am Main after a brief illness.

Sophie von La Roche was by no means the first woman in the German-speaking world to make an appearance as an author. But regardless of the various degrees of success of her works, La Roche was the first woman of the German-speaking world who, as an author, also managed to earn a living from her profession for a long period of time. This distinguishes her from Luise Gottsched, for example, who hardly had to worry about the financial success of her writings and translations, for as the wife of a professor she was financially secure.

La Roche was one of the most important female authors of the eighteenth century, and her literary work exhibits an impressive breadth and diversity. It includes novels, morality tales, journal articles, travel descriptions, and autobiographical pieces. In her texts, she explored fields of action for women, which she described within the typical limits of the times, but while always searching for their potential beyond those limits. In this respect, her texts have a pedagogical dimension. Her body of work also includes numerous letters, a great many of which have survived, but to date they have not been completely catalogued, never mind edited. Her own correspondence and that of others further shows her as an intermediator and organiser in the literary industry, especially during her time in Ehrenbreitstein near Koblenz, when she played a role in the literary development of the young Goethe, among other things. Moreover, as a networker, she acted as the publisher of *Pomoma*, in which she also gave other female authors the chance to publish their work.

Notes

1 Johann Arndt was one of Lutheranism's most important post-Reformation theologians; he was highly esteemed by the founders of

Pietism. August Hermann Francke was a founder of one of the main currents of Pietism.
2 La Roche, S. (1806) *Melusinens Sommer-Abende*, edited by Wieland. C.M. Halle: Societäts-Buchhandlung, pp. VII–VIII.
3 *Pomona für Teutschlands Töchter*. Available at https://opacplus.bsb-muenchen.de/title/BV003900753.
4 Here La Roche wrote: "The *Magazine for Women* and the *Yearbook of Memorable Matters for the Fair Sex*—show my readers what German men find useful and pleasing for us. *Pomona*—will tell you what I as a woman consider worthy of attention." Quoted in Nerl-Steckelberg and Pott, *Sophie von La Roche*, p. 81.
5 See Becker-Cantarino, B. (1993) "Sophie von La Roche (1730–1807): Kommentiertes Werkverzeichnis", *Das achtzehnte Jahrhundert: Mitteilungen der deutschen Gesellschaft für die Erforschung des 18. Jahrhunderts* 17 (1), pp. 28–49.
6 Quoted in Nerl-Steckelberg and Pott, *Sophie von La Roche*, p. 98.

Selected bibliography

Becker-Cantarino, B. (2008) *Meine Liebe zu Büchern: Sophie von La Roche als professionelle Schriftstellerin*. Heidelberg: Winter.

Dawson, R.P. (2002) "The Enabling Effect of Difference", in Dawson, R.P., *The Contested Quill: Literature by Women in Germany, 1770–1800*. Newark: University of Delaware Press, pp. 92–154

Hilliard, K. (2007) "Sophie von La Roche", in Brown, H. (ed.), *Landmarks in German women's writing*. Oxford: Lang, pp. 43–58.

La Roche, S. (1991) *The History of Lady Sophie Sternheim*. Edited by Lynn, J. Translated by Collyer, J. Worcester: Billing & Sons.

Nerl-Steckelberg, C., and Pott, K. (eds.) (2000) *"Das wahre Glück ist in der Seele des Rechtschaffenen": Sophie von La Roche (1730–1807), eine bemerkenswerte Frau im Zeitalter von Aufklärung und Empfindsamkeit*. Bönnigheim: La Roche-Museum.

AMALIE GALLITZIN (1748–1806)

Philosophy, Religion, and Conviviality

Adelheid Amalie von Schmettau was born in 1748 as the daughter of the Prussian General Field Marshal Count Samuel von Schmettau and his wife, Maria Johanna. After her father died when she was just three years old, her mother assumed responsibility for the upbringing of Amalie and her two brothers. However, one should not imagine her childhood environment as an aristocratic estate; the family lived in Berlin, and Amalie's mother's only income came from the father's military pension. Since Johanna von Schmettau was Catholic, at just seven years of age Amalie was sent to an Urseline convent near Wrocław (Breslau), where she received the higher education of an aristocratic girl: reading, writing, religion, French, piano playing, singing, and dancing.

Upon returning to Berlin at age 15, the young woman had no idea about life at court in a major capital and little to show in terms of an education in contemporary literature and art. To maintain her daughter in a status-appropriate manner, her mother immediately pursued an engagement for Amalie, which came about in August 1763. But since the aristocratic marriage candidate had not truthfully represented his financial circumstances, Amalie's guardian soon dissolved the agreement, much to her relief. Instead, Countess Schmettau now tried to find her daughter a place at the court, and she finally managed to arrange for Amalie to be a maid of honour to a Prussian princess.

However, this quite honourable position left Amalie very ill at ease. The moral laxity in the social interactions between men

DOI: 10.4324/9781003252870-27

and women conflicted with her strict monastic education. She felt constrained by the tightly scheduled daily routine, which was primarily organised according to the needs of Princess Anna Elisabeth Luise of Prussia. It becomes apparent from her later letters that over the next few years Amalie escaped into a world shaped by her intensive readings. She dreamed of a famous "prince on a white horse" who would save her from what she felt was a meaningless existence.

It was in this situation of personal distress that Amalie von Schmettau came to know Prince Dmitri Alexeievich Gallitzin in 1768 on a journey of Luise of Prussia to Aachen. He was from an important Russian family and served first in Paris and then in The Hague as the czarina's ambassador. The prince was passionately interested in the natural sciences, literature, and painting of his times. He was also friends with Enlightenment figures such as Voltaire and Denis Diderot, and to the latter owed his acquaintance with the painter Anna Dorothea Therbusch, whom he supported in Paris. As an art agent of Czarina Catherine the Great, Gallitzin repeatedly facilitated art purchases for St. Petersburg.

Despite these numerous merits, in the long run Gallitzin was unable to fulfil his young bride's lofty expectations of marriage as a state of mutual friendship. Amalie's temperament and contrariness overwhelmed the decidedly liberal prince. Her sensitivity made everyday married life difficult for her to bear. This could not be belied either by their trips to St. Petersburg, Dresden, Berlin, and Vienna or by the birth of their two children, Marianna and Dmitri.

Back in the Netherlands—Prince Gallitzin would remain the ambassador at The Hague until 1782—the young princess soon regularly retreated to the countryside, refusing to take part in court society, and instead occupying herself with her studies. In contrast to many other aristocratic ladies, who at least felt well provided for in an unhappy marriage, Amalie soon responded with resolve: she left her husband, taking the children, and began living separately from him around 1774. Prince Gallitzin visited his family every year and financed it, but the conjugal partnership was never resumed.

FIGURE 24.1 Princess Amalie Gallitzin, 1783

Alamy

Georg Oswald May, Porträt der Fürstin Gallitzin, 1783, Privatbesitz

Amalie Gallitzin first lived near The Hague in the Netherlands, then, as of 1779, in Münster in Westphalia and in the village of Angelmodde before Münster's gates. For contemporaries, the fact that the princess lived separately from her husband was not so unusual in and of itself. Amalie caused more of a sensation through her own educational aspirations and because she taught her children herself, which she did on fully equal terms without regard to gender while drawing on the most modern pedagogical standards. Adopting the ideals of Jean-Jacques Rousseau, she understood the physically and mentally challenging education of her two children as her mission in life, and she dedicated her entire strength to this undertaking. When an acquaintance speculated that Amalie primarily wanted her son Dimitri to receive an education socially appropriate for an aristocrat, as would have been usual, she responded, "the main purpose of my education went towards forming him, where possible, into a human being, and his future destiny, which the father had left entirely to me, should be decided by nothing other than through his abilities to be useful to himself and others."[1]

Amalie had been intensely occupying herself with the positions of Rousseau and many other Enlightenment philosophers, along with the art and literature of her times, at least since when she married. Consequently, she quickly acquired a reputation as an educated woman, even though she always construed her studies and readings first and foremost as the further development of her person. She learned Latin and Greek, delved into mathematics and physics, philosophy and theology. Later added motivation for her studies was the desire to be able to educate her children and to lead them in every respect as a role model.

She continued these studies throughout her life, always searching for people who could inspire her in this respect. To begin with, very important to her as of 1775 was her friendship with the significantly older Frans Hemsterhuis, an independent scholar who primarily focused on philosophical studies. Their relationship repeatedly gave rise to gossip, especially since Amalie herself often wrote about "friendship" and "love" in her letters. Throughout her life, she saw both as central values on which she often reflected. But she probably considered her relationship with Hemsterhuis to be an intellectual marriage, an indissoluble bond based on commonalities in thought and emotion, which she had missed in her relationship with Gallitzin.

As time went on, however, Amalie found this relationship became too constrained by the jealousy of her congenial teacher, and she took her distance, at least spatially. They remained connected until Hemsterhuis's death in 1790. But after 1779, when Amalie moved to Münster in Westphalia, Franz von Fürstenberg, also 20 years older than her, became the main person with whom she jointly configured her life as an educated woman and unconventional thinker. Fürstenberg had been a canon in the high diocese of Münster and a curator of the University of Münster from 1780. For a long time, he had been a minister of the bishop, who simultaneously ruled as a prince over a mid-sized territory in Westphalia. As a minister, Fürstenberg had implemented school reforms in the prince-bishopric based on key Enlightenment principles. His activities in this regard were also why Amalie moved to Münster, for she hoped to be able to educate her children in the milieu created by these reforms.

Despite their deep connection, over the long term Fürstenberg too could not entirely satisfy Amalie's aspirations—in her longing for perpetual personal authenticity and unlimited attention, which, however, was never allowed to restrict her, they were no doubt unattainable. But that the princess clearly articulated such aspirations, called for them, and reflected on them, shows her as person who lived her individuality and thus applied new standards to herself and others.

Together, she and Fürstenberg became central figures in the so-called Münster Circle, one of many literary-progressive societies and salons[2] that shaped intellectual life in the Holy Roman Empire around 1800. In this social circle, made up almost exclusively of educated men (officials, teachers, clerics, and authors), people lived out the Enlightenment ideals of friendship and education. Amalie Gallitzin was able to attain central importance in this group not just because of her personality and undoubtedly outstanding education. Her high social rank and financial independence also helped, allowing her to continuously dedicate herself to her intellectual interests.

The conversations in the Münster Circle centred on theology, on the one hand, and the education of broad social classes according to Enlightenment ideas, on the other, both topics that intensely preoccupied Amalie. Philology, political science, literature, and philosophy were other topics for the circle, in which books were read and read aloud, discussed, and exchanged. As temperamental discussants, Fürstenberg and Amalie often dominated the debates. The conviviality also included exchanging ideas about art: the house of the princess, where the circle met, included a "museum" in which ancient cameos and plaster casts of ancient and contemporary sculptures were collected and stored.

After her Catholic education, Amalie had held her distance from the church for many years. But in 1786, after a longer stay in Münster and countless discussions with her religiously committed friends there, she returned to the Catholic Church. Her diaries and letters clearly show that the humility and subordination to the will of God that this required placed quite a demand on her as an active woman who strove for self-determination. But she remained true to her decision until the end of her life. Still today, her motives for this "return" to the Church are not entirely clear. In any case, her intensive Bible readings played a major part, and she immersed herself in them so she could educate her children in religion and at the same time be a role model again.

The princess was a devotee of the quiet, concentrated reading of religious texts in the effort to take in the word of God as directly as possible—and, on the other hand, she was a critical reader of such texts, including the Bible. In this respect, she can stand for the (not only religious) internalisation process of German intellectuals in the period around 1800, which she advanced both in her own way and through her example. This interiority and emotionality clearly come through in many of her letters. For example, Amalie Gallitzin reported on a conversation with Johann Georg Hamann, a Christian-philosophical author of the Lutheran faith who visited Münster in 1787, in which he moved her to tears with a Bible verse because she momentarily felt the presence of God.

The kind of interiority and soul-searching that marked the age of sentimentalism pervaded Amalie's diary and letters. Her private papers, now found in the library of the University of Münster, include some 2500 letters alone, which show that letters for her were an indispensable and direct medium in which she could also represent her sensitivity and self-reflection. In this respect, she does not stand out as an exception in her generation, for the second half of the eighteenth century in particular is indeed considered the "century of the letter", in which men and women used letters with great intensity to exchange ideas, develop self-images, and represent and live out their feelings. This development was related to the gradual formation of a modern individuality, as well as to the need of the educated classes to exchange ideas about knowledge, literature, and philosophy.

They strove for the ideal of a "natural" style of letter writing, and in this respect Amalie Gallitzin was highly skilled. Like few others, she managed in her correspondence to produce an equality and intimacy between the correspondents. While this was generally understood as a clear dissociation from the ceremonial and often very formal letter-writing style of earlier generations, for Amalie it was also a symbol for her own alienation from the court society into which she was born and where she spent the first decades of her life.

Along with her letters, her diaries too—which have survived for the period between 1783 and 1800—provide an opportunity to approach her world of ideas and emotions.[3] More so than the letters, Amalie's diaries served as a medium for self-exploration and religious observation, while everyday events tended to be considered as an aside. Despite her eloquence and literary expressiveness, Amalie Gallitzin evidently did not find it important to get involved in contemporary debates beyond her intimate circles. Only one of her writings was published during her lifetime, and this, moreover, under the name of her long-time spiritual advisor, Bernard Overberg.

In contrast, personal engagements and discussions with people whom she or other members of the Münster Circle valued were absolutely important to her. So in 1785, for example, she travelled with Fürstenberg and Hemsterhuis to Weimar to meet with Johann Wolfgang von Goethe, Johann Gottfried Herder, and other people from the group around Duke Karl August of Saxe-Weimar. In 1787 she visited Frankfurt am Main and Mainz, which was followed by a trip through northern Germany in 1793. And in Münster, visitors were regularly included in the social circle.

As an educated woman, but above all because of her unconventional lifestyle, Amalie was also seen and described as unusual by famous contemporaries. Thus after visiting Münster in the early 1790s, Goethe wrote, "She was one of those individuals whom one cannot imagine if one had not seen her, whom one could not properly assess if one had not observed this very individuality in connection and in conflict with her temporal environment."[4] He thereby conveyed both the princess's impact on her contemporaries and her lifelong controversial position as an independent woman.

Amalie Gallitzin died in 1806 in Münster after a long illness and was buried in the church cemetery in Angelmodde before the city gates. Excerpts from her correspondence and the first biographical sketches began appearing in the nineteenth century. These publications helped keep the memory of the princess alive—albeit a memory that has drawn widely different pictures of Amalie since her death.[5] In the nineteenth century she was pictured above all as a confessing Catholic with heroic, almost saint-like features; the Münster Circle was considered a return to religion after a phase of Enlightenment criticism. However, such portrayals had more to do with conflicts between Catholics and Protestants in the German Empire as opposed to actually doing justice to her person, for they only captured one facet of her life.

In later life, she was undoubtedly marked by a deep, very emotional and pronouncedly Catholic piety. But in general, one would need to remember her more in the way she characterised herself in 1786:

> In the seven years that I have been here [in Münster], my reputation has strangely changed. With regard to religion, I have been considered in turn: as a Greek,[6] an atheist, a deist, a Christian .... With regard to morals, in my first and second years I was considered as a cynic for the reason that I swim and let my children swim, and then again as a strict Pietist, after our swimming also led others to go swimming; as concerns my attitude towards love, I was considered ... as a Platonist, by others as foolish and moonstruck. As concerns philosophy, I was considered as a stoic, an Epicurean, a Leibnitzian, a Hemsterhuysian,[7] -ian, -ian, -ian, into infinity, one after another, and according to my manner, almost always as eccentric and foolish.[8]

With this she pointed to a central aspect of her person and life, to the discrepancy between her striving for an identity and a self-determined life and how she was perceived by her contemporaries. With this ambivalent position, as well as through her striving for self-determination, she also stands as an example for a generation of women around 1800 who broke out of traditional patterns, searched for their own life plans, and implemented them. They also included Dorothea Schlegel, for example, and Princess Dorothea of Courland. Gallitzin said herself that she was an "absurdity", a person who wrestled with her place in the gender order and the world, and who deliberately ignored conventions because she did not accept them. And, notwithstanding all of her deep friendships and regained Christian humility, she never hesitated to energetically argue for her position in debates and to demand what she considered proper and justified.

Contemporaries construed and described this as a "masculine" trait, but it reveals not only a woman who was searching for individuality and lived it, but also that the gender order was being rethought during the revolutionary period around 1800. Admittedly, this did not lead to a fundamental challenge to the traditional gender hierarchy. But women like Amalie Gallitzin made use of this (temporary) phase of the transformation and reconceptualisation of gender roles, while the princess's social position and financial independence provided her with additional freedoms.

Notes

1 Quoted in Schulz, *Gallitzin*, p. 172.
2 See especially the chapter on Henriette Herz.
3 Schlüter, C.B. (ed.) (1874–1876) *Briefwechsel und Tagebücher der Fürstin Amalie von Galitzin* (3 vols.). Münster: Russell.
4 Quoted in Trunz, E., and Loos, W. (eds.) (1971) *Goethe und der Kreis von Münster: Zeitgenössische Briefe und Aufzeichnungen*. Münster: Aschendorff, p. 141.
5 See Hänsel-Hohenhausen, M. (ed.) (2014) *Princess Amalie von Gallitzin: Significance and reception 1806–2006*. Translated by Bowles, L. Frankfurt am Main: August von Goethe Literaturverlag (with bibliography).
6 That is, as a member of the Russian Orthodox Church, which presumably was assumed because of her marriage to Prince Gallitzin.
7 Gottfried Wilhelm Leibniz, German philosopher and scholar of the early eighteenth century; Frans Hemsterhuis, Amalie's close friend, also published philosophical writings.
8 Quoted in Schulz, *Gallitzin*, p. 232.

Selected bibliography

Schulz, P., and Bell, E. (ed.) (1998) *Amalia Fürstin von Gallitzin (1748–1806): "meine Seele ist auf der Spitze meiner Feder"*. Münster: Ardey-Verlag.

MARIA THERESIA PARADIS (1759–1824)

The Blind Pianist

For a number of decades, the Vienna City Library has held a leather-bound book protected by a wooden case. It is a so-called *Stammbuch* (friendship book), hundreds of which exist in libraries and archives throughout the German-speaking world. Starting in the late sixteenth century, it was common among scholars and students, as well as in aristocratic circles, to carry a small book when travelling in which to record new acquaintances and famous contemporaries whom one visited. After these travellers returned home, they frequently continued to maintain their small albums and enjoyed showing them around. Often embellished with poems or drawings, the entries they contain thus document to this day the properly conducted and successful travels through which people made connections and met with renowned personalities of the times.[1]

What makes this *Stammbuch* special is that it was kept by a woman, which until into the nineteenth century happened far less frequently than one might think today, for women travelled much less often than men. Even more unusual is that the little book, with its entries from the period between 1774 and 1821, belonged to a blind woman who, as a musician, composer, and teacher achieved some celebrity among her contemporaries.

Maria Theresia Paradis was born in Vienna in spring 1759 as the daughter of an imperial official, Joseph Anton Paradis, and his wife, Rosalia Maria, a daughter of the imperial dance master, Thomas Levassori della Motta. At age three, the lively girl lost her sight, presumably due to an eye infection. Her worried parents

DOI: 10.4324/9781003252870-28

FIGURE 25.1 Wax portrait bust of Maria Theresia Paradis[2]

Wien Museum

Anonymus, Porträtbüste der Maria Theresia von Paradis, Wien Museum Inv. Nr. 76808, Bild: Tim Tom

had her treated by more or less famous doctors for years, with more or less drastic methods, but without any success. In fact, the treatments only weakened the patient's health and at times left her in chronic pain.

In 1777, her parents finally decided to entrust their daughter to Franz Anton Mesmer, a doctor who was famous but also controversial because of his theories and methods. He began attracting attention in Vienna in 1774 because of his treatments, which used magnetism as a healing method. He achieved several sensational successes with this approach but was fiercely criticised by contemporary proponents of conventional medicine and dismissed as a charlatan. Regardless of how his theory is judged, in the case of Maria Theresia Paradis, his treatment seemed quite successful at first. She probably regained some of her vision, but most significantly the twitching of her eyes substantially subsided. Because of the detailed reports by Mesmer, on the one hand, and Maria Theresia's father, on the other, today we can still trace the efforts to restore this young woman's eyesight.

However, the accounts emerged in the course of a veritable dispute that was fought first in the Viennese salons, then with the involvement of various other doctors, and finally in the arena of Vienna's broader public. Mesmer was suspected to be a fraud who even subjected his patient, who lived at his house for months, to violence. Consequently, Rosalia Paradis forced her way into Mesmer's house and brought her daughter home. As a result of the scandal, which was never resolved, Mesmer ultimately had to leave Vienna in 1777. The dramatic story, which to date constitutes the best-documented episode in the life of Maria Theresia Paradis, was also creatively retold in several literary accounts and movies.[3]

But Maria Theresia Paradis was known in Vienna long before these events—namely, as a musical child prodigy. That too was thanks to her parents, who endeavoured to support their daughter in every regard. Back then, providing an education for a sightless child was beset with major difficulties, for there were hardly any learning aids, and even today's widespread Braille system was not invented until 1825, shortly after Maria Theresia Paradis died. However, her father took the time—apparently this was possible for him as court secretary—to educate the girl himself. In so doing, he read aloud to her and had her trained through memorisation.

Evidently, this is how she became familiar with much of the modern literature of her times: she listened to her father read fables by Christian Fürchtegott Gellert, poems by Gottfried August Bürger, and novels by Sophie von La Roche. In addition, she learned the basics of French, understood Italian, and, by no later than her stay in London in 1784/85, spoke fluent English. However, for a blind person of the eighteenth century, learning how to write was naturally far more difficult than learning through listening. Maria Theresia Paradis benefited here from a mechanical writing machine she received in 1778/79 from its inventor, Wolfgang von Kempelen. With the machine, she could write letters herself by setting up a print template, which someone would print for her, and she would then "sign" using a name stamp. But she was also taught mathematics, geography, and history, effortlessly played the latest card games, was adept at various handicrafts, and enjoyed participating in dances where she was led by a partner, such as the minuet.

Thus, despite her disability, Maria Theresia Paradis received a diverse and decidedly status-appropriate education. Since such an education also properly included music, her pronounced musical talent quickly became apparent, which is why, to begin with, she learned to play the harpsichord as early as six or seven. Over the years, a long line of teachers, including Antonio Salieri, who would later become the imperial court composer and music director (Hofkapellmeister), opened the way for her to learn singing, harmony, and counterpoint. Maria Theresia learned the pieces by ear, as she herself described in 1780:

> I have two excellent grand pianos. Someone plays the pieces for me, and I try to play them back right away. One improves the fingering somewhat, and in one lesson I often learn one and a half solos without much effort ... My hearing is pretty accurate. I can rely on it more than on conducting by hand.[4]

She seems to have taken the stage in Vienna as a child prodigy as early as 1770 with piano and organ concerts, during which she also sang, although she was more of a virtuoso on instruments than as a singer. Her appearance in 1775 in the Augustinian Church in Vienna, the court chapel of the imperial house, also impressed her namesake, Empress Maria Theresa, who consequently offered Paradis a small annual pension that ensured a minimal livelihood.

The question of Maria Theresia's financial security seems have preoccupied the Paradis family, at least after the failure of the last attempt to heal her blindness. They now had to assume that, contrary to contemporary norms, she would never marry and in this way achieve long-term security. Instead, they envisaged a career for her as a musician. Her disability thus created for Maria Theresia the opportunity to work permanently as a musician, a prospect that remained closed to many women (one of the most well known was surely "Nannerl" Mozart) because after they married, they could only dedicate themselves to music as a pastime.

For musicians without any disability, it was clear that the basis for a successful career could only be established by extensive concert tours. They had to establish their intraregional fame by visiting larger cities that in the eighteenth century could support the development of their own musical culture, and by appearing at smaller and larger princely courts. If they were fortunate, they could then secure a stable income through gifts from patrons and income from concerts. Another option was a permanent position as a musician or singer at one of the princely court theatres—with the flourishing opera culture north of the Alps, such venues had steadily multiplied since the late seventeenth century, even in the Holy Roman Empire. But neither of these options could be easily realised for a blind pianist.

But the Paradis family would not be deterred by such difficulties, and they began planning a major concert tour of Europe. The preparations included having Maria Theresia's teacher, Leopold Koželuh, a respected teacher, pianist, and composer living in Vienna, write several piano concertos for his student, which she could perform at her concerts. Her father, Joseph Anton, obtained a letter of recommendation from the imperial state chancellor, Wenzel Anton von Kaunitz, which was supposed to ensure that the travellers received support from all of the imperial diplomats in the empire, France, and England. Then in August 1783, escorted by her mother and a violinist who accompanied her in concerts, Maria Theresia Paradis began her big tour. It led first to Salzburg, where the two women paid a visit to Leopold Mozart, perhaps not least to ask about his experiences from numerous concert tours in the 1760s with his children Wolfgang Amadeus and Nannerl (Maria Anna).

In autumn and winter 1783–1784, they moved on from Salzburg to many of the capitals of the Holy Roman Empire, including Würzburg, Mannheim, Koblenz, Karlsruhe, Stuttgart, and Munich, as well as to the large imperial cities of Frankfurt am Main, Regensburg, and Augsburg. Then they took the route via

Strasbourg, Colmar, and Switzerland to Paris, where Maria Theresia Paradis celebrated major successes from March to October 1784. From Paris, the small group travelled to London, and in March 1785 finally to Brussels, where Archduchess Marie Christine, a sister of Emperor Joseph II, held court as a governess. After another circuit through the capitals along the Rhine, they travelled via Darmstadt and Frankfurt am Main to the north. By way of Kassel, Göttingen, and Hanover, they reached Hamburg. From November 1785 to February 1786, Paradis gave concerts in Berlin, before the group returned via Leipzig, Dresden, and Prague to Vienna.

Along with various newspaper reports and several letters from third parties, the *Stammbuch* of Maria Theresia Paradis is an important source for the itinerary of the tour. It documents, for example, that she stayed in Mannheim three times, and from there visited Sophie von La Roche because she knew and appreciated her books. La Roche wrote about the visit in her journal *Pomona für Teutschlands Töchter*. Mannheim was also important to Paradis because here she met the musician and scientist Ludwig Weissenburg, who was also blind and with whom she had long been corresponding.[5]

Important to her in Paris, on the other hand, was her contact with the notable composer and music teacher Abbé Georg Joseph Vogler. She kept in touch with him afterwards and he would later count among her musical partners in Vienna. In Hamburg, the highly esteemed composer Carl Philipp Emanuel Bach and two famous contemporary poets, Friedrich Gottlieb Klopstock and Matthias Claudius, entered their names in her *Stammbuch*. In Berlin, she not only gave successful concerts at the court but through the recommendation of Fanny von Arnstein, one of the most important women of Viennese society, also found access to the home of the latter's parents, Daniel and Miriam Itzig. As a Jewish court factor, Daniel Itzig was one of Berlin's most affluent entrepreneurs, the elder of the Jewish community, and a close friend of Moses Mendelssohn.

These and many other examples provided by the *Stammbuch* show that Paradis gathered a multitude of contacts on her tour, some of which she cultivated for a longer period and no doubt added to her prominence. The concert tour was evidently also successful in financial terms, but above all it greatly enhanced Paradis's fame. And finally, Mannheim was where Maria Theresia Paradis met Johann Riedinger, the man with whom she would share her life. He accompanied her to some extent on her tour and then followed her to Vienna, where they lived together until Paradis died—albeit without ever getting married. It was also thanks to Riedinger's ingenuity that Paradis had access from the 1790s to a music typesetting machine,[6] which he had constructed for her. With it she could put her own compositions on paper and also study those by others, in that Riedinger or a student would transfer them to the music composition board.

Composing became more important to Maria Theresia Paradis after her return to Vienna, for she could further exploit her newly acquired European fame by selling sheet music. Her most well-known pieces were no doubt the *Zwölf Lieder auf ihrer Reise in Musik gesetzt* (Twelve songs set to music on her journey),[7] which she probably composed on her tour and were published by Breitkopf in Leipzig in 1786. In the following years and decades, Paradis also wrote choir music, cantatas, musical comedies, and operas (1797 *Rinaldo und Alcina*)—a contemporary praised her "inexhaustible wealth of ideas".[8] Although many of her works have been lost, a few are found in the archive of the Society of Friends of Music in Vienna.

After her journey, Maria Theresia rarely appeared in large concert halls, perhaps because, as also noted by a number of contemporaries, she felt insecure about the quality of her playing. On the other hand, she regularly performed concerts in smaller venues—for example, in Viennese salons such as those of Caroline Pichler or Fanny von Arnstein. There were also regular music events in the Paradis household itself, which continued to be held even after the death of her parents in 1794 and 1808, respectively. One can probably say that, on the basis of her musical talents and social skills, Maria Theresia Paradis established a musical salon that was frequented by Viennese music lovers and travellers alike. Many of these visitors entered their names into the aforementioned *Stammbuch*, which has therefore become an important source for studying the artist's social milieu after her return to

Vienna. At the same time, it shows that Maria Theresia Paradis remained an integral part of the diverse Viennese music scene of the late eighteenth and early nineteenth centuries.

In 1808, the year of her father's death, Paradis finally founded a music school, where she taught girls and boys, blind and sighted. Although she no doubt had taught individual students before, a substantial reason for institutionalising her teaching was economic in nature, for after her father's death Maria Theresia only had the small imperial annuity at her disposal. This and the income of her life partner, who worked at the customs office, were just barely enough to live on. That she also found teaching to be a source of great personal enrichment and joy is reflected not least by a description of the school routine, published in 1817 in the *Allgemeine musikalische Zeitung*.[9] Paradis was evidently very patient and had an intense, affectionate relationship with her students. Starting in 1809, regular student concerts took place at the Paradis household in the Rotenturmstraße, which saw the performance of works by Mozart, Salieri, Haydn, and Beethoven, as well as those by Johann Nepomuk Hummel, Ignaz Franz Pleyel, and Louis Emmanuel Jadin.

Maria Theresia Paradis died in winter 1824, after having written her will in 1821. Admittedly, she had no riches to allocate, for her financial situation remained rather constrained. Important to her, however, were the stipulation that she be interred in the grave of her father at the St. Marx Cemetery in Vienna, on the one hand, and the provisions she made for her housekeeper, Maria Anna Diwald, and for Paradis's life partner, Johann Riedinger, whom she named as sole heir. However, he essentially inherited debts, which he just barely managed to settle by selling the bequeathed music library.

Even while she was alive, Maria Theresia Paradis's fame and her work as a musician were based on the fact that she took an active part in social life as a blind person. Her professional life and her disability were always inextricable. However, in the nineteenth century she was remembered more as a pioneer in the education for the blind—a Viennese doctor who had dedicated himself to the support of the blind wrote the first biography about Paradis, a short text published in 1876. The first comprehensive treatment of her life and work as a composer did not appear until 1989 in the dissertation of the Japanese musicologist Hidemi Matsushita. In the wake of his study, the musical work of Paradis has (again) been taken into the canon of music history.

It is true that female composers had existed in the Holy Roman Empire prior to Paradis. But into the second half of the eighteenth century, these were predominantly woman of princely or aristocratic origin who never pursued composition as a way to earn their daily bread but rather as part of their status-appropriate education. They include Wilhelmine Friederike of Brandenburg-Bayreuth, for example, or Maria Antonia Walpurgis of Saxony. Professional singers and—in smaller numbers—instrumentalists, on the other hand, are known to have started appearing at the courts of the Holy Roman Empire in the sixteenth century. Among them, one could name Franziska Lebrun or Gertrud Elisabeth Mara, for example. But Maria Theresia Paradis was one of the first women in the empire who worked professionally as a musician and composer. Much more noteworthy, however, is that she managed, as a blind woman, to lead a largely self-determined life and, as a teacher, to pass the skills and attitudes this required on to others.

Notes

1 Wiener Stadt- und Landesbibliothek, Handschriftensammlung H.I.N.-92659: Stammbuch of Maria Theresia Paradis.
2 This object was acquired by a Nazi agency. Thus far it has not been possible to identify its previous owners.
3 See, for example, the novel *Am Anfang war die Nacht Musik* by Alissa Walser (2012), made into a movie entitled *Licht* (2017), and the opera *Maria Paradis* by Bo Holten (1999), the movie *Mesmer* by Roger Spottiswoode (1994), the novel *The Strange Case of Mademoiselle P.* by Brian O'Doherty (1992), and as early as 1931, Stefan Zweig's essay *Heilung durch den Geist*.
4 *Rheinische Beiträge zur Geschichte der Gelehrsamkeit* (1780), p. 245. Available at http://resolver.sub.uni-goettingen.de/purl?PPN 732374502
5 Durand, S. (2019) "Parole et musique d'aveugle. La correspondance de Maria-Theresia von Paradis (1759–1824) avec Johann-Ludwig Weissenburg (1752–1800)", in Roussel, C., and Vennetier, S. (eds.), *Discours et représentations du handicap: Perspectives culturelles*. Paris: Garnier, pp. 101–118.

6 For a description of this machine, see *Allgemeine musikalische Zeitung* (1810), no. 57. Available at https://alex.onb.ac.at/cgi-content/anno?aid=aml&datum=18101031&zoom=33
7 Today the sheet music is available online at https://imslp.org/wiki/12_Lieder_auf_ihrer_Reise_in_Musik_gesetzt_(Paradis%2C_Maria_Theresia_von)
8 "Fräulein Marie Therese Paradis: Eine biographische Skizze", *Wiener allgemeine musikalische Zeitung* (1813), no. 32, pp. 483–489, p. 496; see also no. 33, pp. 493–498. Available at https://archive.org/details/WienerAllgemeineMusikalischeZeitung1813/mode/2up?view=theater.
9 *Allgemeine musikalische Zeitung mit besonderer Rücksicht auf den österreichischen Kaiserstaat* (1817), no. 38, pp. 322–323. Available at https://anno.onb.ac.at/cgi-content/anno-plus?aid=amz&datum=1817&page=194&size=45

Selected bibliography

Fürst, M. (2005) *Maria Theresia Paradis: Mozarts berühmte Zeitgenossin*. Cologne: Böhlau.

Matsushita, H. (2006) "The Blind Composer Maria Theresia Paradis: Facts, Fictions, and Speculations", in Ostleitner, E., and Dorffer, G. (eds.), *"Ein unerschöpflicher Reichthum an Ideen ..." Komponistinnen zur Zeit Mozarts*. Vienna: Vier-Viertel-Verlag, pp. 29–39.

HENRIETTE HERZ (1764–1847)

A Salon in Berlin

Henriette de Lemos was born in 1764 into a Jewish family in Berlin. Her father Benjamin was a doctor in the city's Jewish community and came from Hamburg, where his ancestors had immigrated from Portugal. Her mother Esther de Charleville was, for her part, the daughter of a Jewish doctor. According to Henriette's own statements, her parental home was "fully set up according to Jewish laws and customs", but the girl nonetheless received lessons in piano playing, reading, writing, and arithmetic, and she learned Hebrew and French. Looking back, Henriette took a very critical view of the Jewish approach to raising girls, especially with regard to religion; but she herself received a very socially appropriate bourgeois education. She already had literary interests at an early stage, which manifested in an irrepressible passion for reading and was initially directed towards popular novels. This was theoretically forbidden to her as a Jewish girl, but her parents indulged her. With evenings spent reading aloud from books that Henriette brought from a lending library, they actually participated in her reading.[1]

In this respect, the de Lemos family can be considered representative of the small but culturally important segment of the educated Jewish middle class that was strongly influenced by the Enlightenment. In Henriette's youth, this group was experiencing a golden age in Berlin, associated in particular with the work of Moses Mendelssohn. Living in Berlin, the philosopher counted among the most renowned representatives of the empire's Jewish Enlightenment, the Haskalah. Educated people of Christian and

DOI: 10.4324/9781003252870-29

Jewish origin met in reading societies and discussion circles. This was linked to the gradual increase in the scope of action for men and women of the Jewish faith who, still prior to legal equality, sought acculturation in Christian society, which at the same time paved the way for Jewish emancipation in the future. Henriette was friends with Mendelssohn's daughter Brendel (later Dorothea) from childhood.

Notwithstanding the gradual transformation of the lifestyle of these enlightened Jewish citizens, Henriette was already engaged in a traditional manner at 12 years old (as had also been the case more than a century earlier with Glikl bas Judah Leib). At age 15, she married the substantially older Jewish doctor

FIGURE 26.1 Henriette Herz as a 15-year-old, portrayed as Hebe, the goddess of youth, 1778. This is a work by the painter Anna Dorothea Therbusch

Alamy

Anna Dorothea Therbusch, Henriette Herz dargestellt als Hebe, die griechische Göttin der Jugend, 1778, Berlin, Nationalgalerie

Markus Herz in autumn 1779. The vivacious Henriette hoped to thereby escape her strict and intolerant mother. The marriage her parents arranged for her proved to be sustainable: Herz treated Henriette affectionately and indulgently, providing her with diverse intellectual stimulation, and in this way participated in his young wife's further education. In the process, Henriette dealt with the natural sciences, among other things, but above all she learned languages. Despite their age gap and superficial differences, husband and wife seem to have had a harmonious relationship.

Whereas Markus Herz was rather small, his young wife was tall, lively, and extremely charming, and was considered a beauty from early on. This all led to a situation where above all older men, whom she met among her husband's acquaintances, quickly fell to her feet, but so too did the students who came to her husband's house for lessons. Already in her first year of marriage, Henriette effectively found herself pressured by the advances of various men and probably decided early on not to let herself be captivated by passions and to keep at a distance the men who idolised her.

This distinguished her from several of her adolescent girlfriends and acquaintances, who rebelled against the practice of parentally arranged marriages by divorcing or leaving their husbands. The fact that Henriette Herz came to terms with her marriage, however, does not mean that she unconditionally accepted all of the rules of Jewish life. This is demonstrated by her criticism of girlhood education, as well as by her persistent and ultimately successful struggle against the rules that allowed Jewish wives to leave the house only if they covered their hair—thus, they wore a hood or wig.

As a young wife, Henriette was able to visit literary-philosophical reading societies in other Jewish houses, which would not have been possible for her as a girl, and this definitely influenced her education and her attitude towards Jewish traditions. Among other things, she was regularly a guest of Moses Mendelssohn, about whom she later wrote, "Without even becoming aware of it, the interactions with this house no doubt had a very great influence on me, and the splendid Mendelsohn bore my youthful and truly boisterous gaiety with great patience."[2]

Her beauty, which was admired throughout her life[3] and which also played a major role in Henriette's memories of youth and her self-image and her literary and scholarly interests, as well as her innate social skills were important prerequisites for what is still today presented and remembered as the central aspect of the first half of her life, namely, her role in the "salon" at the Herz household. The heart of this social circle was the scholarly discussion group organised by Markus Herz, which primarily focused on philosophical subjects (Herz had studied with Immanuel Kant) and experimental physics. The group met mostly on Fridays at the Herz house, and the lectures and discussions acquired a bit of a reputation in Berlin society. Guests included not only scientists and philosophers but also, for example, the young Alexander and Wilhelm von Humboldt. Later their tutor also brought renowned scholars to the Herz household to expand the circle's education in the natural sciences.

Henriette wrote about the two Humboldts and the evolving social gatherings:

> They [Alexander and Wilhelm] already distinguished themselves very early on through their intellect and knowledge; they were lively, witty, courteous, and very likeable—and I often saw them with us—and certainly one evening each week in a reading society that had been arranged and which consisted of the brightest, most distinguished people back then ... and us associated women. ... In the summer we were in Bauer's garden, in the winter in the castle. We younger people played all kinds of games outside, which, however, were often joined by the older ones, but every time there was also reading, smaller and larger essays, theatrical things, etc., we women read too, and because I was beautiful, one also found that I read beautifully.[4]

This comment in Henriette's *Jugenderinnerungen* (Memories of youth) already implies that the socialising included men and women. However, it does not make clear that the initiative actually came from Henriette herself. In parallel with her husband's lectures, she invited people to tea, namely, her (mostly married) Jewish girlfriends, such as Dorothea (Brendel) Veit, née

Mendelssohn. They were joined by young aristocrats, including the Humboldts who initially played a special role, as well as by authors and visitors to the city. As alluded to in the quote, the evenings began with readings and the discussion of current literature at the tea table. Henriette quite clearly preferred the fashionable literary trend of *Sturm und Drang*, whereas her husband clung to somewhat older Enlightenment literature.

Along with having a passion for literature and the study of languages, Henriette was also interested in natural sciences, in which she was educated by her husband; she herself said that she had particularly applied herself to physics. For non-Jewish guests, the fact that a Jewish scholar with the title of privy counsellor (which Herz received in 1785 from the prince of Waldeck) was holding public lectures and gathering a scholarly discussion circle around him was intriguing in and of itself, but his beautiful young wife with her diverse interests was an even greater fascination. Where could one actually find a woman who enthusiastically studied foreign languages and thus in her way could take on a linguistically gifted young man such as Wilhelm von Humboldt?

Thus, even as a young woman, Henriette Herz became the focal point of a social circle in Berlin that today is mostly referred to as a "salon". Characteristic of these salons was that people regularly met once or several times a week in a private home, although the participants changed. They usually featured the shared reading or reading aloud of literary, philosophical, or scientific texts, but most important was the discussion—the extensive, spirited discussion about the widest range of topics.

In Berlin and Vienna around 1800, it was notably several Jewish women who gathered such groups around themselves as meeting places for Jewish and Christian, aristocratic and bourgeois persons of both sexes. These "Jewish" salons only flourished for the relatively brief period of a few decades, effectively like an "experimental" open society, which on a large scale would admittedly still be a long time coming. Yet even though women often acted as hosts and initiators of these social circles, this does not mean that they played a decisive role in salons in terms of arranging or dominating the debates. This applied not only to Henriette Herz but also to Amalie Gallitzin in Münster and Henriette's girlfriend, the famous Berlin salonnière Rahel Varnhagen, as well as to the glamorous Dorothea of Courland and to Fanny von Arnstein, who hosted a salon in Vienna but was actually from Berlin.

The salon was not an emancipatory project in the sense of gender equality. Instead, it was a place where women and men, aristocrats and bourgeoisie, Christians and Jews came together outside family ties for discussions and intellectual exchange. But this commonality alone was already seen by contemporaries as an innovation, for just a few decades earlier general doubts about women's educability had still prevailed,[5] not to mention the marginalised position of Jewish women back then.

This commonality was especially pronounced at times in the "League of Virtue" that emerged from Henriette's salon, founded in 1789 by Henriette Herz, Dorothea (Brendel) Veit-Mendelssohn, Wilhelm von Humboldt, and around a dozen other people, including Carl von La Roche, the son of the writer Sophie von La Roche. Its members were supposed to be bound to one another in love and equality. However, the experiment soon came to an end because Wilhelm von Humboldt gradually distanced himself from Henriette Herz, and by the time of his marriage in 1791 to Caroline von Dacheröden, who also belonged to the League of Virtue, the group had fallen apart.

The "salon" in the Herz household survived, however, and repeatedly brought Henriette into contact with literati, scientists, and philosophers, including those who were just passing through Berlin. This is how she met the theologian and philosopher Friedrich Schleiermacher in 1794, with whom she would have a close, trusting friendship until his death in 1834. Like Amalie Gallitzin, in Henriette's case too, her personal connection with Schleiermacher led to long-standing assumptions and suspicions about their relationship, but for the rest of their lives both Henriette and Schleiermacher insisted they were joined by a purely platonic yet all the more heartfelt friendship. In 1798, for example, they spent the summer together in a house in the Berlin Tiergarten, where she taught him Italian and he taught her Greek; they read Shakespeare and contemporary German literature. Schleiermacher's essay *Toward a Theory of Sociable Conduct*, published in 1799, should also be read as the product of this commonality.

The close connection to Schleiermacher no doubt helped Henriette Herz overcome her husband's death in 1803. The passing of Markus Herz not only meant the loss of a long-time confidant, it also had serious consequences for her social position. She now had to live as a widow from his pension as a professor and at the same time provide for her mother and an unmarried sister. This also meant the end of her salon, since a prerequisite for this type of sociability was not least the ability to finance it. Her situation grew even worse in 1806, when, as a result of Prussia's collapse after being defeated by French troops under Napoleon, the pension was no longer paid.

To be sure, conviviality remained an important part of Henriette Herz's daily life, but she now had to pay more attention to functionally structuring her affairs and to her financing. To this end, she decided to work as a teacher or educator. This was unusual and courageous because, as a Jewess, she faced many restrictions in this regard, and affluent families who could afford a tutor often backed off from her, no doubt because of her religious affiliation.

Charlotte von Kathen, however, who had a friendly relationship with Herz, hired her as a teacher for her children, despite social opposition. Hence, as of 1807 Henriette Herz lived for some time on the island of Rügen. She worked as a teacher afterwards, as well, above all teaching languages, and also philanthropically looked after the upbringing and care of young girls and students without means. However, until now her work as an educator and translator (at Schleiermacher's suggestion) has been much less well known than her role as a salonnière.

The anxious years of the Napoleonic Wars were also reflected in Henriette's biography. After her time on the Baltic Sea, she returned to Berlin in 1809. In 1811, she stayed in Vienna for several months with Fanny von Arnstein, a childhood friend from Berlin who in the meantime had come to run the imperial capital's most important salon and who was one of the few Jewish women accepted into high-aristocratic society. Then during the Wars of Liberation, Henriette worked together with Rahel Levin (soon to be Varnhagen von Ense) in a military hospital in Wrocław (Breslau).

Herz took a personally very decisive step in 1817 when she converted to Christianity[6] by having herself baptised according to the Lutheran rite. This move had been in preparation for a long time—Schleiermacher's *On Religion: Speeches to its Cultured Despisers*, published in 1799, played a major role here. But Herz did not convert until after her mother's death and, in a certain sense, she thereby sealed her own independent religious development. She undoubtedly retained her ideas on religious tolerance in the Enlightenment tradition, but her need for religious sentiment was probably what ultimately led her to take this step. As Henriette herself wrote:

> Reason, which the more educated take as support and aid, is not sufficient to carry them in severe suffering. Happy is the one for whom, later in life, the beautiful light of faith arises within, and who does not die without having been permeated by that sublime, exhilarating feeling of devotion—it is thanks to God's grace that this blessedness also became mine.[7]

To understand this decision, it is important to consider that, by converting, Henriette Herz took a step that many other women of Berlin's enlightened Jewish society had already taken before her, including her friend Dorothea Schlegel-Veit-Mendelssohn. Furthermore, the decision reflected the general post-1815 Zeitgeist, shaped by Romanticism, in which the return to faith played a significant role.

Her conversion in 1817 was also the prelude to a long-desired educational journey to Italy. She travelled to Rome via Nuremberg, Munich, Verona, Venice, and Florence, accompanied by a girlfriend. Henriette Herz then sojourned in Rome for around one and a half years, where she met several old acquaintances, including Dorothea Schlegel, with whom she jointly ran another (small) salon, meeting once again at the tea table. Aside from that, she also had contact with numerous German artists in Rome, who belonged to the new romantic-religious "Nazarene" art movement. Not until 1819, after having accompanied the famous Danish sculptor Bertel Thorwaldsen to Naples, did she travel over Switzerland, Stuttgart, and Bonn back to Berlin.

In her later years, she continued pursuing her charitable work in Berlin and was frequently a guest of Rahel Varnhagen at her salon but, in the end, she outlived almost all of her friends from the days of her own salon. Henriette Herz died in October 1847 in Berlin at an advanced age.

Henriette Herz's enduring familiarity and the intensive preoccupation with her are based not least on her ostensible memoirs,[8] which appeared in print in 1858. Their authenticity is more than debatable today, but the text certainly helped keep alive the memory of Herz's role in Berlin society of the late eighteenth century. Quite a few of her letters have survived, although they were very dispersed in various private archives; she herself destroyed most of her correspondence. The fragment of her memories of youth, which was not published until later, is the only larger continuous text that we still have by Herz, if one disregards two texts she translated from English.[9]

She is still remembered today as one of Berlin's first salonnières[10] and as an inspirational friend or at least discussion partner of notable poets, literati, painters, and philosophers, as well as a symbolic figure for "the" Jewish salon of the period around 1800. Only recently has it been pointed out that Henriette Herz was clearly more than that, namely, also a teacher and translator. However, this aspect of her career, and thus above all the second half of her life, still largely needs to be explored.

Notes

1 Hahn, H. (ed.) (1896) "Jugenderinnerungen von Henriette Herz", *Mittheilungen aus dem Litteraturarchive in Berlin* 5, pp.141–184, p. 151. Available at http://sophie.byu.edu/sections/jugenderinnerungen-von-henriette-herz.
2 Hahn, "Jugenderinnerungen", p. 179.
3 Goozé, M. (2003) "Posing for posterity: The representations and portrayals of Henriette Herz as 'beautiful Jewess'", in Henn, M., and Pausch H.A. (eds.), *Body Dialectics in the Age of Goethe*. Amsterdam: Rodopi, pp. 67–95.
4 Hahn, "Jugenderinnerungen", p. 182.
5 See for example the chapter on Dorothea Erxleben.
6 For detail on this, see Hertz, D. (2017) "Henriette Herz as Jew, Henriette Herz as Christian: Relationships, Conversion, Antisemitism", in Lund and Schneider, *Henriette Herz*, pp. 117–139.

7 Hahn, "Jugenderinnerungen", p. 148.
8 Fürst, J. (ed.) (1858) *Henriette Herz: Ihr Leben und ihre Erinnerungen*. Berlin.
9 Park, M. (1799) *Reise in das Innere von Afrika*, Berlin: Haude and Spener 1799; Weld, I. (1800) *Reisen durch die Vereinigten Staaten von Nord-Amerika*. Berlin: Oehmigke.
10 Schmitz, R. (ed.) (2013) *Henriette Herz in Erinnerungen, Briefen und Zeugnissen*. Berlin: Die Andere Bibliothek.

Selected bibliography

Hertz, D. (2005) *Jewish High Society in Old Regime Berlin*. Syracuse, NY: Syracuse University Press.

Lund, H.L., Schneider, U., and Wels, U. (eds.) (2017) *Die Kommunikations-, Wissens- und Handlungsräume der Henriette Herz (1764–1847)*. Göttingen: V&R Unipress.

INDEX

Aachen 269
Acquaviva d'Aragona, Andrea Matteo (c. 1570–1634) 108
Acquaviva d'Aragona, Franziska of (1569–1626) 108
Aesop (c. 620–564 BC) 83
Africa 16, 66, 153, 251
Agathenburg (manor) 179, 182, 185
Alba Iulia 100
Albert I of Prussia, Duke (1490–1568) 77–8, 115
Albert II Frederick of Prussia, Duke (1553–1618) 115–18
Albert V of Bavaria, Duke (1528–1579) 94–5, 125
Alberti, Michael (1682–1757) 224
Albrecht of Brandenburg, Elector of Mainz (1490–1545) 72
Allgäu 259
Alps 70, 281
Alsace 14, 52
Altenhohenau (abbey) 131–32
Altona 159
Amalie Elisabeth of Hessen-Kassel, Landgravine (1602–1651) 33
Americas 16, 26, 63, 153, 155, 251, 265
Amsterdam 148, 150, 152–56, 161–62
Amstetten 137

Andernach, Felicitas von (d. 1562) 57
Angelmodde 270, 274
Anhalt, House of 111
Anna Dorothea of Saxe-Weimar, Abbess of Quedlinburg (1657–1704) 181, 184
Anna Elisabeth Luise of Brandenburg-Schwedt (1738–1820) 268–69
Anna Maria of Prussia, Duchess (1532–1568) 72, 77
Anna Maria of Württemberg, Duchess (1526–1589) 91
Anna of Austria, Duchess of Bavaria (1528–1590) 94
Anna of Austria, Queen of Poland (1573–1598) 97, 99–100
Anna of Bohemia and Hungary, Queen (1503–1547) 61–2, 236
Anna of Brandenburg, Electress (1576–1625) 10–1, 19, 33, 88, 115–24, 229, 236
Anna of Denmark *see* Anna of Saxony
Anna of Palatinate-Neuburg, Duchess (1552–1632) 118
Anna of Prussia *see* Anna of Brandenburg
Anna of Saxe-Coburg, Duchess (1567–1613) 84

Anna of Saxony, Electress (1532–1585) 11, 19, 23, 27, 30–1, 33, 83–92, 94
Anna Sophie of Saxony, Electress (1647–1717) 182
Annaburg 86, 89–90
Antoinette Amalie of Brunswick-Bevern, Duchess (1696–1762) 236
Anton Ulrich of Brunswick-Wolfenbüttel, Duke (1633–1714) 144
Arndt, Johann (1555–1621) 259
Arnim, Bettina (Elisabeth Catharina) von (1785–1859) 263
Arnold, Christoph (1650–1695) 201
Arnstein, Fanny von (1758–1818) 282–83, 292–93
artists: literature 23, 159, 137–47, 179, 210–17, 259–67; music 23, 28, 70, 277–85; painting 23–4, 148–57, 178, 217, 238–47, 255, 294
Asia 63
Auernhammer, Josepha Barbara (1758–1820) 33
Augsburg 2, 12, 17, 27, 30–1, 56, 86–7, 210, 250–55, 260, 281
August of Saxony, Elector (1526–1586) 27, 84, 86–8
Augustusburg 86
Austria 93–101, 137, 139–41, 144, 146, 173, 227, 235

Bach, Carl Philipp Emanuel (1714–1788) 282
Baltic Sea 30, 161, 210, 293
Bamberg 162
Bassi Veratti, Laura (1711–1778) 224
Bavaria 4, 94, 100, 125, 127, 132–33, 135
Bayle, Pierre (1647–1706) 213
Becker-Cantarino, Barbara 142
Beethoven, Ludwig van (1770–1827) 284

Beila bas Nathan Melrich (d. 1704) 159
Belgrade 62
Berka z Dubá, Zbyněk, Archbishop of Prague (1551–1606) 111
Berlin 17, 21, 120, 122, 162–63, 185–86, 200, 203, 205–06, 224–25, 238–42, 244–46, 268–69, 282, 287, 290–95
Berlin, Judah 164
Bethmann, Elise (Katharina Elisabeth) von (1753–1813) 264
Bianconi, Giovanni Ludovico (1717–1781) 260
Biberach 260–61
Binche 69–70
Birken, Sigismund von (1626–1681) 137, 139–45
Blankenburg (duchy) 231
Block, Agneta (1629–1704) 156
Bohemia 10, 15–6, 20, 28–9, 31, 56, 61–3, 105–13, 173, 228, 231–33
Bonn 294
Bora, Katharina von see Luther
Bordeaux 266
Brandenburg 10, 15, 75, 115, 117–21, 123, 178, 185, 222, 236
Brandenburg-Bayreuth (margraviate) 141
Bratislava (Pressburg) 62–3, 140–41
Brean, Franz Xaver SJ (1678–1735) 175
Breidbach zu Bürresheim, Emmerich Joseph von, Elector of Trier (1707–1774) 261
Breisgau 54
Brentano, Clemens Wenzeslaus (1778–1842) 263
Brentano, Pietro Antonio (1735–1797) 263, 265
Brunswick 162–63
Brussels 29, 61, 64–6, 68–70, 244, 282

Bucer, Martin (1491–1551) 60
Buda 62
Bugenhagen, Johannes (1485–1558) 83, 86
Bürger, Gottfried August (1747–1794) 279
Burgundy (duchy) 11, 61, 63

Caetani, Enrico, Cardinal (1550–1599) 98
Calenberg (duchy) 72, 75–7
Caligari, Giovanni Andrea, papal Nuntio (1527–1613) 94
Calvinism 18–9, 110, 121–22
Capito, Agnes (d. 1531) 54
Capito, Wolfgang (1478–1541) 54, 56
Caribbean 16
Carinthia 95
Castell, Counts of 10
Catherine II (the Great), Czarina (1729–1796) 245, 269
Catholic confession 18, 20–1, 28, 33, 56, 75, 77–8, 94–6, 98–101, 105, 108–09, 111–13, 122, 127–30, 137, 143, 169, 250, 260, 268, 272, 275
Catholic reform 18, 79, 94–6, 101, 112–13, 127–30
Celtis, Conrad (1459–1508) 43
Chajim ben Joseph (d. 1689) 31, 160–62, 164
Chambord 183
Charlemagne, Emperor (747–814) 130
Charles V, Holy Roman Emperor (1500–1558) 11, 16, 27, 56, 61, 63–70, 75, 77, 79
Charles VI, Holy Roman Emperor (1685–1740) 10–1, 170, 174, 227–28, 230–31
Charles VII Albert, Elector of Bavaria, Holy Roman Emperor (1697–1745) 231
Charles XI King of Sweden (1655–1697) 180
Chiemgau 131
Chiemsee (lake) 125, 127

Christian I of Anhalt-Bernburg, Prince (1568–1630) 110
Christian I of Saxony, Elector (1560–1591) 84
Christian II King of Denmark (1481–1559) 68
Christian II of Anhalt-Bernburg, Prince (1599–1656) 110–11
Christian II of Saxony, Elector (1583–1611) 118
Christian III King of Denmark (1503–1559) 83
Christian of Brandenburg-Bayreuth, Margrave (1581–1655) 116
Christiane Eberhardine of Saxony, Electress and Queen of Poland (1671–1727) 182
Christine Luise of Brunswick-Wolfenbüttel-Blankenburg, Duchess (1671–1747) 230–31
Christine of Lorraine, Duchess (1521–1590) 67, 69
Cigalés 70
Clark, Christopher 123
Claudia Felicitas, Holy Roman Empress (1653–1676) 168, 170
Claudius, Matthias (1740–1815) 282
Clemens Wenzeslaus of Saxony, Elector of Trier (1739–1812) 263, 265
Clement VIII, Pope (1536–1590) 100
Cleves (duchy) 65–66
Cochin, Charles-Nicolas (1715–1790) 242
Colmar 282
Cologne 7, 64, 256
Commelin, Caspar (1668–1731) 153
confessions see catholic confession, Lutheran confession, Calvinists, Moravian church, Pietism
Contarini, Gasparo (1483–1542) 62

Copenhagen 83, 85–6, 161–62, 200
coronation 2–3, 62, 84, 86, 109, 231–33
correspondence 12, 22, 28–9, 43–4, 57, 59, 65–6, 68, 77–8, 85, 87–8, 99, 110, 119–20, 129, 135, 137, 139, 145, 170–171, 174, 211–13, 217, 266, 273–75, 285, 295
Corvinus, Antonius (1501–1553) 76
Cosimo II de' Medici, Grand Duke of Tuscany (1590–1621) 100
Cosmerovius, Susanna (d. 1702) 256
Counter Reformation *see* catholic reform
Courland 183

Dacheröden, Caroline von (1766–1829) 292
Darmstadt 282
daughter-heir *see* heiress
Dawson, Ruth 25
Denmark and Norway (kingdom) 16, 68, 72, 80, 86–7, 89, 159–60
Diderot, Denis (1713–1784) 242–43, 269
diets *see* territorial estates or imperial estates
Diwald, Maria Anna 284
Dorothea Biron of Courland (1761–1821) 275, 292
Dorothea of Brunswick-Lüneburg-Celle, Duchess (1546–1617) 83
Dorothea of Brunswick-Wolfenbüttel, Duchess (1563–1587) 84
Dorothea of Denmark (1520–1580) 67
Dorothea of Denmark, Queen (1511–1571) 83, 86
Dorothea of Prussia, Duchess (1504–1547) 91

Dorothea Sophie of Parma, Duchess (1670–1748) 172
Dresden 28, 84–5, 88, 181–83, 185–86, 269, 282
Dürer, Albrecht (1471–1528) 43, 50
Düsseldorf 116, 169, 171
Dynasty 9–11, 63–4, 69, 97, 99, 116–17, 123, 168–70, 176, 228–29, 232, 236

Ebersdorf 21, 193–94, 197–98
education 5, 7, 21–7, 41–2, 58–9, 83, 97, 106, 122, 125, 138, 143, 145, 148–50, 170, 178, 182, 192, 194, 197, 205–07, 210–11, 214, 216–17, 219–24, 228, 235, 238–39, 246–47, 259–61, 264, 268–70, 272, 279, 280, 284–85, 287, 289–90, 294
Ehrenbreitstein 262, 266
Eichstätt 41
El Escorial 70
elector, electorate 2–3, 9–10, 14, 80, 84–5, 87–8, 115, 120, 123, 127, 171, 173–75, 231–33, 260
Eleonora Gonzaga-Nevers, Holy Roman Empress (1630–1686) 170–71
Eleonora Magdalena of Palatinate-Neuburg *see* Eleonora Magdalena, Empress
Eleonora Magdalena, Holy Roman Empress (1655–1720) 1–3, 11, 16, 33, 168–77, 184
Eleonora of France, Queen (1498–1558) 68–70
Eleonore of Brandenburg, Electress (1583–1607) 116
Elisabeth Amalie of the Palatinate, Electress (1635–1709) 168–70
Elisabeth Christine, Holy Roman Empress (1691–1750) 227–28
Elisabeth of Brandenburg *see* Elisabeth of Brunswick-Calenberg

Elisabeth of Brandenburg, Electress (1485–1555) 72–3, 80
Elisabeth of Brunswick-Calenberg, Duchess (1510–1558) 11, 19, 72–82, 96
Elisabeth of France, Queen (1554–1592) 108
Elisabeth of Henneberg (1526–1566) 72
Elisabeth of Palatinate-Simmern (1552–1590) 84, 86
Elizabeth I of England (1533–1603) 94
Emser, Hieronymus (1478–1527) 45
England 28, 30, 63, 65, 210, 251, 265, 281
Enlightenment 21–8, 203, 210–13, 216–17, 221–22, 225, 245, 261–62, 264, 269, 271–72, 275, 287–88, 291, 294
Epidemics 16, 28, 55, 91, 132–33
Erasmus of Rotterdam (1466–1536) 43
Erbach, Counts of 10
Erdmuthe Benigna of Reuß-Ebersdorf (1670–1732) 11, 21, 191–99
Erich I of Brunswick-Calenberg, Duke (1470–1540) 72–3, 75, 77, 80–1
Erich II of Brunswick-Calenberg, Duke (1528–1584) 72, 75, 77–9, 81
Ernst August of Brunswick-Hanover, Elector (1629–1698) 181
Erxleben, Dorothea Christiane (1715–1762) 17–8, 23–4, 208, 219–26
Erxleben, Johann Christian (1697–1759) 223, 225–26
Essen 15
Ettal (abbey) 132
Europe 1, 3, 7, 10, 13–7, 21–2, 26, 29–30, 49, 68, 113, 115, 123, 133, 153, 156, 163, 171–72, 180, 185–86, 224, 227–28, 230–32, 235–36, 281, 283

female regency 11, 61, 64–6, 73–8, 97, 173–74, 194–98
Ferdinand Albrecht II of Brunswick-Bevern, Duke (1680–1735) 236
Ferdinand I, Holy Roman Emperor (1503–1564) 27, 61, 63, 65–8, 75, 94, 116
Ferdinand II, Holy Roman Emperor (1578–1637) 20, 95, 97–101, 108–11, 126, 137
Ferdinand Maria of Bavaria, Elector (1636–1679) 126
Ferrara 100
Feuerstein, Martin OSB 129
Florence 100, 230, 294
Fonte, Moderata (1555–1592) 8
France 14, 16, 23, 28, 63, 65–6, 69, 165, 169, 183, 197, 224, 230, 235, 242, 251, 264, 281
Francis I of France, King (1494–1547) 68–9
Francis I of Lorraine, Duke (1517–1545) 69
Francis I Stephan, Holy Roman Emperor (1708–1765) 229–35
Francke, August Hermann (1663–1727) 197, 202–03, 259
Frankfurt am Main 9, 12, 21, 27, 30, 86, 109, 148, 150–52, 159, 162, 191–92, 198, 210, 231–32, 263, 265, 274, 281–82
Franz Ludwig of Palatinate-Neuburg, Bishop of Breslau (1664–1732) 171
Frauenaurach 141
Frauenchiemsee 19, 125–35
Frederick II of Prussia, King (1712–1786) 215, 222, 224–25, 227, 230, 245
Fredrick III of Brandenburg, Elector and King of Prussia (1657–1713) 2, 184–85, 203
Friedrich August I of Saxony, Elector and King of Poland (1670–1733) 182–84, 186
Friedrich August of Anhalt-Zerbst, Prince (1734–1793) 238

Friedrich I of Denmark, King (1471–1533) 83
Friedrich I of Prussia, King *see* Friedrich III of Brandenburg
Friedrich II of Denmark, King (1534–1588) 83, 87, 94
Fürstenberg, Albrecht von (1557–1599) 108
Fürstenberg, Elisabeth von (1557–1610) 108
Fürstenberg, Franz Friedrich Wilhelm von (1729–1810) 271–72, 274
Fürstenberg, Vratislav von (1584–1631) 108
Fyodor I Ivanovich, Czar (1557–1598) 100

Gallitzin, Amalie (1748–1806) 21, 23, 26–8, 33, 268–76, 291–92
Gallitzin, Dmitri (1770–1840) 269–70
Gallitzin, Dmitri Alexeievich (1728–1803) 244–45, 269–71
Gallitzin, Marianne (1769–1823) 269
Gandersheim, Hrotsvitha von (c. 935–973) 43
Gans von Putlitz, Adam (c. 1562– c. 1621) 120
Gars (abbey) 132
Gasc, Anna Rosina de *see* Matthieu
Gasc, Ludwig de (1718–1793) 238
Gdańsk (Danzig) 161, 206, 210–11
Gellert, Christian Fürchtegott (1715–1769) 279
gender, gender roles 3–9, 24–5, 59, 80–1, 140–42, 145–46, 150, 153, 163–64, 168, 172–76, 180, 182, 186, 205, 207, 211–13, 216, 221, 231–33, 240–42, 247, 266, 270, 275–76, 292
gender guardianship 4, 6, 55–6, 195–96, 253

Geneva 250
Georg Friedrich of Brandenburg-Ansbach, Markgrave (1539–1603) 116
Georg Ludwig of Brunswick-Hanover, Elector (1660–1727) 172–73
George Sand (Amantine Aurore Lucile Dupin de Francueil) (1804–1876) 186
George William of Brandenburg, Elector (1595–1640) 119, 122
German Empire 275
Ghent 66
Gignoux, Anna Barbara (1725–1796) 31, 249–58
Gignoux (Emmerich), Felicitas Barbara (1751–1814) 251, 253, 255
Gignoux, Jean François (1691–1761) 250, 252
Gignoux, Johann Friedrich (1724–1760) 31, 250–52, 255
Gignoux, Johann Friedrich (d. 1777) 251, 253–54
Gleich, Anna Barbara *see* Gignoux, Anna Barbara
Gleich, Georg Christoph 31, 250, 252–55
Glikl bas Judah Leib (c. 1647–1724) 27, 31, 158–67, 256, 288
Goethe, Johann Wolfgang von (1749–1832) 28, 260, 262, 265–66, 274
Gohl, Johann Christian (1743–1825) 246
Gomperz, Kosman (d. 1730) 163
Gonzaga di Castiglione, Bibiana of (1579–1616) 108
Gonzaga di Castiglione, Francesco (1577–1616) 108
Gonzaga di Castiglione, Giovanna (1612–1688) 111
Göttingen 76, 222, 282
Gottsched, Johann Christoph (1700–1766) 27, 210–17

Gottsched, Luise Adelgunde (1713–1762) 17, 24, 27, 29, 33, 209–18, 227, 233, 266
Graff, Dorothea Maria (1678–1743) 149, 151–55
Graff, Johann Andreas (1637–1701) 149, 151–52
Graff, Maria Sibylla *see* Merian, Maria Sibylla
Graz 20, 93–9, 101
Great Britain 16, 23
Gregory XIII, Pope (1502–1585) 96
Greiffenberg, Anna Regina von (d. 1651) 137, 139
Greiffenberg, Catharina Regina von (1633–1694) 16, 20, 23, 28, 137–47
Greiffenberg, Eva Maria von (d. 1675) 28, 138–40, 143–45
Greiffenberg, Hans Rudolph von (c. 1606–1677) 138–43
Greiffenberg, Johann Gottfried von (1575–1641) 137–38
Großenhain 254
Grumbach, Argula von (1492–1554) 58
Gsell, Georg (1673–1740) 155
Gstadt am Chiemsee 127, 132
Guben 202–03
Guelders (duchy) 16, 65
Guild 5, 7, 9, 30–1, 250–51
Gustav II Adolf of Sweden, King (1594–1632) 122, 131
Güstrow 86
Gutermann, Georg Friedrich von (1705–1784) 259–60
Gutermann, Regina Barbara von (d. 1748) 259–60
Gutermann, Sophie von *see* La Roche, Sophie von

Habsburg Hereditary Lands 11, 15–6, 143–44, 174, 228, 230, 232
Habsburg, House of 10, 11, 15, 20, 64, 68–70, 97, 99, 101, 105, 168, 172–74

Hackert, Jakob Philipp (1737–1807) 245
Haderslev 83
Haidenbucher, Maria Cleophe OCist (1576–1657) 125, 131–33
Haidenbucher, Maria Magdalena (Salome) OSB (1576–1650) 17, 19, 125–36
Haidenbucher, Reinhard (d. 1585) 125
Halle 197–98, 202–03, 208, 222, 224
Hamann, Johann Georg (1730–1788) 273
Hamburg 30, 144, 158–65, 178, 180, 185, 244, 257, 282, 287
Hamburger, Mordechai (c. 1660–c. 1730) 161
Hameln 76, 160
Hameln Goldschmidt, Löb (c. 1673–1701) 164–65
Hameln Goldschmidt, Mordechai (c. 1670–1709) 162
Hameln Goldschmidt, Nathan (c. 1663–1744) 163–64
Hannoversch Münden 74–6, 78–81
Hanover 28, 80, 180–82, 206, 282
Hanseatic towns, Hanseatic League 4, 30, 159, 161, 210, 250–51, 254–55
Harrach, Ernst Adalbert von, Archbishop of Prague (1598–1667) 112
Harz 181, 219
Haskalah 26, 287
Haslang, noble family 135
Haydn, Joseph (1732–1809) 284
Hedio, Caspar (1494–1552) 73
Hedio, Margarethe 55
Heinrich Julius of Brunswick-Wolfenbüttel, Duke (1564–1613) 84
Heinrich the Younger of Brunswick-Wolfenbüttel, Duke (1489–1568) 74–5, 77, 80

Heiresses 10, 115–19, 123, 162, 227, 229–30, 234–36
Hemsterhuis, Franz (1721–1790) 271, 274–75
Henckel, Johannes (d. 1559) 64
Hendriks, Philipp (d. 1711) 154
Henneberg, Elisabeth of *see* Elisabeth of Brunswick-Calenberg
Henneberg, Poppo XII of (1513–1574) 78–81
Henry II of France, King (1519–1559) 69
Herberstein, Georg von (1529–1580) 94
Herder, Johann Gottfried (1744–1803) 260, 274
Herolt, Jacob Hendrik (c. 1660–1715) 154
Herolt, Johanna Helena (1668–1730) 149, 151–52, 154–55
Herrenchiemsee (abbey) 128, 132, 134–35
Herrnhut 198
Herschel, Caroline Lucretia (1750–1848) 206
Herz, Henriette (1764–1847) 17, 21, 23, 26–7, 29, 33, 287–96
Herz, Markus (1747–1803) 288–91, 293
Hessen (landgraviate) 76, 192
Hoffmann, Johann Heinrich (1669–1716) 205
Höfler, Konstantin (1811–1897) 49
Hohberg, Wolf Helmhard von (1612–1688) 144
Hohenfeld, Christoph Philipp von (d. 1822) 263
Hohenlohe, Counts of 10
Hohenlohe-Langenburg, Anna of (1522–1594) 89, 91
Hohenlohe-Langenburg, Magdalena of (1547–1633) 91
Hohenzollern, House of 10, 15, 115–117, 120–123
Hohnstein, Wilhelm von, Bishop of Strasbourg (c. 1470–1541) 54

Holland 152, 162, 164, 197, 251, 265
Holy Roman Empire, institutions 2–3, 9, 12–5, 79, 97, 109, 174, 176, 184, 225
Holzen (abbey) 131
Horn, Claes Gustav (c. 1663) 180–81
household 5, 6, 8–9, 42, 53–5, 60, 86, 112, 142, 153, 160, 165, 192, 194, 207, 212, 223, 239, 251, 253, 259, 283–84, 290, 292
housewife 6, 9, 33, 53, 88, 91, 109–10, 142, 149, 160, 194, 223–24, 239
humanism 21–3, 41–4, 47, 49
Humboldt, Alexander von (1769–1859) 290–91
Humboldt, Wilhelm von (1767–1835) 290–92
Hummel, Johann Nepomuk (1778–1837) 284
Hungary 10, 15–6, 62–5, 67, 109–10, 173–74, 183, 228, 232–33
Hus, Jan (1369–1415) 56
Hutton, John 69

Ilmenau 80
imperial cities 2, 29, 56, 281
imperial estates 2, 9, 14–5, 27, 56, 64, 67, 86, 97, 109–10
India 16, 161
Ingelheim, Anselm Franz von, Elector of Mainz (1634–1695) 2
Ingolstadt 98
Inn (river) 131
Inner Austria *see* Austria
Innsbruck 61–63
Irmengard von Chiemsee, Abbess (831/33–866) 130, 132
Isabella of Demnark, Queen (1501–1526) 68
Isenburg-Büdingen, Counts of 191
Italy 14, 22–3, 27, 29–30, 41–2, 66, 69, 79, 86, 89, 98, 106, 108, 144, 149, 174, 224, 235, 251, 260, 294

Itzig, Daniel (1723–1799) 282
Itzig, Mirjam (1727–1788) 282

Jablonski, Johann Theodor (1654–1731) 205
Jadin, Louis Emmanuel (1768–1853) 284
Jerusalem, Friederike (d. 1836) 264
Jews 21, 26, 31, 158–66, 282, 287–95
Joachim I of Brandenburg, Elector (1484–1535) 72–3, 80
Joachim II of Brandenburg, Elector (1505–1571) 75, 77
Joanna of Austria, princess of Portugal (1535–1573) 90
Joanna of Spain, Queen (1479–1555) 61, 236
Johann Casimir of Palatinate-Simmern (1543–1592) 84
Johann Casimir of Saxe-Coburg, Duke (1564–1633) 84
Johann Georg I of Saxony, Elector (1585–1656) 116
Johann Georg III of Saxony, Elector (1647–1691) 3
Johann Georg of Brandenburg, Elector (1525–1598) 116
Johann of Brandenburg-Küstrin, Duke (1513–1571) 73
Johann of Denmark (1518–1532) 68
Johann of Saxony, Elector (1468–1532) 72
Johann the Younger of Holstein-Sonderburg, Duke (1545–1622) 83, 87
Johann Wilhelm of Jülich-Cleves-Berg, Duke (1562–1609) 115–16, 118
Johann Wilhelm of the Palatinate, Elector (1658–1716) 171–72, 174
Johanna Elisabeth of Anhalt-Zerbst (1712–1760) 212

John Sigismund of Brandenburg, Elector (1572–1620) 115–23
Joseph Clemens of Bayern, Elector of Köln (1671–1733) 2
Joseph I, Holy Roman Emperor (1678–1711) 2, 170, 173, 228, 231
Joseph II, Holy Roman Emperor (1741–1790) 232, 282
Juda Joseph ben Nathan (c. 1595–1670) 159
Juliane of Hessen-Kassel, Landgravine (1587–1643) 88
Jülich-Cleve-Berg (duchy) 10, 116, 118–19, 123
Julius Caesar (100 BC–44 BC) 83
Juncker, Johann (1679–1759) 224–25

Kant, Immanuel (1724–1804) 290
Karl August of Saxe-Weimar, Duke (1757–1828) 260, 265, 274
Karl Eugen of Württemberg, Duke (1728–1793) 240
Karl II of Inner Austria, Archduke (1540–1590) 11, 20, 93–8
Karl of Austria, Archduke (1590–1624) 97, 100
Karl Philipp of Palatinate-Neuburg (1661–1742) 171
Karl Theodor of the Palatinate, Elector (1724–1799) 241
Karlsruhe 281
Karsch, Anna Louisa (1722–1791) 33
Kassel 86, 200, 282
Kathen, Charlotte von (1777–1850) 293
Kaufbeuren 259
Kaufering 125
Kauffmann, Angelica (1741–1807) 247
Kaunitz, Wenzel Anton von (1711–1794) 281
Kelly-Gadol, Joan 25
Kempelen, Wolfgang von (1734–1804) 279

Kenzingen 54
Keuslin, Albert, Abbott of St. Peter OSB (1591–1657) 134
Kirch, Christfried (1694–1740) 202–03, 206
Kirch, Christine (1697–1782) 202–03, 206
Kirch, Gottfried (1639–1710) 201–04
Kirch, Margaretha (c. 1703–c. 1744) 202–03, 206
Kirch, Maria Margaretha (1670–1720) 20–1, 23–4, 200–08
Kleve 163
Klopstock, Friedrich Gottlieb (1724–1803) 282
Koblenz 262, 266, 281
Kolb, Honorat, Abbott OSB (1603–1670) 135
Kolding 86
Königsberg (Kaliningrad) 78, 115, 117–18, 122
Königsegg-Rothenfels, Maximilian Friedrich von, Prince-Bishop of Münster (1708–1784) 271
Königsmarck, Hans Christoph von (1605–1663) 178
Königsmarck, Konrad Christoph von (1634–1673) 178
Königsmarck, Maria Aurora von (1662–1728) 15, 23, 28, 33, 178–87
Königsmarck, Maria Christine von (1638–1691) 178, 180
Königsmarck, Otto Wilhelm von (1639–1688) 178
Königsmarck, Philipp Christoph von (1665–1694) 178, 180–82
Konstanze of Austria, Queen of Poland (1588–1631) 100
Koppmair, Andreas 250, 252
Koppmair, Anna Barbara see Gignoux, Anna Barbara
Koppmair, Sabina 251
Kostrzyn nad Odrą (Küstrin) 86
Koželuh, Leopold (1747–1818) 281
Kraków (Krakau) 100

Krosigk, Bernhard Friedrich von (1656–1714) 206
Kufstein 132
Kulmus, Johann Georg (1680–1731) 210
Kulmus, Katharina Dorothea 210
Kulmus, Luise Adelgunde see Gottsched, Luise Adelgunde

La Guêpière, Pierre de (1715–1773) 242
La Roche, Carl von (1766–1839) 265, 292
La Roche, Franz Wilhelm von (1768–1791) 264–65
La Roche, Georg Michael Frank von (1720–1788) 260–61, 263, 265
La Roche, Maximiliane von (1756–1793) 262–63, 265
La Roche, Sophie von (1730–1807) 23, 27–8, 259–67, 279, 282, 292
Lake Constance 259
Lambert Wilstadt, Mirjam (c. 1686–1749) 165, 166
Landsberg am Lech 125
Laßberg, Potentiana von (d. 1689) 144
Laubach 192–94, 198
Lebrun, Franziska (1756–1791) 285
Lech (river) 125, 131, 250, 254
Leibniz, Gottfried Wilhelm (1646–1716) 204–05, 212, 275
Leipzig 12, 17, 30, 161–62, 185, 201–02, 210–12, 214–16, 221, 227, 282–83
Lemos, Benjamin de (1711–1789) 287, 289
Lemos, Esther de (1742–1817) 287, 289, 293–94
Lemos, Henriette de see Herz, Henriette
Leopold I, Holy Roman Emperor (1640–1705) 2, 142–43, 168, 170–73, 175–76, 184, 228

Leopold Joseph, Archduke (born and died 1716) 228
Leopold of Austria, Archduke (1586–1632) 100
Leporin, Anna Sophia (d. 1757) 219
Leporin, Christian Polycarp (1689–1747) 219–23
Leporin, Christian Polycarp the Younger (1717–1791) 219, 222
Leporin, Dorothea Christiane *see* Erxleben, Dorothea Christiane
Leporin, Johann Christian 219
Leporin, Marie Elisabeth 219
Levant 68
Levassori della Motta, Thomas (d. 1757) 277
Levy, Hirsch (Cerf) (d. 1712) 165–66
Liebmann, Jost (c. 1639–1702) 163
Linck, Wenzeslaus (1483–1547) 47–8
Lindau 259
Linnaeus, Carl (1707–1778) 148
Linz 63
Lisbon 29
Lisiewski, Anna Dorothea *see* Therbusch, Anna Dorothea
Lisiewski, Christian Friedrich (1725–1794) 238, 245
Lisiewski, Elisabeth (d. 1733) 238
Lisiewski, Georg (1674–1750) 238–39
Listhenius, Georg (1532–1596) 87
Litomyšl (Leitomischl) 106
Lobenstein 196
Lobkowicz, House of 108, 111–12
Lobkowicz, Polyxena of (1566–1642) 11, 20, 28–9, 31, 33, 105–14
Lobkowicz, Václav Eusebius Popel of (1609–1677) 108, 112
Lobkowicz, Zdeněk Vojtěch Popel of (1568–1628) 108–11, 113

Lodron, Paris, Prince-Archbishop of Salzburg (1586–1653) 128
London 161, 200, 206, 279, 282
Lorraine (duchy) 94, 165, 230, 236
Louis II of Bohemia and Hungary, King (1506–1526) 61–2
Louis XIV of France (1638–1715) 168
Louis XVI of France (1754–1793) 235
Löwenhaupt, Amalie Wilhelmine (1663–1740) 178–81, 183
Löwenhaupt, Karl Gustav (1662–1703) 179, 183–84
Lower Austria *see* Austria
Lower Saxony 72
Ludwig Anton of Palatinate-Neuburg, Grand Master of the Teutonic Knights (1660–1694) 171–72
Luise Dorothea of Saxe-Gotha, Duchess (1710–1767) 33
Luther, Katharina (1499–1552) 33, 54
Luther, Martin (1483–1546) 17, 18, 33, 44, 45, 47, 54, 58–9, 64, 72–3, 83
Lutheran confession 18–21, 45–8, 53–60, 64, 66, 73, 75–9, 81, 83, 87, 94–6, 98, 112, 121–22, 132, 137, 139–44, 151–52, 159–60, 194–95, 202, 212, 273, 294

Madrid 100, 106, 113
Magdalene Sibylla of Saxony, Electress (1586–1659) 116
Magnus of Denmark (1540–1583) 83
Mainz 261–62, 274
Mainz (electorate) 14, 233
Malaspina, Germanico, papal Nuntio (1547–1603) 99
Mannheim 241–42, 281–83
Mansfeld, Anna Maria of, widowed Pernštejn (d. 1636) 105–06

Index

Mansfeld, Dorothea of (1493–1578) 89, 91
Manteuffel, Ernst Christoph von (1676–1749) 212
manufactory 30–31, 162, 250–57
Mara, Gertrud Elisabeth (1749–1833) 33, 285
Margaret of Savoy, Duchess (1480–1530) 61, 64, 68
Margarethe of Spain, Queen (1584–1611) 98, 100
Margarita Teresa of Austria, Holy Roman Empress (1651–1673) 168
Maria Amalia of Austria, Archduchess (1724–1730) 228
Maria Amalia of Bavaria, Electress, Holy Roman Empress (1701–1756) 231–32
Maria Anna of Lorraine (1718–1744) 228
Maria Anna of Spain, Queen (1667–1740) 171–72
Maria Anna of the Palatinate-Neuburg (1654–1689) 171
Maria Antonia of Bavaria, Electress (1669–1692) 168
Maria Antonia Walpurgis of Saxony, Electress (1724–1780) 285
Maria Christina of Transylvania (1574–1621) 100
Maria Elisabeth of Holstein-Gottorf, Abbess of Quedlinburg (1678–1755) 225
Maria Magdalena of Tuscany, Grand Duchess (1587–1631) 100
Maria of Austria, Holy Roman Empress (1528–1603) 90, 100, 105–06
Maria of Bavaria *see* Maria of Inner Austria
Maria of Burgundy, Duchess (1457–1482) 236
Maria of Hungary, Queen (1505–1558) 11, 16, 22, 27, 29, 32, 61–71, 235
Maria of Inner Austria, Archduchess (1551–1608) 11, 16, 19–20, 33, 93–102
Maria of Jülich-Cleves-Berg, Duchess (1531–1581) 116
Maria Sophie of Portugal, Queen (1666–1699) 171
Maria Theresa, Holy Roman Empress (1717–1780) 10, 17, 32, 214, 227–37, 280
Marie Antoinette of France, Queen (1755–1793) 235
Marie Christine of Austria, Archduchess (1742–1798) 282
Marie Eleonore of Prussia, Duchess (1550–1608) 115–18, 121
Marie Eleonore of Sweden, Queen (1599–1655) 122
Marie of Brandenburg-Bayreuth, Markgravine (1579–1649) 116
Mariemont 70
Marigny, Abel François Poisson de Vandières, Marquis de (1727–1781) 242
Marinella, Lucretia (1571–1653) 8
Mark (Jülich-Cleves-Berg), House of 123
Marquard, Johann Philipp (d. 1727) 192
Marrel, Jacob (1614–1681) 148–49, 151
Martinic, Georg Adam von (1602–1651) 111
Martinic, Jaroslav Bořita von (1582–1649) 111
Mathesius, Johannes (1504–1564) 83
Matsushita, Hidemi 285
Matthias, Holy Roman Emperor (1557–1619) 109
Matthieu, Anna Rosina (1713–1783) 238, 246
Maurice of Saxony, Elector (1521–1553) 84, 87

Maximilian Ernst of Austria, Archduke (1583–1616) 100
Maximilian I of Bavaria, Duke, later Elector (1573–1651) 126
Maximilian I, Holy Roman Emperor (1459–1519) 61
Maximilian II Emanuel of Bavaria, Elector (1662–1726) 2
Maximilian II, Holy Roman Emperor (1527–1576) 86, 94
Mediterranean 30
Melanchthon, Philipp (1497–1560) 47–8, 73
Mendelssohn, Moses (1729–1786) 282, 287–89
Merian, Caspar (1627–1686) 152
Merian, Johanna Catharina (d. 1690) 148, 151–52
Merian, Maria Sibylla (1647–1717) 20–1, 23–4, 27, 148–57
Merian, Matthäus the Elder (1593–1650) 148
Mesmer, Franz Anton (1734–1815) 278–79
Metz 162, 165–66
Meusel, Johann Georg (1743–1820) 239
Meyer, Amelia 55
Meyer, Jacob (d. 1567) 56
migration *see* travels
Milan 98
Mohács 62
Moravian Church 12, 21, 197–98
Morhart, Magdalena (d. 1574) 256
Moritz of Saxony (1696–1750) 183
Moscow 161
Mozart, Leopold (1719–1787) 281
Mozart, Maria Anna (1751–1829) 281
Mozart, Wolfgang Amadeus (1756–1791) 281, 284
Munich 86, 94–5, 127, 131–35, 281, 294

Münster 28, 133, 270–75, 291
Münster (prince-bishopric) 271
Muslims 26

Naples 294
Napoleon Bonaparte (1769–1821) 293
Nassau, Counts of 10
Naumburg 162
Neefe, Appolonia (d. 1578) 89
Neefe, Johann (1499–1574) 89
Netherlands 11, 14, 16, 21, 30, 61, 63–4, 66–7, 70, 79, 148, 151–52, 154, 174, 183, 210, 235, 244, 269–70
Neuber, Friedrike Caroline (1697–1760) 33, 211
Neuburg an der Donau 169
Niederschönenfeld (abbey) 125, 131, 133
North Sea 30, 66, 161
Northeim 76
Nuremberg 12, 18, 22, 28, 30, 41–6, 48–9, 53, 78, 139–41, 144–45, 149–50, 152, 155–56, 202, 210, 294
Nützel, Caspar (1471–1529) 45–8

Offenbach 265–66
Oppenheimer, Samuel Wolf (1630–1703) 163–64
Ore Mountains 31, 256
Orsbeck, Johann Hugo von, Elector of Trier (1634–1711) 2
Osiander, Andreas (1496/98–1552) 78
Osman II, Sultan (1604–1622) 110
Osnabrück 133
Ostein, Johann Friedrich Karl von, Elector of Mainz (1689–1763) 233
Ottomans 16–7, 28, 62–3, 66, 68, 75, 95, 106, 110, 140, 143–44, 168, 170, 174–75
Overberg, Bernhard Heinrich (1754–1826) 274

Palatinate-Neuburg, House of *see* Wittelsbach
Panitzsch 201
Paracelsus (1493–1541) 89
Paradis, Joseph Anton (1733–1808) 277–81, 283–84
Paradis, Maria Theresia (1759–1824) 23, 26–8, 277–86
Paradis, Rosalia Maria (1739–1794) 277–81, 283
Paris 69, 241–45, 247, 269, 282
Passau 63, 100, 168
Pavia 79
Perici, Petrus, Bishop of Seckau (d. 1572) 94
Pernštejn, Frebonia of (1596–1646) 111
Pernštejn, Hedwig of (1559– after 1625) 108
Pernštejn, House of 106, 109, 111
Pernštejn, Jan of (1561–1597) 106
Pernštejn, Luisa of (1574–1641) 106, 108, 113
Pernštejn, Maria of (1538–1608) 105–06, 109, 112
Pernštejn, Polyxena of *see* Polyxena of Lobkowicz
Pernštejn, Vratislav Eusebius of (1594–1631) 109, 111
Pernštejn, Vratislav of (c. 1530–1582) 105
Pesne, Antoine (1683–1757) 239
Petersen, Johanna Eleonora (1644–1724) 33, 191
Pfaffenhofen 127
Philip II of Spain, King (1527–1598) 69–70
Philip III of Spain, King (1578–1621) 100
Philip of Burgundy, Archduke (1478–1506) 61
Philipp I of Hessen (1504–1567) 75, 77
Philipp Ludwig of Palatinate-Neuburg, Duke (1547–1614) 118
Philipp Wilhelm of the Palatinate, Elector (1615–1690) 2, 168–72

Pichler, Caroline (1769–1843) 283
Pietism 12, 20–1, 25, 191–98, 202–03, 259, 275
Pirckheimer, Barbara (d. 1488) 41
Pirckheimer, Caritas (Barbara) (1467–1532) 18, 22–3, 41–51, 53
Pirckheimer, Clara (1480–1533) 42, 49
Pirckheimer, Hans (1417–1492) 41
Pirckheimer, Johannes (d. 1501) 41–2
Pirckheimer, Katharina (Caritas) (1498–1563) 49
Pirckheimer, Katharina (d. 1484) 41
Pirckheimer, Willibald (1470–1530) 42–4, 47–8
Pizan, Christine de (1364–1431) 8
Pleyel, Ignaz Joseph (1757–1831) 284
Poland 89, 100, 115, 117, 122, 183, 210
Pope, Alexander (1688–1744) 214
Popp, Susanna (d. 1683) 139, 144
Portugal 69, 100, 108, 159, 171, 287
Potsdam 246
Prague 28, 62, 86, 106–13, 131, 159, 161, 282
Preyndorfer, Sabina OSB (d. 1609) 125–26
Preysing, noble family 135
Prussia (duchy, later Kingdom) 10, 15–7, 80, 115–17, 120–23, 210, 215, 222–23, 230–31, 236, 238–39, 245, 268, 293

Quedlinburg 15, 181, 183, 185–86, 219–20, 223, 225

Rabus, Ludwig (1523–1592) 57, 59
Racine, Jean-Baptiste (1639–1699) 179
reading society 23, 261, 288–90

Recke, Elisa von der (1754–1833) 264
reformation 9, 17–9, 21, 25–6, 44–5, 47, 49, 53–4, 56, 58–9, 64, 72, 75–6, 81, 87, 96, 116, 125, 181, 191, 195
Regensburg 15, 27, 86, 109, 139, 144, 281
Religion *see* catholic confession, Lutheran confession, Calvinists, Moravian church, Pietism
renaissance 21–2, 25, 49, 70
Reuß, House of 195–96
Reuß-Ebersdorf, Heinrich X of (1662–1711) 193–94
Reuß-Ebersdorf, Heinrich XXIX of (1699–1747) 193–94
Reuß-Ebersdorf, Sophie Theodora of (1703–1777) 197–98
Reuß-Schleiz, Heinrich XXIV of (1681–1743) 195–97
Rhine (river) 9, 16, 116, 118, 236, 282
Rhineland 116
Richardson, Samuel (1689–1761) 261
Riedinger, Johann (1751–1827) 283–84
Roman Curia 171
Rome 44, 94–5, 105, 266, 294
Rosenberg, Katharina of (1534–1559) 72, 80
Rosenberg, Polyxena of *see* Polyxena of Lobkowicz
Rosenberg, William of (1535–1592) 106–07
Rosenheim 127
Roudnice and Labem 107–109, 111–13
Rousseau, Jean Jacques (1712–1778) 261, 270–71
Rudolf II, Holy Roman Emperor (1552–1612) 97–100, 105, 107, 118
Rügen (island) 293
Ruhr (river) 256

Rulership 10, 14–5, 65, 97, 99, 101, 117, 174, 183–84, 194, 196, 232, 235
Rumschottel, Anna 73, 80
Runckel, Henriette Dorothea von (1724–1800) 212–13, 216
Russia 16, 155, 210, 244–45, 269

Saar (river) 256
Saint Petersburg 155, 269
Salieri, Antonio (1750–1825) 280, 284
Salon, salonnière 17, 21, 23–4, 26, 261, 272, 279, 283, 290–95
Salzburg 127–29, 133–34, 281
San Clemente, Guillén de (1550–1608) 106
Sandrart, Esther Barbara von (1651–1733) 156
Sandrart, Joachim von (1606–1688) 149
Sangerhausen 89
Saxony 16–7, 21, 45, 72, 76, 84, 86–9, 91, 118, 181–83, 192, 201–02, 210, 212, 215, 254
Scandinavia 210
Schallaburg (castle) 139
Schellersheim, Paul Andreas von (d. 1781) 224–25
Schiller, Friedrich von (1759–1805) 260, 263
Schlegel, Dorothea (Brendel) (1764–1839) 33, 275, 288, 290–92, 294
Schleiermacher, Friedrich (1768–1834) 292–94
Schleusingen 80
Schmettau, Amalie von *see* Gallitzin, Amalie
Schmettau, Maria Johanna von (1718–1771) 268
Schmettau, Samuel von (1684–1751) 268
Schönebeck an der Elbe 265
Schurman, Anna Maria van (1607–1678) 33
Schütz, Jakob 53

Schütz, Katharina *see* Katharina Zell
Schütz, Lucas 56
Schwab Krumbach, Esther 165–66
Schwab Krumbach, Moses (1665–1736) 165–66
Schwarz, Johann Conrad 253
Schwarzburg-Sondershausen, Juliane of (1546–1588) 91
Schwenckfeld, Caspar von (1490–1561) 57
science 23–5, 41, 89–91, 146, 148, 150, 152–56, 201–08, 210, 216, 220–21, 224, 264, 269, 271–72, 289–91
Seckendorff, Clara Dorothea von (1674–1757) 212
Seckendorff, Friedrich Heinrich von (1673–1763) 212
Seebruck 132
Seeon (abbey) 129, 132, 135
Seisenegg (manor) 137, 139, 141–42, 144
Seligenthal (abbey) 131
Selnecker, Nikolaus (1530–1592) 87
Shakespeare, William (1564–1616) 215
Sicily 68
Siena 139
Sigismund III of Poland, King (1566–1632) 99–100
Silesia 16, 31, 57, 230–31
Simanowitz, Ludovike (1759–1827) 246
Skilled crafts and trades 5–8, 30–1, 238, 250–52, 255–57
Sobieski, Hedwig Elisabeth (1673–1722) 172
Sobieski, Jakub Ludwig (1668–1737) 172
Solms-Laubach (county) 192
Solms-Laubach, Benigna of (1648–1702) 191–94, 198
Solms-Laubach, Carl Otto of (1673–1743) 192, 195
Solms-Laubach, Counts of 191

Solms-Laubach, Erdmuthe Benigna of *see* Erdmuthe Benigna of Reuß-Ebersdorf
Solms-Laubach, Johann Friedrich of (1625–1696) 191, 192–93
Sommerfeld 201
Sophie Charlotte of Prussia, Queen (1668–1705) 205
Sophie Dorothea of Brunswick-Hanover (1666–1726) 181
Sophie Kettler of Courland, Duchess (1582–1610) 116
Sophie of Saxony, Electress (1568–1622) 84
Sopron (Ödenburg) 110
Spain 16, 29, 61, 63, 69–70, 79, 98, 105–06, 108–13, 159, 171, 174, 228
Spanish Netherlands 174, 210, 244
Spener, Philipp Jacob (1635–1705) 191–92
Speyer 9, 79, 263
Stade 178, 181, 185
Stadion, Anton Heinrich von (1691–1768) 260–61
Stahl, Georg Ernst (1659–1734) 224
Steinbühl (manor) 145
Stockholm 178–79
Stolberg, Counts of 10, 191
Stolpen 86
Stralsund 257
Strasbourg 12, 17, 52–8, 60, 73, 261, 282
Stubenberg, Johann Wilhelm von (1619–1663) 139–40
Stuttgart 239–42, 281, 294
Styria 10, 94–5
Suleiman I, Sultan (1494–1566) 62
Suriname 27, 152–55
Swabia 31, 131, 133
Sweden 87, 122, 174, 178, 180
Switzerland 14, 89, 133, 264–65, 282, 294
Szczecin (Stettin) 161
Székesfehérvár (Stuhlweißenburg) 62

Teplice (Teplitz) 185
Territorial estates 75, 79, 96, 98, 121
The Hague 269–270
Therbusch, Anna Dorothea (1721–1782) 23, 26–7, 33, 238–48, 269, 288
Therbusch, Ernst Friedrich (1711–1773) 239, 245
Therbusch, Georg Friedrich 239, 245
Therbusch, Karl August 239, 245
Thirty Years War 16–7, 20, 109, 118, 127, 131–35, 140, 178, 250
Thorn 15
Thorwaldsen, Bertel (1770–1844) 294
Thukydides (c. 460–c. 400 BC) 83
Thuringia 21, 80
Töllner, Justinus (1656–1718) 201
Töllner, Sara Elisabeth 201
Tordesillas 61
Torgau 84, 86
Törring, noble family 135
trade 12, 16, 27, 29–32, 158–59, 161–63, 165–66, 210–11, 251, 255–57
Transylvania 100
travels 9, 11, 26–8, 61, 64, 86, 88, 98, 100–01, 109, 118, 120, 140, 142, 148–49, 152, 154, 163–64, 180–82, 232, 240–44, 246, 260, 264–66, 274, 277, 281–82, 294
Tübingen 256, 260
Tucher, Sixtus (1459–1507) 43
Tunis 29, 68–9
Tuscany (grand duchy) 100, 230, 232
Tyrol 127

Ulrich, Arsenius OSB, provost of Herrenchiemsee (d. 1653) 128, 134
Ulrika Eleonora of Sweden, Queen (1656–1693) 179

Ungnad von Sonnegg, Hans (1493–1564) 89
Upper Lusatia 198
Upper Palatinate 110
Utrecht 148

Varnhagen von Ense, Rahel (1771–1833) 292–93, 295
Vasa, House of 122
Venice 294
Verona 294
Verospi, Fabrizio, papal Nuntio (1571–1639) 105
Vienna 9, 16, 27, 29, 61, 63, 86, 94, 105, 108–10, 142, 144, 159, 162–63, 169–71, 173–75, 184, 214–15, 227, 229, 233, 244, 256, 269, 277–84, 291–93
Villahermosa, Fernando de Aragón y Borja, Duque de (1546–1592) 106
Villahermosa, Johanna Duquesa de (1556–1631) 106, 108
Vladislaus II of Bohemia and Hungary, King (1456–1516) 61
Vogler, Georg Joseph (1749–1814) 282
Volckamer, Johann Georg (1662–1744) 155
Voltaire (François-Marie Arouet) (1664–1778) 185, 269

Waldeck, Counts of 191
Waldeck-Pyrmont, Friedrich Karl of (1743–1812) 291
Waltha (manor) 151–52, 154, 156
wars 15–7, 28, 32, 53, 67, 78–9, 87, 106, 140, 153, 160, 174–75, 183, 215, 231–32, 265, 293; *see also* Thirty Years War
Warthausen 261
Wasserburg 131–33
Watzdorf, Margarethe von OSCl (d. 1570) 89
Weimar 28, 260, 265, 274
Weißenfels 84, 89

Weissenburg, Ludwig 282
Wertheimer, Samson (1658–1724) 163
West Indies 154–55
Westphalia 270–71
Wettin, House of 10
Wetzlar 9
widowhood 4–7, 9, 16, 31, 62–4, 67–8, 74–7, 79–80, 97–100, 106, 108, 110, 112, 143–45, 158, 162–65, 173, 178, 194–95, 204, 212, 250–54, 256–57, 264–65, 293
Wieland, Christoph Martin (1733–1813) 260–63, 265
Wieland, Regina Katharina (1715–1789) 260
Wieuwerd 151
Wildenfels 192
Wilhelm Kettler of Courland, Duke (1574–1640) 116
Wilhelm V of Bavaria, Duke (1548–1626) 95, 97, 99
Wilhelm V of Jülich-Cleves-Berg, Duke (1516–1592) 66, 116
Wilhelmine Friederike of Brandenburg-Bayreuth, Markgravine (1709–1758) 285
Winckelmann, Maria (d. 1683) 202
Winckelmann, Maria Margaretha *see* Kirch, Maria Magaretha
Winckelmann, Matthias (d. 1682) 201

Witsen, Nicolaas (1641–1717) 153
Wittelsbach, House of 10, 171–72, 175
Wittenberg 54, 56, 59, 64, 73, 87
Władysław IV of Poland, King (1595–1648) 122
Wolfenbüttel 28, 86, 180–81, 185–86
Wolfenbüttel (duchy) 236
Wolff, Christian (1679–1754) 212
working couple 8, 11, 18, 31, 55, 120, 170, 202–04, 211–15, 217, 233
Wrangel, noble family 178
Wrocław (Breslau) 100, 171, 202, 268, 293
Wunder, Heide 8
Würzburg 281

Zell, Katharina (1497/98–1562) 17–8, 33, 52–60, 81
Zell, Matthäus (1477–1548) 17–8, 53–7, 59–60
Zemon Davis, Natalie 159
Ziegler, Christiana Mariana von (1695–1760) 211, 221
Zinzendorf, Erdmuthe Dorothea von (1700–1756) 197–98
Zinzendorf, Nicolaus Ludwig von (1700–1760) 197–98
Zwickau 192

For Product Safety Concerns and Information please contact our EU representative GPSR@taylorandfrancis.com
Taylor & Francis Verlag GmbH, Kaufingerstraße 24, 80331 München, Germany

www.ingramcontent.com/pod-product-compliance
Lightning Source LLC
Chambersburg PA
CBHW071812230426
43670CB00013B/2433